Dear Reader:

The book you are about to read is the latest bestseller from the St. Martin's True Crime Library, the imprint *The New York Times* calls "the leader in true crime!" Each month, we offer you a fascinating account of the latest, most sensational crime that has captured the national attention. St. Martin's is the publisher of bestselling true crime author and crime journalist Kieran Crowley, who explores the dark, deadly links between a prominent Manhattan surgeon and the disappearance of his wife fifteen years earlier in THE SURGEON'S WIFE. Suzy Spencer's BREAKING POINT guides readers through the tortuous twists and turns in the case of Andrea Yates, the Houston mother who drowned her five young children in the family's bathtub. In Edgar Award-nominated DARK DREAMS, legendary FBI profiler Roy Hazelwood and bestselling crime author Stephen G. Michaud shine light on the inner workings of America's most violent and depraved murderers. In the book you now hold, THE PROM NIGHT MURDERS, acclaimed author Carlton Smith takes a closer look at a twenty-year-old tragedy shrouded in mystery.

St. Martin's True Crime Library gives you the stories behind the headlines. Our authors take you right to the scene of the crime and into the minds of the most notorious murderers to show you what really makes them tick. St. Martin's True Crime Library paperbacks are better than the most terrifying thriller, because it's all true! The next time you want a crackling good read, make sure it's got the St. Martin's True Crime Library logo on the spine—you'll be up all night!

Charles E. Spicer, Jr.
Executive Editor, St. Martin's True Crime Library

Other True Crime Titles From

CARLTON SMITH

Poisoned Love
Mind Games
The BTK Murders
Vanished
Cold Blooded
Reckless
Death of a Doctor
Shadows of Evil
Hunting Evil
Bitter Medicine
Murder at Yosemite
Death in Texas
Dying for Daddy
Death of a Little Princess
Seeds of Evil

Available From St. Martin's True Crime Library

THE PROM NIGHT MURDERS

A Devoted American Family, Their Troubled Son, and a Ghastly Crime

Carlton Smith

St. Martin's Paperbacks

THE PROM NIGHT MURDERS

For information address St. Martin's Press, 175 Fifth Avenue, New York, NY 10010.

ISBN: 0-312-94724-0
EAN: 978-0-312-94724-8

Printed in the United States of America

St. Martin's Paperbacks edition / May 2009

St. Martin's Paperbacks are published by St. Martin's Press, 175 Fifth Avenue, New York, NY 10010.

10 9 8 7 6 5 4 3 2 1

ACKNOWLEDGMENTS

Trying to reconstruct—or even deconstruct—a series of events that took place over thirty years is an endeavor fraught with difficulties. A researcher can try to reassemble records, but the past is like the beach—each daily wave erodes a little bit more, and makes it that much harder to know what the landscape looked like back then. Historians can assemble, collate, analyze, infer—guess—but the psychological reality is, no one can really know what someone who lived in the past really thought or felt. It's all only educated conjecture.

So it was with the Pelleys. Just what happened in the parsonage on April 29, 1989, may never be known. As Judge Chamblee observed to some of the jurors, after the event, there were only five or possibly six people who knew what had really taken place, and four of them were dead.

Still, some fragmentary records remain, along with some similarly fragmented memories. In the course of preparing this book, I made two trips to South Bend and Indianapolis, Indiana; another trip to Fort Myers, Florida; and separate stops in Washington, D.C.; Cincinnati, Ohio: and Detroit, Michigan. Along the way I encountered a great many people who were very generous with their time and patience in answering questions and helping me unearth documents.

First and foremost of these was Maura Pierce, then the spokesperson for the Indiana Court of Appeals, who labored diligently to provide me with access to the entire Pelley court file, all 2,000 some–odd pages of it, as well as the opportunity to inspect a number of photographic exhibits from the trial. Also in Indianapolis, defense appellate lawyer Stacy Uliana and Staci Schneider of the Office of the Indiana Attorney General were both of great assistance.

In South Bend, both John Botich and Mark Senter very kindly made themselves available for interviews, and thereafter patiently answered new questions by both telephone and email. Tim Harmon and Pablo Ros of the *South Bend Tribune* were very helpful, as was Dave Hathaway.

In Fort Myers, Florida, I owe particular thanks to Sheldon Zoldan of the Fort Myers *News-Press* for allowing me to rummage through his paper's library of old clippings, and Tom Kontinos, for his recollection of his investigation into the still-unsolved murder of C. Eric Dawson. In Fort Lauderdale, I owe thanks to Peter Franceschina, for his recollection of the same events. Also in Florida, I am grateful to Biff Lagan of the state Department of Insurance's fraud division for his assistance.

I am likewise grateful to Alan Baum, of Los Angeles, for his kind assistance throughout the preparation of this book.

Most of all, though, I wish to thank Jacque Pelley for her faith and her frequent emails, in which she attempted valiantly and honestly to resolve so many questions, and whose faith in the innocence of her brother remains undiminished.

Carlton Smith
Reno, Nevada
August 2008

CONTENTS

AUTHOR'S NOTE

Over the past twenty years since the murder of the Pelleys, a number of the characters' names have changed—most frequently because of matrimony. Although many people testified at the trial under their married names, I have chosen to refer to them throughout the text by their maiden names, simply to avoid confusion.

In a different way, I have avoided using Jacque Pelley's last name, out of respect for her desire for privacy, and have chosen not to use the name of Jeff's wife and mother-in-law for the same reasons.

PREFACE

The murder of a minister's family near South Bend at the end of April 1989 was, at the time, the worst case of mass murder in the history of northern Indiana. Police very quickly focused on Robert Jeffrey Pelley, the son of the minister, Robert Lee Pelley, and within a matter of hours concluded that he had to be the killer.

But was Jeff Pelley, as he was called, really the murderer? The case of the Pelleys fascinated Indiana for almost two decades—for every fact that seemed to suggest that Jeff Pelley had murdered his father, stepmother and stepsisters, there were other facts that seemed to show he was innocent.

It took Indiana authorities years to charge Jeff Pelley with the murders of his family, and still more years to bring him to trial. And the story isn't over yet . . .

But the truth of what really happened on April 29, 1989, remains a mystery.

THE PROM NIGHT MURDERS

I. LAKEVILLE, INDIANA

Sunday, April 30, 1989

CHAPTER 1

The cars began arriving a little after nine that morning. Of all years, makes and sizes, they rolled into the graveled parking lot of the Olive Branch United Brethren Church in Christ, on Osborne Road, just five miles south of South Bend, Indiana. It was a beautiful spring morning—the sun was out, the skies were clear and blue—and as the members of the congregation assembled in their whitewashed, steepled sanctuary, dressed in their Sunday finest, none had the faintest idea of the horror that lay only yards away. It was the last day of April, and the year was 1989.

The Olive Branch United Brethren Church in Christ had perhaps a hundred members, most drawn from the surrounding neighborhood of prosperous farms. Mothers, fathers, grandparents and children—the church had been the center of their lives for generations, something that linked them all, in birth, life and death, no matter what happened in the outside world. It was a small church, but the members were devoted to their faith, their families, to their church, and to one another.

But that morning, their pastor, the Reverend Robert Lee Pelley, was missing.

Well, it had happened before. The reverend, after accepting the post, had once arrived unshaven, dressed in a T-shirt and blue jeans, then for some minutes had desultorily perused the newspaper from a seat in a front pew, while his parishioners wondered what was up. The idea, as he explained later, was that church time wasn't casual—you were either in church when it was time, or you weren't. You either dressed respectfully to worship the Lord, or you didn't. You could be indifferent to God, or you could read the comics—you could be on time and ready to praise Him, or you could be lukewarm, as the Bible said.

Point taken, the congregants had agreed, appropriately chastened. But now, on this fine spring morning on the last day of April 1989, the pastor was absent, and there were those who said, *Well, Bob is just making another point*, although this time no one was quite sure what it was.

At about 9:15 A.M., the father of 11-year-old Stephanie Fagan sent her over to the nearby parsonage to see what was holding up the pastor. Located just east of the church, the parsonage was a white-washed house with a full basement, provided to the appointed clergyman rent-free by the church board. Its garage door and a concrete slab driveway were connected to the gravel church parking lot, along with a basketball hoop used by church boys of all ages. The garage door was down, Stephanie saw—that was odd. There were two cars in the driveway—the same vehicles usually driven by the pastor, Bob Pelley, and his wife, Dawn.

Stephanie approached the small side door into the garage, the one that faced the long cornfield to the south. The door was locked. Stephanie was surprised again—that door was *never* locked on Sundays. She moved east past the kitchen windows facing the cornfield, then to the sliding glass door that led into the adjacent dining room. It, too, was locked, and all the curtains were drawn.

Seeing the closed curtains and drapes, another oddity for the parsonage, Stephanie had a creepy feeling. It was too quiet, and she knew something had to be wrong. She ran back to the church, and told her father that it looked as though the pastor and his family were still asleep, even while knowing in her stomach that something was—well, very, very off. After hearing this from Stephanie's father, several church ladies went over to the parsonage and knocked on the doors. No one answered. They returned to the church, mystified by the pastor's absence. It was now just after 9:20 A.M.

While this was going on, a member of the church board, Sunday school superintendent David Hathaway, was trying to get things organized—it was his job to make sure the right Bible teachers had the right teaching rooms in the church basement, so Sunday school could take place as scheduled at 10:30. That was when he heard from some of the church ladies that the Reverend Pelley and his family might still be asleep, or possibly even absent from the parsonage, although the Pelleys' cars were in the parsonage driveway, in front of the closed garage doors.

Well, that's odd, Hathaway thought. But services were supposed to begin at 9:30 that morning, in just ten minutes, and if, for some reason, Bob Pelley wasn't going to make it, someone else would have to step in.

Hathaway found a young student pastor-in-training, Richard Wygant, who sometimes preached. Would Richard be willing to take over for Bob? The young man agreed to pinch-hit for the pastor, and with that, Hathaway went over to the parsonage to see what was up, and why the Reverend Pelley was a no-show.

From the front doors of the church, the long rectangle of the white-painted parsonage could be seen end-on, the closed garage door facing the church parking lot, and the front door of the church. Ordinarily, the two cars of Reverend Pelley and his wife, Dawn, were parked on the concrete slab in front of the garage, next to the basketball hoop, and sure enough, both cars were there. The garage door was down—usually, Hathaway knew, it was open.

Well, maybe Bob is giving us another joke, Hathaway thought, although he, like the congregants, couldn't for the life of him figure out what it was.

Hathaway walked all the way around the parsonage, trying the doors, trying to look into the windows, finishing at the front door, the one facing Osborne Road on the north. Every door was locked. All the curtains were drawn. Hathaway knew this was strange—the Pelleys habitually kept their doors unlocked, and their curtains open, as far as Hathaway knew. It was a symbol of their accessibility, their belief in the collective faith of the Olive Branch Church, in which spiritual honesty was paramount, and in which personal secrets, especially of sins, were anathema.

Hathaway had been a member of Olive Branch for more than thirty years, and as a member of the church's administrative board, had been one of those who'd agreed to hire Bob Pelley, a little more than two years earlier. So, as he made his way around the parsonage, testing every door and trying to look in every window, he felt a little miffed that Bob hadn't called to tell him that he wouldn't be available for the morning's services.

While no one seemed to be home, the presence of the two cars in the driveway gnawed at Hathaway. If Bob and his family had left, why were their cars still parked in front of the garage? And why wouldn't Bob have phoned him, if he wasn't going to show up that morning? It didn't seem right to Hathaway.

Hathaway returned to the church and slipped into a rear pew. The congregation was singing a hymn. Hathaway joined in, but something kept telling him he had to get into the parsonage. He had a feeling there was trouble there. Later, he put his uneasiness down to a message from the Lord.

When the hymn was over, and Wygant was supervising the taking up of the offering, Hathaway told another church member, Wilmot Tisdale, that he had a bad feeling—something was very wrong: they had to get into the parsonage to see about Bob.

But first, he had to go home to get the key, he told Tisdale. As a member of the board, Hathaway thought he might have a spare.

Hathaway's house was about a mile away to the east, also on Osborne Road. It took him about ten minutes to find the key and get back to the parsonage. He met Tisdale at the small door on the south side of the garage, the one Stephanie Fagan had tried first. The key worked to unlock that door. But once they were inside the garage, the same key wouldn't work on the door from the garage to the kitchen.

"I'll try the front," Hathaway told Tisdale. But his key wouldn't work on that door, either.

"It looks like they changed the locks on the doors," Hathaway told Tisdale, once he'd returned to the rear of the parsonage. "We have to find someone with a new key." By now, Wygant had launched into his extemporaneous sermon. Hathaway was increasingly convinced that there was something very, very wrong inside the parsonage.

At that point, church member Lydia Mae Easterday came out of the church. Lydia Mae said *she* had a key to the parsonage—her husband was on the church's property board, which controlled the church as well as the pastor's residence.

But once inside the garage, Lydia Mae's key wouldn't work on the inside kitchen door either. Hathaway took Lydia Mae's key and said he'd try it in the front door. If it worked, he'd let them in through the kitchen door from the garage. If not, they'd have to figure out something else—by then, Hathaway was convinced that something bad had to have happened. Why else would Bob Pelley have been a no-show at the morning services? Why were all the doors locked, the curtains drawn, the Pelley cars still in the driveway?

Lydia Mae's key fit the front door. Hathaway went in and made his way down the entrance hall, heading toward the dining room and kitchen, directly ahead. But near the end of the hall, Hathaway noticed a pair of eyeglasses lying on the floor.

Uh oh, there's been a fight, Hathaway told himself. As he moved closer to the eyeglasses, he glanced to his left, down a second hallway. He saw Bob Pelley, lying faceup on the floor. Bob wasn't moving. Hathaway saw dried blood on Bob's chest and arms, as well as some on the baseboard of the hallway. He knew without even checking that Bob was dead.

Hathaway backed out the hallway, into the dining room and then into the kitchen. He let Wilmot and Lydia Mae in from the garage.

"We have a problem," Hathaway told them. "It looks like Bob is dead." He cautioned them not to touch anything. He advised Lydia Mae to stay where she was, not to look: it was too gory. He led Tisdale into the front hall to show him what he was talking about. Lydia Mae ignored Hathaway's warning and followed them. The trio looked at Bob's dead body, and then Hathaway shooed them back into the kitchen, telling them again not to touch anything.

"We've got to call 911," Hathaway said. But by then, Lydia Mae was already on her way out the back door of the kitchen, heading for the church with the news. Tisdale, a bit rattled, picked up the telephone and made the call, but when the dispatcher asked him for the address, Tisdale drew a blank. Hathaway took the telephone from him and provided the information.

By that time people were streaming out of the church because of Lydia Mae's alarm. Hathaway realized he had to keep people out of the house to preserve what was almost certainly a murder scene. He and Tisdale shut the side door and kept everyone out. Paramedics arrived at the house within a very few minutes.

"It just seemed like I hung up the phone," Hathaway said later, "and they were there."

The medics checked Bob and saw that he was definitely dead. They looked through the other rooms on the first floor—three bedrooms, two bathrooms, a living room, as well as the combination kitchen and dining room. Besides Bob, there were no other victims.

"We want to check the basement," one of the paramedics told Hathaway. They started down the stairs from the kitchen, trailed by Hathaway and Tisdale. Someone turned on the stairwell lights as they went down. As they neared the bottom of the steps, one of the paramedics saw something on the basement floor.

"There's a body there," he said. Hathaway, the second paramedic and Tisdale froze on the third step up from the basement floor. The first paramedic went ahead and disappeared into the dim light cast from the stairwell.

"I think I see *three* bodies," Hathaway said.

Afterward, Hathaway, Tisdale and Lydia Mae waited outside the parsonage, along with the rest of the congregation, as officers from the St. Joseph County, Indiana, Police Department, arrived. All the church members were in a state of shock, not least Hathaway, Tisdale and Lydia Mae. The scene in the house was gruesome in the extreme, particularly in the basement, where blood seemed to be everywhere—on the walls, even on the ceiling. For Hathaway, it was World War II all over again.

The numbing reality began to sink in: at some point over the previous twenty-four hours, someone inside the parsonage had slaughtered Reverend Pelley, his wife, Dawn, and Dawn Pelley's two youngest daughters, Janel, 8, and Jolene, 6. It had been Dawn Pelley's body the paramedic had first seen on the basement floor. And it had been Janel and Jolene whom Hathaway had noticed on the floor next to her, the younger child clasping her mother as all three waited for an inevitable execution—"six legs," as Hathaway later described it. It was beyond gruesome—it was bestial.

CHAPTER 2

In many ways, the Reverend Robert Pelley seems, at least in retrospect, a rather contradictory personality. Described by many who knew him as a joyful, engaging, charismatic man, he also seems to have had something of a dour, even angry side. A minister of the gospel, he was also said to have "loved guns," particularly the sort most useful in hunting varmints of the two-legged variety, including shotguns and a .44 magnum Smith & Wesson pistol—the same weapon Clint Eastwood, playing Dirty Harry Callahan, once famously described on film as "the most powerful handgun in the world," when asking a bank robber if he felt lucky.

Seemingly a man who put his family first, who was so morally straight he once turned his own son into the police for a minor burglary, he nevertheless had connections to others who had a history of skirting close to the edge of the law. He'd given up a remunerative job with a major Florida bank to accept the pastorate of a small church in a rural town in northern Indiana that paid a little over $1,200 a month—plus the parsonage—yet had life insurance policies worth over $150,000.

As it turned out, he told things to some people that were contradicted by what he told others. On the morning before his death, he'd been at a gun shop in Lakeville inspecting handguns. That afternoon, he was to receive a religious certification of his qualifications as a pastor—a graduation of sorts—but did not bother to collect it. All in all, Bob Pelley was a hard man to figure out.

Born in northern Kentucky, raised in Ohio, Bob had, as his sister, Jon Boso, later recalled, an early call to the ministry. But after changing his mind and deciding to attend Youngstown State University in the late 1960s, he'd reversed himself yet again and enrolled in a religiously affiliated school. While attending Mount Vernon Nazarene University in Ohio, he'd met and married Ava Joy Armstrong, whose parents, Jack and Mary Armstrong, lived across the Ohio River from Cincinnati in Kenton County, Kentucky. A year or so after the marriage, Joy Pelley, as she was called, gave birth to Robert Jeffrey Pelley in Kenton County on December 10, 1971. A little less than three years after that, a daughter followed, Jacqueline Kay Pelley, known as Jacque. By that time, Bob Pelley had gone into the growing field of computer networking.

Both Bob and Joy were members, as were their respective families, of the Church of the Nazarene, an evangelical, missionary sect that believes that perfection of the soul is possible, in that Original Sin can be erased by the heartfelt acceptance of and perfect obedience to the Holy Spirit. As such, repudiation of one's prior sins, with sincere repentance, can cleanse the soul completely—one can be reborn in this life in the spirit of Jesus. The Nazarenes represent an offshoot, or refinement, of the ideas of the founder of Methodism, John Wesley. The church filled an important role in the Pelleys' lives, and that of their small children.

By the late 1970s, the Pelley family had relocated first to Orlando, Florida, and by 1979 or 1980 to Cape Coral, near Fort Myers. City directories there from that time show that Bob was employed as a "tech" for the local telephone company, United Telephone, until about 1984. Around that year, Bob changed jobs, taking a position with Landmark Bank, a South Florida financial institution. Bob worked in the bank's data processing headquarters in Fort Myers, a solid, fortress-like building with high security a mile or so east of the city's historic downtown district. Exactly what Bob did in the center wasn't entirely clear, later, but it appears that he had some role in keeping the bank's data network connected, so that the various branches' computers could talk to each other.

In the summer of 1983, Bob and Joy bought a small house in Cape Coral, just across the Caloosahatchee River estuary from Fort Myers, for a little over $64,000. The future seemed bright. Then tragedy struck: Joy Pelley was diagnosed with breast cancer.

On February 24, 1985, Joy Pelley died in the hospital in Fort Myers, at the age of 34. Bob Pelley was 33, Jeff was 13 and Jacque was 10.

Bob wouldn't let them cry, Jacque said later.

"That's the way we were raised," she said. "The day that Mom died, prior to her death, Dad sat us down on the couch. And he said, no matter whether she lived or died, we had to go on with our lives, and we weren't to be crying about it. And he told Jeff to go do his homework, and he told me that [a friend from church] was going to pick me up and take me to church with her, and I had to spend the night with her and go to school the next morning. And that was typical of Dad. I begged to stay at the house, and he made me go.

"I went to the church and the pastor met us at the door, and my mom had passed away . . ."

Jacque was sent to the bathroom at the church—apparently to compose herself—and when she emerged, she was put in a car and sent home.

"And I knew the whole way home that she had died. But we weren't allowed to cry about it. Dad came home to tell us later."

Six months later, that summer, at a family gathering in Ohio, Bob met Dawn Hayes Huber, a widowed mother of three daughters, Jessica, then 6, Janel, 5, and Jolene, 3. Dawn's first husband, Ed Huber, had died in an accident in Ohio, although some said it was actually suicide. By November 1985, Bob and Dawn had married.

The merger of the two families was not without difficulties. Jeff, for one, thought his father had been precipitate in joining with Dawn. The pain of losing his mother and seeing her replaced as the object of his father's affection so soon after Joy's death created resentments—of Dawn, and of

Bob. In Jeff's mind, his father seemed to have abandoned his original family for a new one. And in place of his mother was another, younger woman, who seemed diffident, altogether incapable of asserting herself, at least with Bob's children. Dawn was only thirteen years older than her stepson, who clearly wasn't happy with her sudden appearance in the previously close-knit lives of the Pelley family.

Then, sometime later, something happened—something that would be shrouded in mystery, confusion and rumor for the next two decades. As Jacque was to recall the story—fragmentary though it was to someone who was only 12 years old at the time she first heard about it—there was a problem at the bank. Money had gone missing, so the story went, perhaps as much as a million dollars. Or possibly there was a problem with money-laundering—Jacque never knew the details. But one night in the fall of 1986, as she recalled, her father got a telephone call summoning him to the bank's fortress-like computer headquarters in Fort Myers. The following night, according to Jacque, the Pelleys were leaving Cape Coral.

As Jacque put it later, they left in the middle of the night, for a place they had never been before; and even more significantly, they changed their religious denomination—no longer were they of the Church of the Nazarene, now they were members of the United Brethren. The next thing Jacque knew, they were all in Lakeville, Indiana, just a few miles south of South Bend, where her father had taken a position as the pastor of the Olive Branch Church on Osborne Road. Bob had transformed himself from a promising computer maven into a fairly impoverished, evangelical preacher, in a small, out-of-the-way place in northern Indiana.

What had caused her father to abruptly take his family out of Cape Coral? Over the years, there were bits and pieces, fragments of whatever had happened that no one really talked about. There was something about some sort of dispute with superiors at the bank . . . the bank had recently been acquired by a larger bank, but not before some employees of the old bank had been caught up in a fifty-million-dollar money-laundering scandal involving a Colombian, who was washing cocaine proceeds for the Cali cartel. The Colombian had been arrested just a month before Joy Pelley died. Three bank employees were arrested for cooking the bank's books to permit the laundering. Was this why her father had suddenly pulled up stakes in Southwest Florida, to move to, of all places, Lakeville, Indiana? Was this why he'd abandoned his career in the then-burgeoning computerized banking field to become a pastor in such an out-of-the-way place as Lakeville, Indiana—and at a church of a different denomination, at a fraction of his former salary? Did Bob Pelley know too much? Was someone willing to kill the entire family to keep Bob's mouth shut?

Jacque didn't know. But the seeds of doubt and suspicion—of Florida, of the banks, of the drug pushers and later, even of the police in both Indiana and Florida—were sown. And when, many years later, the effort to find out just who had so callously murdered the Pelley family bore fruit in a criminal prosecution, Jacque would have some ideas of her own.

CHAPTER 3

Lakeville, Indiana, is a spot on the road transversing a mostly flat plain cut by numerous sloughs running down to the banks of the north-flowing St. Joseph River, which rolls through northern Indiana on its way to Lake Michigan. It represents a divide of sorts—waters south of Lakeville drain to the Ohio-Mississippi watershed, while those to the north owe their allegiance to the Great Lakes. Travelers through the region will occasionally encounter a sign: the Continental Divide, not that of the Rocky Mountains, but of the lesser-known division between the origin waters of the Atlantic and the Caribbean, some to the north, others to the south.

In earlier centuries, the St. Joseph River provided a useful portage for the French *coeur de bois*—the woodsmen of the fur-trapping trade, linking the Great Lakes to the Mississippi. In later years, the site of the portage trail grew into the commercial-industrial city of South Bend, more familiarly known to all America as the home of the University of Notre Dame. Although Notre Dame is one of America's finest academic institutions, when Americans think of South Bend and its university, they are apt to think first of Knute Rockne, Grantland Rice, the Four Horsemen of the Apocalypse, the Gipper (the original, not his on-screen imitator, Ronald Reagan), or even Ara Parseghian—the Fighting Irish, as they are called.

South Bend is also the home of the College Football Hall of Fame, as well as a museum dedicated to the late, now often lamented Studebaker automobile. But apart from its nationally known university, South Bend is mostly a working-class town, held together by railroads that long ago replaced the birch-bark canoes of those intrepid, mosquito-bitten, cursing French paddlers, the intrepid woodsmen of an earlier age.

South of South Bend, on the crown of the watersheds of Indiana, in places like Lakeville, the real cash crops have always been corn, soybeans, hay and wheat, not touchdowns. Football has always been a matter of pride in South Bend, but south of town, it doesn't pay the bills.

Osborne Road is a small thread of blacktop that veers off U.S. Highway 31, also known as the Dixie Highway, the central link between northern Indiana and the capital of Indianapolis in the mid-southern portion of the state. About five miles south of South Bend, and running east and west across Highway 31, Osborne Road passes expansive fields that rise and fall gently with the contours of the land. Anyone who stops to look will see hundreds of acres of fertile farmland, separated by two-hundred-year-old trees planted by pioneers back in the day when Tippecanoe had Tyler, too.

In fact—actually, a little-known fact—the area was once an early haven for African Americans desirous of establishing their own free community, well beyond the penumbra of the oppression of slavery to the south in Kentucky, and . . . Dixie.

Slightly to the west of Highway 31, a small lane, Maple Road, runs north and south, dead-ending at State Route Four. About a mile farther west, just past the Olive Branch United Brethren Church, another north-south road, Mulberry, all of twenty-five feet of weather-debilitated blacktop, runs all the way to Quinn Road, a mile or so south of State Route Four. Quinn Road in turn runs east, back to Highway 31, at the south end of Lakeville. Between these two rural lanes, Maple and Mulberry, on the south side of Osborne Road, separated by expansive fields of newly planted corn and hay, was the killing ground for Bob Pelley, his wife, Dawn, and Dawn's two youngest daughters, on the next-to-last day of April 1989. And it was this geography, or at least the time and distance to traverse it, that was to prove crucial as the next two decades unfolded.

* * *

Like many rural areas around the country, St. Joseph County had to maximize its police resources when it came to some crimes. As some put it later, the county was the place to dump victims of murder from the city of South Bend, usually the nexus of the original crime. The St. Joseph County police—equivalent to the sheriff's department in other jurisdictions—had to do little in the way of murder, other than to process the bodies, identify the victims, and then call upon their compatriots in the city to figure out just who had done what to whom.

But as a result, both the city and the county knew how to work with each other; and both agencies could draw on help from the Indiana State Police, as well as the St. Joseph County Prosecutor's Office, if needed. Experts from all of these agencies were sometimes called together when a major crime occurred.

The murder of four people—a man, his wife and two young girls—was by any definition a major crime in St. Joseph County, probably the worst in the history of northern Indiana. By late morning on Sunday, April 30, 1989, a deputy district attorney, Jack Krisor, and an Indiana State Police investigator, Mark Senter, were already on their way to Osborne Road. As it happened, Senter was already familiar with the Pelley family.

Meanwhile, just before noon on the same day, a St. Joseph County detective, Sergeant John Botich, was at a house he was building for himself and his family in east Lakeville. A dispatcher from the county department directed him to an address on Osborne Road a few miles away. The killings had occurred at a church, Botich was told, and the scene was particularly ugly.

At the house, Botich was met by several uniformed deputies from the county police, who briefly described the carnage—one adult male, dead from apparent gunshot wounds in an upstairs hallway, one adult female, dead in the basement from another gunshot wound. Lying in close proximity to the adult female were the bodies of two young girls, who, like the adults, had also been shot in the head. It could not have been a murder-suicide, Botich was informed—there was no gun near any of the bodies. In fact, there weren't even any shell casings.

Based on a cursory visual inspection of the injuries, it looked as though all had been killed with blasts from a shotgun firing lead slugs—deer slugs, as they were called, usually used to hunt large game in the woods of northern Indiana.

While waiting for the county's crime-scene technicians to arrive, Botich assembled some additional facts from the patrol deputies, who had been talking to some of the church members, and Indiana State Police Investigator Senter, who had just arrived. There were three other Pelley children, he learned—Jessica, Jacque and Jeff. Where were they? Botich soon learned that 9-year-old Jessica had been spending the weekend with a friend in La Paz, another small town south of Lakeville; that Jacque had been visiting friends at Huntington University in Huntington, Indiana, some miles away; and that Jeff was with a group of fellow students who'd attended the LaVille High School prom the night before, and were even then on their way to Six Flags Great America amusement park in Gurnee, Illinois, north of Chicago.

Calls were made to La Paz and Huntington, and soon Jessica and Jacque were on their way back to Lakeville, while other efforts were made to see which group of teenage promgoers Jeff might be riding with. But Botich soon learned from Senter and others that there might be more to Jeff's movements than had first appeared.

Jeff, it seemed, had been grounded by his father some weeks before. At first, he had been so angry at his 17-year-old son that Bob had forbidden him to attend the prom. After hearing that Jeff's girlfriend, Darla Emmons, had bought a new dress just for the event, he'd relented—but said he would drive Jeff and his date to the dance, and pick them up afterward. Jeff would not be allowed to attend the after-prom party at a nearby bowling alley, and under no circumstances would he be allowed to go with his friends to the amusement park the following day.

Bob, according to his confidants in the church, was adamant: his eldest child, his only son, had to pay the price for his transgressions: he had lost the privileges of adulthood, at least temporarily—letting Jeffrey loose on the roads and highways with a girlfriend, to Bob, was an invitation to disaster. And Bob had told Jeff exactly how he felt.

Jeff had felt angered and belittled by this—father and son had been squabbling over the issue for days, according to some of the congregation. As late as Saturday afternoon, some church members said, Bob was insistent—under no circumstances would Jeff be allowed to drive his own car, a 1984 silver Ford Mustang, to the prom, which was to be held in an Elks Lodge in South Bend on Saturday night. In fact, Bob had cancelled the insurance on the car, hidden the keys, and even removed parts from the car so it could not be driven.

Yet on this Sunday morning, Jeff's car was missing.

The crime-scene technicians soon arrived and entered the house, Botich keeping back until they had finished their work. One expert took still photographs of each of the rooms, while another wielded a video camera. Others measured distances between victims and walls, while still others looked through the dwelling for anything that might shed light on what had happened.

Finally, Botich entered the house, through the rear door, to see for himself. Accompanied by Senter, he noticed what appeared to be an unwashed bowl with a spoon in it on the kitchen counter. He saw the eyeglasses at the corner of the entrance to the kitchen, at the end of the hallway leading directly to the front door. He saw Bob Pelley's supine body, right arm curled halfway up, left arm extended down, a packet of folded papers, a small notebook, and a ballpoint pen near his head, down the east hallway.

The pen, in fact, was standing on one end, its top resting against the side of Bob's head. It looked as though Bob might have had the pen behind his left ear when he was shot, while carrying the papers and notebook in his left hand. These had fallen to the floor just over his left shoulder. The gap between the papers and notebook, and the downstretched left arm, seemed peculiar, a contradiction. But perhaps, in his last seconds of life, Bob's left arm had flopped forward, his right arm curled backward. Who could say? In any scene of violent murder, Botich knew, it was often impossible to draw conclusions as to what had happened from the position of the body alone; violence tends to change things unexpectedly, and the act of dying confounds logic.

There were two large wounds, almost certainly from a small-bore shotgun, one in Bob's right chest area, and a second to his neck and chin. It looked like the killer had hit Bob in the chest first, knocking him flat on his back, in the process casting the glasses toward the front entrance hall, and then had fired a second shot directly into his neck and jaw from a few feet away. Whoever had shot Bob, this was definitely up close and personal, indicating, possibly, a passionate rage.

From Bob's outstretched feet—he was wearing rubber-soled sneakers—there was a distance of perhaps four or five feet to the end of the hall, where there were four doors: one to the left that led to a bedroom, a closet door directly at the end of the hall, another bedroom to the right, and a bathroom immediately to the right of Bob's waist. Inside the bathroom, Botich noticed three washcloths draped over the side of the tub. One was dry, one was slightly damp and one was wetter, although not dripping. Inside the tub, Botich could see water droplets still shining on the bathmat.

Botich made his way back down the hall to the kitchen-dining area, then to the door that led to the basement. From the top of the stairs, Botich could see two adult-sized feet, clad in white socks. As he descended, the rest of the horror came into view: Dawn Pelley, lying mostly on her right side, with little Jolene on the left, bent at the knees with her arms around her mother; and Janel, lower legs near Dawn's left-turned face, with her own head off to the side near the west wall. A sofa along the north wall was fronted by two small coffee tables just past the bodies.

Both girls were clad in shorts and T-shirts, while Dawn was wearing blue jeans and a white sweater with lettering—"Chicago," it read, or at least as much as Botich could see. Blood spatter covered the west wall and the ceiling. Brain matter, forced out of the heads of the victims by the gunshots, was found to the north and west of the bodies. It appeared that each had been shot at close range, almost certainly with a shotgun. From the configuration of the three victims, it looked like Dawn had been shot first, falling to the floor. Then, as the two girls knelt down beside her, each had been shot in turn, execution-style.

More blood spatter could be seen on the coffee tables, and on books lying atop the tables. One book, in fact, held a portion of what looked to be a solid lead, half-inch deer slug fired from a shotgun.

A plastic container of popped popcorn was on the desk to the east that Bob Pelley normally used as his office. Altogether, it looked as though the killer or killers had fired at least five shots, possibly six, and maybe even seven.

It was gruesome.

CHAPTER 4

After Botich had looked over the murder scenes, he consulted again with the evidence technicians, who filled him in on what they had found. In a large storage room just south of the basement office–family room, a washing machine held a very small number of recently washed garments. The clothing was still affixed to the drum of the washer, as if it had been spun-dried and left. An empty nylon case for a long gun was found behind a pile of rolled-up sleeping bags.

Upstairs, a gun rack hung from the wall of the bedroom shared by Bob and Dawn. Other than a bow and a few arrows, it was empty. In the open top drawer of a bureau in the same room, there was a single shotgun shell, buckshot and two tarnished rifle cartridges of fairly large size. The rest of the bureau top and drawer was composed of the normal detritus of life—a bottle of English Leather cologne, an empty key ring, a prescription bottle, a tin of Tylenol, shoelaces, an old pocket watch, a small screwdriver, an eraser, a few pens and scraps of paper, the envelope from a recent telephone bill.

The small living room upstairs contained two plaid-covered armchairs, a matching sofa, a coffee table and a wall unit containing a television, VCR and stereo. On an end table next to the sofa there was another empty plastic Tupperware bowl with a spoon in it; it appeared that someone might have been eating cereal, possibly cornflakes. Next to the empty bowl was a white sock with a lacy top. An identical white sock was on the coffee table. Underneath, a newspaper was folded over, a local free advertiser. In the two other bedrooms, Botich observed other things: in one, a camera in its case lay on the bed; in a second, the one that had apparently been occupied by Jeff Pelley, was a book, also on the bed: *Our Baby's First Seven Years*.

Sometime around two that afternoon, Dr. Rick Hoover, a forensic pathologist employed on contract by the county, happened to drive by the parsonage and noticed all the emergency vehicles. As it happened, Hoover lived about a mile west of the church, also on Osborne Road. Out of curiosity, he stopped his car to see what was going on.

Told of the murders, Hoover gained admittance to the scene, thinking he might be able to help the detectives by interpreting the blood spatter on the walls, a comparatively new area of interest for Hoover. He first examined the area where Bob had been found. Here, the blood drops along the baseboard and nearby wall were small—less than a millimeter. The near–mist-like pattern told Hoover that Bob had been down on the hallway floor when the second shot was fired—that was the only way a mist-like pattern on the baseboard could have been cast.

Downstairs, Hoover examined the blood spatter on the walls of the basement, and the spatter on the ceiling. It was clear from the patterns, as well as the brain matter that had been expelled from the heads of the victims, that the killer had been quite close to the victims when he fired—in the case of little Jolene, less than a foot away.

But Hoover did not inspect the bodies. In fact, he did not touch them at all.

"I did not want to contribute to anything that might disturb the crime scene," he said later. He had only come to look at the blood spatter evidence, and even that was only on the sufferance of the police—having a forensic pathologist conduct an on-site examination of murder victims wasn't part of accepted police procedure, at least in St. Joseph County. (In all fairness, it usually isn't normal procedure in other counties, either—not even in large metropolitan areas like Los Angeles County, where professional medical personnel are usually the last to know about a murder.)

"So my role there was kind of one that, we were just feeling our way," Hoover said later. "So I really, as I recall, did not even touch the bodies. I was there to basically observe, and I was there primarily to observe blood spatter."

Yet this segregation of responsibilities would have profound consequences. Because Hoover was only inspecting the blood spatter—in an effort to gain experience in that rather specialized field—no one took responsibility for performing one of the most fundamental tasks in any homicide investigation: attempting to determine the approximate time of death. This would be a critical oversight, as matters later developed.

Ordinarily, there are several anatomical indicators of time of death. While pinpointing the time within hours or even minutes is a staple of detective fiction—particularly of the English variety, in which the time of a murder is often the linchpin of the mystery's solution—it doesn't work that way in real life.

That's why many pathologists today refuse to officially specify a time of death, either in writing or in court testimony. Often, in fact, a pathologist will testify that the time of death is between the time a person was last seen alive and the time they were found dead, which can cover a rather wide span.

Nevertheless, there are biological indicators that, taken together and placed into environmental context, can narrow the time rather considerably. And in cases where a window of opportunity to commit murder is very small, making at least some attempt to perform these anatomical estimates on-site can be crucial. The complete absence of any such efforts to estimate the time of death was to prove critical to the Pelley case over the next decade-and-a-half.

One method of assessing the time of death, often referred to in fiction or on television, is the assessment of rigor mortis—the stiffening of muscles that generally begins within, say, six hours of death, and begins to abate around twelve hours later. Determined by touch and manipulation, the extent of rigor can give a clue as to the time of death.

Another, related method involves lividity, that is, the pooling of blood in the lower portions of the body. Pulled by gravity once the heart stops beating, blood tends to sink. The extent of lividity, indicated by the degree of reddish or purple coloring of skin on the parts of the body closest to the ground or floor, can suggest the length of time a body has lain undisturbed.

A third method is to take samples of the body's temperature. As a general rule, a body loses its heat after death at a rate of approximately one and a half degrees an hour. Often a diligent on-site pathologist will extract a reading from the victim's liver in order to calculate an approximate time of death. A figure above the ambient room temperature indicates a fairly recent death, while one equivalent to room temperature suggests one that took place many hours earlier—after all, descending from over 98.6 to, say, 70 degrees can take a number of hours.

A fourth method involves examination of the condition of the eyes, particularly the chemical composition, which changes as time elapses after death.

All of these indicators are then combined, and placed into the context of the environment—chiefly, what the room or area temperature has been over the time preceding discovery of the body. Cooler temperatures retard rigor mortis, while speeding up loss of body heat. Warmer temperatures act in the opposite way.

Despite these techniques of narrowing down the time of death of the four Pelleys, no one at the parsonage conducted any of these examinations. Had they been undertaken—had they demonstrated that it was more likely the murders had been committed less than, say, six hours before their discovery—the outcome of the Pelley case might have been very different.

Sometime that Sunday morning, Jessica arrived from La Paz, driven to the parsonage by the family she'd been spending the weekend with. One of the detectives asked her if she knew where Jeff was.

"Great America," Jessica said. Now this was a contradiction—hadn't Bob told several church members on Saturday afternoon that Jeff would not be allowed to attend the after-prom party at the bowling alley, or go to Great America? And hadn't Jessica been out of the house since Friday afternoon? How could she know that Jeff was at Great America unless Bob had relented by Friday afternoon? Had he then reversed himself by Saturday? Had something else happened between Jeff and his father after Jessica had left for La Paz?

Or was Bob saying one thing to Jeff and the family, and another thing entirely to church members, even that same afternoon? The contradictions were piling up. It wasn't supposed to work that way in the textbook on how to investigate murder. In the book, once the prime suspect was identified, all the evidence was supposed to point to his guilt, not undermine it. It was becoming imperative to reconstruct the last hours of the Pelley family—who had seen them, and what they'd said.

A few hours after Jessica's arrival at the parsonage, Jacque also returned, driven back to Lakeville by a United Brethren church official affiliated with Huntington University. Jacque could hardly believe what had happened. It was simply too bizarre. But then the rumors about the missing bank money, or the money-laundering, or whatever it was that had happened in Florida, came to her mind, and she began to wonder if her father, stepmother and stepsisters had been murdered by some sort of cabal of organized crime.

By late afternoon, Jack and Mary Armstrong, Joy Pelley's father and mother and Jeff and Jacque's maternal grandparents, arrived from Kentucky. Police assured them they'd find Jeff at Great America, notify him and bring him back to Lakeville. The Armstrongs took Jacque with them, and checked in to a South Bend hotel. Edward and Lara Hayes, Dawn Huber Pelley's father and mother, and Jessica's maternal grandparents, also arrived from Eaton Rapids, Michigan, and took custody of Jessica.

By early that afternoon, even before Jacque and Jessica returned to the parsonage, Botich, Senter, Krisor, Botich's supervisor Lieutenant Jerry Rutkowski, and Sergeant John

Pavlekovich, the supervising criminalist, were seated around the Pelley dining room table, discussing what to do next.

Senter, who had known the Pelley family, filled the others in.

He'd known Bob casually, Senter said—the Lakeville Lions Club held its monthly meetings in the church. Then one day in early April, he continued, he'd seen a crime report about a residential burglary of a young man who lived on Osborne Road, near its intersection with Highway 31. According to the report, the young man claimed that his house had been robbed in mid-March, and that Jeff Pelley, a friend of his younger brother, had admitted being in the house around the time the stuff was taken.

It hadn't been a large rip-off—less than $100 in cash, some coins, and about forty compact discs, which were just then coming into popular use.

Since he knew Bob Pelley, Senter continued, he called him up to tell him of the allegation. A few days later, Bob brought Jeff to the state police barracks in Bremen, Indiana. Jeff was contrite, and readily confessed to the burglary. It turned out that this hadn't been Jeff's first trouble, either—about a year before, he'd been caught shoplifting, breaking into cars at a mall, smoking marijuana and had later forged a check from the church ladies' fund that had been administered by Dawn. Dawn had made him stand up before the assembled ladies and apologize.

A few days after Jeff's confession in Bremen, Senter said, he'd met with Bob and Dawn in the church, and the three of them discussed Jeff, and what to do. Bob was anxious about his son's record—he thought a formal arrest and court proceeding might ruin Jeff's life.

Jeff, it appeared, was a very smart kid, but someone who was obviously in conflict with his father, and, particularly, his stepmother. Angry at his father's remarriage, at the move from cosmopolitan Florida to small-town Indiana, resentful at parental restrictions, he was torn between a boy's desire for his father's support and affection, and a conflicting adult desire to make his own way in the world.

Jeff's relationship with his girlfriend, Darla Emmons, worried the parental Pelleys. The family had been in counseling in South Bend for more than a year, and at one point, distraught over the rapid changes in his life and the distancing he felt from his father, Jeff had threatened to commit suicide.

In the end, Senter agreed not to bring charges against Jeff, as long as Bob agreed to repay the young man who had been burgled, and Jeff apologized to his victim. In addition, Bob promised to monitor Jeff far more closely—in fact, Bob said, he'd take away Jeff's car until the fall by cancelling the insurance, and disabling it.

But Jeff's car was now missing from the crime scene.

There were a few other things also missing from the crime scene. A weapon, for instance. Or bloody clothing, or shoes. And shell casings. Still, a theory of the crimes quickly formed in the minds of those around the dead Pelleys' kitchen table: Jeff, angry at being treated as a kid by his father, forbidden to drive his date to the prom, had used a small-bore, pump-action shotgun to shoot his father twice, then his stepmother and two stepsisters downstairs. Next, after calmly stripping off his clothes, dropping them into the washing machine and starting it, he'd picked up three or four shell casings from the basement floor.

Then, naked, he would have gone back upstairs, picked up two more shell casings from the hallway, perhaps washed himself in the bathroom, maybe even taken a shower, then put on more clothes. Then he would have drawn all the curtains, turned out all the lights, locked all the doors, and taken his prom tuxedo, the shotgun and the shell casings out to his car.

Somewhere on the road to pick up his prom date, Jeff would have ditched the shotgun and the casings, then driven on to pick up Darla, where he would have changed into his tuxedo, then gone to the dance for his alibi.

The consensus around the table was that Jeff, in the phrase that had then recently come into vogue, was at least "a person of interest" in the murders of his own family. But first, they would have to canvass the nearby neighbors to see if anyone had seen or heard anything unusual the night before.

The main priority, Botich and the others decided, was to sit down with Jeff Pelley and see what he had to say. Then came word: police in Gurnee, Illinois, asked a few hours earlier for assistance by the St. Joseph County authorities, had located Jeff, Darla and other post-prom party attendees at the amusement park. They were holding the entire group, waiting for Botich and Rutkowski to drive up and collect them.

CHAPTER 5

The word that four members of a family had been murdered in Lakeville quickly spread, and even as Botich, Senter and the others in the parsonage were discussing what to do next, the South Bend news media were already on the scene.

As usual, the television people were the most aggressive. One camera crew was already inside the church itself, panning over the altar.

Dave Hathaway was horrified.

"What are you doing?" he demanded.

"We're getting a picture of the church," he was told.

"No, you're not," Hathaway said. "I'll give you to the count of ten to get your fannies out of here."

The television people saw that Hathaway meant what he said. They pulled back and went after the church members who remained in the parking lot.

Hathaway was then 66 years old. A veteran of the Battle of Okinawa in World War II, where he'd helped to build airstrips on the small island of Iejima, he'd seen more than his share of carnage and death. At one point, while spending the night in a foxhole in the midst of an intense firefight on the small island, he'd made a promise.

"I said, 'Lord, if you can get me out of this, I'm yours,' " Hathaway recalled, more than half a century later. He'd made it through the night, then the battle and the war, and then come back from the Pacific, married, fathered children and taken up a trade delivering heating oil near South Bend, his promise to God unredeemed. Then, in 1957, the board at the church—

Hathaway attended sporadically, while his wife attended without fail—asked Hathaway if he wouldn't mind being the Sunday school superintendent.

Hathaway temporized. Then he heard a voice:

"What'd you tell me back when you were in that foxhole?"

So Hathaway agreed to be the Sunday school superintendent, and once he got involved in the church, it began to grow: from fewer than 30 members, to more than 120 in five years.

So Hathaway felt very protective of the Olive Branch United Brethren Church in Christ, and he wasn't about to let some sensation-seeking television creeps profane it.

Later, Hathaway worried that he might have been too hard on them; it was probably bad public relations, Hathaway knew that much. The church's conference chairman, based in Michigan, called him for an update after hearing the news about the murders on television. Hathaway ended by explaining that he'd chased the television people out of the church, expecting at least gentle criticism, if not a reprimand.

"Dave," the chairman told him, "you did exactly right."

After the shock of discovering the bodies, Dave Hathaway also called his son Keith, who was a police officer in a nearby Indiana town. He told Keith what had happened at the parsonage. Keith rushed over to see if he could help. As the afternoon progressed, Keith talked to many church members, most of whom he'd known his whole life.

That night, Keith had turned to his father. "If they don't solve it within twenty-four hours," he told Dave, "they can kiss it goodbye."

At 9:30 that morning, even as Stephanie Fagan had been trying to get into the parsonage, Jeff and Darla were on their way to the amusement park north of Chicago, accompanied by another couple, Tony Springer and Sonya Swan. The trip to Great America was to cap the previous night's festivities, which had begun with a dinner at an upscale restaurant in South Bend and continued with the prom dance at the Elks

Lodge in South Bend, followed by the after-prom party at a nearby bowling alley.

About a dozen kids wound up at the house of one of Jeff and Darla's classmates, Kim Oldenburg, where most grabbed a few hours' sleep in the basement, before heading north for the amusement park at about 8 on Sunday morning.

Darla drove her car, with Jeff, Tony and Sonya as passengers, while Kim and her date, David Shoemaker, drove with another couple in Jeff's Mustang. Two other cars followed them; altogether, the car caravan included about fourteen people, evenly divided between girls and boys, most of whom had known each other for years.

Reaching the amusement park about 11, all bought tickets and went in to enjoy the rides. But at one point, just before noon, Jeff grew quiet.

"What's wrong?" Darla asked. She thought that Jeff looked a little pale. Her first thought was that he was just tired from getting too little sleep, or perhaps that one of the rides had upset his stomach.

But it wasn't that, Jeff told her.

"I've got a bad feeling," he said.

"Like what?"

"I don't know, I can't explain it. It's like something's wrong."

"*What*'s wrong?"

"I don't know, but . . ." Jeff dropped the subject, and Darla decided not to pursue it.

Then, a few hours later, Jeff, Darla, Tony and Sonya were in the park's gift shop when several men approached them, some in the uniform of park security officers.

"Are you Jeff?" one of the uniformed men asked.

Jeff acknowledged that he was.

Jeff and Darla were escorted to a back room of the gift shop, leaving Tony and Sonya out in front. In the back, a man in plain clothes who identified himself as a Gurnee police detective frisked both Jeff and Darla for weapons.

"What time did you leave home this morning?" the detective asked.

"I wasn't home all night," Jeff said. "What's this about?" But the detective wouldn't say.

The next thing Jeff and Darla knew, they were being taken with Tony to the park's security office. Sonya was asked to help other police officers round up the remainder of their group. At the security office, the Gurnee detective told Jeff that his father, stepmother and stepsisters were dead, but would give him no details. Jeff did not say anything to this news, and apparently, according to later accounts, asked no questions. Then they set off for the Gurnee police station to wait for the Indiana authorities to arrive.

On the way to the station, Jeff was "very quiet," Darla recalled later—"very sad."

By 6 that night, Botich and Rutkowski were on their way to Gurnee to pick up Jeff and Darla.

"We were kind of shocked they found him so fast," Botich recalled later. "We figured it would be like looking for a needle in a haystack." But the Gurnee police had license plates for some of the cars in the caravan, and it wasn't long before they'd seen two of the group approaching one of the listed cars in the parking lot. One identification had led to another, and within a few minutes, the Gurnee police found Jeff and Darla in the park itself.

Based on Senter's background on the Pelley family and its recent tensions, and the way the victims were shot—particularly the fact that Bob had been shot by someone standing at the bedroom end of the hallway, which implied intimate familiarity with the house—Botich and Rutkowski had already formed an idea about the motive for the murders.

Jeff, they believed, had made up his mind to drive his own car to the prom, no matter what, and if he couldn't convince Bob to let him use his Mustang, he was prepared to kill his father, his stepmother, and anyone else who was in the house. The crimes, they thought, were so cold-blooded as to stagger the imagination. Four murders, just to go to a dance.

Botich and Rutkowski arrived in Gurnee shortly after 9 P.M. Jeff and Darla were being held in separate interview rooms, while the rest of the Lakeville group were together in a larger room. By this time, some of the other teenagers were losing their patience. The Gurnee police wouldn't tell them why they were being held.

"All they told us, it had something to do with Jeff, and we didn't know what," Mark Berger, one of the group, recalled later. "Then I got mad and I pretty much told them I had a three- or four-hour drive home, and somebody better start telling me what is going on."

Besides that, Berger added, they were all hungry. With that, the Gurnee police treated them to pizza. But they still weren't letting anyone leave.

Botich and Rutkowski talked to Jeff first, once they arrived, and for the first time, he was told that his father and stepmother had been murdered, along with the two little girls.

"He really didn't say anything to that," Botich recalled. "He didn't even ask how they had been murdered." Botich explained that they weren't going to ask any questions at that point, that they were just going to escort Jeff and Darla back to South Bend, where Jeff's grandparents and Darla's parents were waiting. The cars would have to remain in Gurnee for the time being.

The two detectives talked to Darla separately, telling her that Jeff's father and stepmother had been shot to death.

"She was shocked," Botich recalled. "She didn't say much." But Darla remembered the strange incident with Jeff earlier in the day, when Jeff had told her that he had a "bad feeling," that something was wrong.

"When was this?" Botich asked.

"About eleven-thirty," Darla said.

That fits, Botich thought—*That's just about the time that Jeff would know that the bodies would have been found.* Well, of course, the bodies had been found an hour or so earlier; but Botich believed that the enormity—the reality—of what he had done, and the fact that the police would soon be questioning him, hadn't actually registered with Jeff until just before noon. The idea that someone by then had almost certainly discovered his father, stepmother and stepsisters shotgunned to death had made Jeff queasy with the expectation of the ordeal of investigation he would now be facing—or so Botich believed.

Botich and Rutkowski talked to a few others from the caravan from Lakeville. Had anyone made any unscheduled stops on the trip north, or had they gotten separated at any point? Anyone see anybody throw anything away? But the answers were all negative.

Finally, about 10, the group was released. Darla was allowed to call her parents, who offered to drive to Gurnee to pick her up, but Darla said no, the police were going to drive them back to Lakeville.

On the way home, in the rear of the car driven by Botich and Rutkowski, Jeff and Darla sat for the most part in silence.

"I didn't do this," Jeff finally said. "You believe me, don't you?"

"I don't know," Darla said.

CHAPTER 6

By around 3:30 in the morning of May 1, Botich and Rutkowski had returned to South Bend with their teenage passengers. They went to the county jail, which housed the police detective bureau in the basement. Jack and Mary Armstrong had been summoned from their hotel, and Darla's parents had also arrived. After some brief additional questioning, Darla was allowed to go home with her parents.

Jack and Mary had a private talk with Jeff. Then, just after 4:30, Botich began a formal interview with Jeff—this one videotaped, and witnessed by Rutkowski and Deputy Prosecutor Krisor.

"Looking back," Botich said later, "I made a bad mistake, with Grandma and Grandpa being there, on either side of him. With them there, he felt safe." But because Jeff was a minor and entitled to have a guardian present for any interview, Botich had little choice. That was Krisor's advice to the police. Krisor assumed that Jack Armstrong was a viable legal guardian for Jeff. And why not? Jack Armstrong was the only adult within conversational distance of Jeff at that point, the Hayes side of the family having taken Jessica back to Michigan.

Botich began by proffering a written Miranda waiver, one specially tailored for a juvenile. He advised Jeff and the Armstrongs that Jeff had a right to consult with a lawyer before answering any questions.

"How long it will take to get a lawyer here, in case we want one?" Jack Armstrong asked. Jack was no fool—he knew that the police had already decided his grandson had to be the murderer. Not that he believed it—he was sure the cops wanted to close the case as fast as they could by laying it on the most vulnerable suspect.

Botich didn't answer the question directly, noting only that any time they felt a lawyer was necessary, he would stop the questioning. Apparently satisfied with this, Jeff signed the waiver. So did Jack and Mary Armstrong.

For someone who had been up for the better part of forty-eight hours, with only a few hours' sleep, Jeff seemed remarkably alert. His eyes focused directly on Botich. His responses were crisp and cogent. By this point he could have had little doubt that Botich and Rutkowski believed he was the killer—a 4-in-the-morning interview made *that* much clear. Yet he answered all of Botich's questions forthrightly, maintaining eye contact with the detective. Jack and Mary sat silently on either side of him, Jack looking faintly sick, while Mary periodically dabbed at her eyes. As with Jacque, who had been left at the hotel, the entire situation seemed too bizarre for them to fully comprehend.

But the overwhelming impression left by the video was of Jeff Pelley's extreme youth—his reedy teenage voice wavered, not yet completely matured; his face was blemished, his bushy hair too long, his physique that of a boy who had yet to turn into a man. Botich wasn't sure whether he was dealing with a cold-blooded murderer or a displaced child. Yet Jeff's callowness was contradicted by his skill at articulation—he wielded his verbosity as the deftest of shields, his brainpower nascent below the surface of his youth.

"When was the last time you were home?" Botich asked Jeff.

"At about quarter to five, Saturday afternoon."

Botich made a note, then asked Jeff to describe his activities from Saturday morning.

He'd gotten up early on Saturday to go to work, Jeff said. He had a job as a cook at a local McDonald's, north on Highway 31. His shift supervisor, Brenda Hale, had picked him up around 4:30 A.M. He'd worked at the McDonald's until 11

A.M., when his father, Bob, had come to pick him up. They'd returned to the parsonage shortly thereafter. Just before noon, he'd washed his car, with Janel and Jolene helping him. Then he, Bob, Janel and Jolene had gone inside the parsonage for lunch. Dawn had left earlier that day to go to a Girl Scout meeting—she was active in the local organization.

After lunch, Jeff continued, his father had visited several church families in the immediate area, as he often did. After Bob had left, Jeff got his clothes ready for the after-prom activities, and put them into the trunk of his car. Then he'd watched the Cardinals and Dodgers play baseball on television.

His father had returned around 4 P.M., Jeff went on, and Dawn had come in about ten minutes after that. Just before 5, he said, he'd put his tuxedo in his car, and driven off to pick up Darla to go to dinner and the prom.

"Before you left, did anyone come over to your house?"

"Yes, Kim Oldenburg came over with David Shoemaker," Jeff said. "Because I used to date Kim Oldenburg, and my dad and her are real good friends, and my dad wanted to see her in her dress."

"Just the two of them came over?"

Jeff shook his head slightly. "Her mom, and her brother and her brother's friend were with them, and then Matt Miller stopped by while they were there." Miller was also attending the prom, as the date for Kris Holmgren, who lived with her family farther west on Osborne Road. But seeing Kim Oldenburg's corsage, Matt suddenly remembered that he'd left Kris's flowers at home in his refrigerator, so he rushed back to his house in La Paz to retrieve them. "He was just there for one minute, and he had to run back out because he forgot the flowers for his date, so he had to go back home." Jeff chuckled, remembering Matt Miller's oversight.

"This about four-thirty?" Botich asked.

It was, Jeff said.

"Were they still there when you left?"

"No—they left about quarter 'til, I suppose. I must've left

four or five minutes after them. I put my tux in the car, I put my radio in the car, and I left right after they did."

He'd driven south to La Paz to pick up Darla at her friend Lynette Greer's house. When he arrived, Darla was already there—Lynette's mom had helped Darla fix her hair. Lynette's date, Mark Berger, was also already there. Jeff changed into his tuxedo, Lynette's sister took some pictures, then Jeff and Darla left in Jeff's Mustang, stopping to pick up another couple, Jenny Barton and Eric Gockle, on the way.

Mark and Lynette had gone ahead to the restaurant, the Emporium, which was on the bank of the East Race of the St. Joseph River in downtown South Bend. His supervisor at McDonald's, Brenda Hale, had given him a $50 gift certificate for the Emporium on Friday night to enable him to pay for the dinner.

After dining at the restaurant, he and Darla, accompanied by Eric and Jenny, had gone to the prom at the Elks Lodge. About midnight, Tony Springer and Sonya Swan had joined Jeff and Darla in Jeff's car, while Eric and Jenny found another ride home. Jeff's group had driven to Tony Springer's house, where they changed out of their tuxedos, and left them there for someone in Tony's family to return to the rental shop in Lakeville the next day.

The foursome next drove to Sonya's house, where the girls changed out of their prom dresses. They then went to the after-prom party at Chippewa Bowl. They left at about 3 in the morning, and drove to Kim Oldenburg's house, where people were gathering for the trip to Great America. There, most had slept for a few hours on the floor of the basement.

The next morning, Jeff had driven Darla back to Lynette's house in La Paz so she could pick up her car. They'd then gone on to Darla's house so Darla could change her clothes again, and pick up some money for the amusement park. They'd returned to Kim Oldenburg's house at about 8, and then had set off for Great America, with Kim driving Jeff's Mustang, arriving at the park at around 11 A.M.

Botich's objective in getting this account was to determine

whether Jeff at any time had been alone during the preceding night—was there any opportunity for him to have gotten rid of the murder weapon and shell casings without anyone knowing? But it seemed as if Jeff had been with some other person the entire time—all except for the short period beginning at quarter to 5 on Saturday afternoon, until he'd arrived at Lynette Greer's house around 5:30 Saturday evening.

That meant that if Jeff was the killer, he had to have shot the four victims, then ditched the weapon and the shell casings somewhere on the road to Lynette's house in La Paz between 4:50 and 5:30 P.M., when he'd arrived at Lynette's. The driving time between the parsonage and Lynette's house was at least twenty to thirty minutes—which meant that if Jeff was the killer, the incriminating evidence couldn't be too far off the route from Osborne Road to Lynette's house. Jeff simply didn't have enough time to make a good job of ditching it, Botich thought. So that meant it could be recovered—it had to be fairly easy to find.

Working back from Jeff's arrival at Lynette's in La Paz, there could only be an extremely small window of opportunity to commit the four murders—about twenty minutes, at most, say between 4:50 and 5:10 P.M., given the fastest travel time of twenty minutes, which also had to include the disposal of the evidence. That was, Botich knew, an extremely narrow window of time to shoot four people, then clean up.

But narrow as the window was, as far as Botich could see, there was only one candidate for the perp—it had to be the troubled teenager, Jeff Pelley.

CHAPTER 7

Was it really possible that a 17-year-old boy could murder four family members, including 8- and 6-year-old stepsisters, with a shotgun, then pick up the shell casings, put his clothes in the washing machine, perhaps even take a shower (if the water beads on the bath mat meant anything), dress in clean clothes, close all the curtains, lock all the doors, put his tuxedo in his car, maybe even fix the car so it could run after Bob's disabling of it, all within twenty minutes, then drive 20 miles, dumping the murder weapon, the casings and any bloody shoes or clothing along the way, to arrive at his girlfriend's friend's house miles away by half past 5, even as most of his family lay dead? To arrive, calm, cool and collected at his girlfriend's friend's house, without a speck of blood on his clothes, or without the least anxiety?

It seemed, on the surface, absurd. But Jeff was Botich's most viable suspect—the only person, as far as Botich could see, with the motive, the means and the opportunity.

Of course, that was only if the murders had occurred on Saturday afternoon—it was the only time Jeff could've committed them, according to his own accounting of his movements, for which he'd given many corroborating witnesses. But this was exactly where the lack of a better time of death was to prove so problematical, later.

St. Joseph County Sheriff Joseph Nagy later claimed that his detectives had a time of death, but officials from the county coroner refused to be more specific beyond simply "Saturday afternoon."

Of course, "Saturday afternoon" covered a multitude of times, and therefore suspects. But the statement evaded the truth: no one could say for sure exactly when the murders had taken place, whether in the afternoon or evening, or even the following morning.

If the murders could be shown to have taken place *after* 5:30 P.M.—say, that night, or even on the morning of Sunday, April 30, Jeff *couldn't* be the killer—his alibi was rock-solid, and backed up by literally scores of people.

It was a strange puzzle—not unlike the locked-room mysteries so beloved of the authors of English detective stories. But unlike those entertainments, this was real—and unlike Agatha Christie, there was no bonging cuckoo clock to help pinpoint the time of death. There wasn't even an adequate on-site medical examination of the bodies of the victims.

But without a more accurate time of death, Botich was forced to conclude that the killings had occurred in that small window of opportunity between 4:50 and 5:10 P.M. Saturday afternoon—the only time that Jeff Pelley could possibly have shotgunned to death his father, stepmother and two little stepsisters, one of whom was still clutching her mother as she waited to have her brains blown out.

After establishing Jeff's movements on Saturday afternoon, Saturday night and early Sunday morning, Botich moved to the subject of Jeff's background, and his recent difficulties with his father. Jeff fielded the transition cleanly, without hesitation.

"Were you in any kind of trouble recently?" Botich asked.

"Yeah, it started about a year ago, I got picked up for shoplifting at Target," Jeff said. "And what happened there was, I took some items, and they turned it over to a probation officer, and she sent me to four shoplifting clinics, I believe. And I went to those, and I didn't have to meet with her any time after that. And just a month or two ago, I started stealing a little bit again. I stole some CDs from Jon Herczeg. And I forged a check from the church. And I stole some miscellaneous other items."

Jeff didn't mention the cash he'd taken from Herczeg, about $80 by his own estimate to Senter three weeks before. He shrugged, seemingly waiting for a more specific query from Botich. But Botich didn't oblige.

"Did the police find out about this?"

"Yeah. My dad talked to the police, 'cause he keeps in touch with some of the undercover people or something, I don't know, he doesn't tell me everything. But he said the sheriff's department, whatever, was getting ready to bust me. And he turned me in to Mark Senter, 'cause he knew Mark. He knew Mark would be fair with me."

"And Mark Senter's an Indiana State Trooper, correct?"

"Correct. He's a detective, I believe. And . . . so he took me in and we talked to Mark, and I admitted everything to Mark . . ."

"Was this in the last couple of weeks?"

"Um, three weeks ago, I believe. It happened on a Tuesday or a Wednesday, about three weeks ago."

"So, were you put on probation, or—?"

"Well, I talked to— We went over everything with Mark. And Mark said that— Mark wanted me to get the CDs back to Jon, and I got some of them back, and we were going to order the rest, me and my dad—my dad was helping me take care of it all. But I wasn't really on probation, I was grounded by my dad. Basically, I was turned over to my dad's custody."

The main motive for the burglary, Jeff acknowledged, was to help finance his spring break trip to Florida—he'd driven the Mustang down to Fort Myers, accompanied by Joe Herczeg, the younger brother of Jon, the man he'd burgled. Once down in Fort Myers, Joe had gone his own way, and Jeff connected with four girls from Lakeville, among them Darla Emmons. He'd returned to Lakeville a week later with the four girls.

"Did you get into any trouble while you were down there?" Botich asked.

Yes, Jeff said. He's gotten a speeding ticket in Georgia on the way down to Florida, and another ticket in Fort Myers for running a red light. He'd been driving around in Cape

Coral, late at night, revisiting his old high school, the house where his family had lived, just checking out all the changes, when a patrol cop stopped him.

He didn't think he'd really run the red light, Jeff added—he thought it was only a pretext on the part of the police officer.

"The cop thought I was loitering," Jeff told Botich. "You know, a kid out by himself, late at night." To Botich, given Jeff's admissions so far, this sounded like Jeff was casing some place to burgle—maybe to get more money, to get back to Indiana.

Now Botich threw a change-up, veering abruptly away from the background, jumping hard into the foreground. Botich knew that shifting subjects without warning was a highly effective way of eliciting damaging admissions from a subject—caught by the sharp change of topic, the guilty often let loose with fragments of the truth, which could later be mined for further admissions.

"When you were at Great America, and the detective, the policeman had you in the room there, and told you that your parents had been murdered, what was your reaction to that?"

"I was shocked . . ." There was a small catch in Jeff's voice, just the slightest hesitation as a lump arose in his throat. He went on: "Started cryin' . . . I mean . . . It stunned me, I didn't know how it could happen, I didn't know why it would happen."

In turn, this response shocked and stunned Botich. To the detective, it was as if the brutal facts of four murders had already passed through Jeff's mental system, had been digested, analyzed, calibrated, and had then produced the most distancing, artificial, formalistic of responses. Jeff had said he was shocked, stunned, but you couldn't tell that from his demeanor. He might have been discussing a precipitate fall in the Dow Jones, as far as Botich could see. It simply wasn't the sort of behavior that one might expect from someone who had learned only hours earlier that his father, stepmother and two stepsisters had been murdered, or so Botich thought.

Where was the grief? Where was the demand for justice? Outside of a small catch in the voice, where was the outrage? In Botich's view, Jeff seemed rehearsed in his response—far, far too placid, under the circumstances. And in that instant, Botich had a short flash on Senter's earlier take on Jeff's personality—both Botich and Senter had grown up on *Leave It to Beaver*, and if anything, Jeff Pelley was coming across as . . . *Eddie Haskell.*

It was just too smooth—"smarmy," as both Botich and Senter put it later. But on the other hand, both of them had grown up twenty years before Jeff Pelley. As working-class kids of their own time, they had the deepest suspicion of people who were glib, like Eddie Haskell. That Jeff was so contained over the murders, so calm, set all their alarm bells off—that wasn't the way innocent people reacted to the slaughter of those they loved.

Botich tried again:

"Do you know of anyone who might want to harm your family?"

Jeff barely hesitated. He looked back at Botich, and seemed to be sincere. *Eddie Haskell*, Botich recognized.

"The only thing I can think of . . . The only reason I can think of, at all, and I don't know all the details, but my dad knew there was a lot of stealing and stuff going on by other students in the community, and he was really getting involved in it . . ."

Jeff suggested that some young people in Lakeville had been involved in habitual petty thievery; that Bob had discovered this—even had evidence of it—and had resolved to do something to stop it.

"Mark Senter would probably know more about it, he's really been talking to Mark a lot," Jeff added.

Botich, impassive, made notes of this, then opened another subject.

"Were there any weapons in your house?"

"Um, there was a bow and arrow . . . We used to have other weapons, but my dad got rid of them. And he had a shotgun, but, for a long time he had it hanging right underneath the bow in his bedroom, but then it wasn't there anymore, I'm not sure if he kept it in the house, or what he did. Usually he had a lock on it, a trigger-guard–type thing, but I'm not sure what he did with it."

He'd once had a .22 pistol, Jeff added, that had belonged to his mother.

"But we had an incident happen last year, where I tried to commit suicide—and my dad sold all the guns in the house, and he kept that one, he gave it to somebody, I don't know who it was . . . I don't know if he did the same with the shotgun, later. He bought the shotgun later, for hunting and stuff. I'm not sure if he gave the shotgun to somebody else to keep also or not, I haven't seen it in a while."

"Do you know what kind of shotgun it was?"

Jeff squinted, apparently trying to visualize the shotgun. "I . . . think it was a Mossberg, twenty-gauge, I'm pretty sure that's what it was."

"Was it an automatic, single-shot . . . pump?"

Jeff seemed confused by the question. "Uh, what do you mean by 'automatic'? Pull the trigger once and it keeps firing?"

"Right."

"Um, I think it was a pump . . . Held like five shots or something."

"And when was the last time you'd seen that?"

"I don't know, it's been quite a while since he's had it hanging up. I don't . . . It's been at least a month since he's had it . . . Well, it's been at least three weeks. I know it was gone when I started talking to the police again and stuff. When he found out I was doing some stuff, and when he started talking to Mark Senter, when he turned me in, I know it was gone then."

"Why would he get rid of it then?"

"Um, just because of what had happened last time. Because of me trying to commit suicide last time, when this happened. I guess he maybe thought I'd try it again or something."

"And why'd you try to commit suicide?"

He hadn't actually tried to kill himself, Jeff explained—he'd only threatened to do it. After he'd been arrested for shoplifting the year before, his father had grounded him "for the whole summer." So in retaliation, he'd said he was going to kill himself. "[I was] basically trying to get my own way, an attention-getting–type thing, you know what I mean?"

Botich asked if Bob was unusually strict with him.

Not really, Jeff said. His father would get mad, but "lighten up" as time went on.

But there were a lot of things that weren't discussed in the Pelley family, Jeff added. "We never really talked to each other."

It wasn't that he didn't like Dawn, Jeff said. It was more like he didn't know her—but then, he didn't really *want* to know her.

"Kind of like, I had guilt feelings about my mother dying, like I couldn't care about Dawn or something," Jeff told Botich. "Like my mom would be upset. They were weird feelings, I didn't understand them, I knew they weren't the right feelings, I knew it was dumb reasoning. But it wasn't something I really wanted to get rid of.

"I mean, I didn't hate her or anything, but we just tolerated each other." Jeff shrugged, unable to express himself further.

"Did she ever come down on you?"

Not really, Jeff said. Whenever he did something wrong, Dawn might say something briefly to him, but then she'd tell his father, and it was Bob who handled it, or decided what the punishment should be.

"I didn't accept her—it wasn't that I didn't *like* her. It was forced on me. When they got married, they wanted us to call Dawn 'Mom' and stuff, and it was really hard to accept, having all that pushed on me at once."

But he really liked the little girls, Jeff said.

"I got along with the girls great, I just love the girls." Jeff's shift to the present tense, with "love" as opposed to "loved"—as if the girls were still living—might have been psychologically significant. It could suggest denial, a refusal to accept responsibility for their murders, or alternatively, ignorance—in other words, innocence. The change in tense from past to present seems to have eluded Botich, who didn't follow up. He swerved back to the guns.

Jeff ran down the list of weapons that his father had either sold or given away: a 12-gauge shotgun, a 16-gauge shotgun, a .22 rifle, two .22 pistols—one of them a semiautomatic with interchangeable barrels and a 25-round clip. This was in addition to the 20-gauge shotgun, which Jeff said had disappeared from the parsonage only three weeks before, when he'd gotten into trouble again.

Botich asked Jeff when he'd last fired a shotgun.

"I haven't shot shotguns for more than a year."

"What kind of shot?"

"Pellet."

"Did you ever shoot, like, deer slugs?"

"No. Oh, Kurt Schafer has a twelve-gauge and I shot slugs out of his one time. Just one slug. We were out in his woods and he had a big old pile of junk. There was a lawn mower in there. I shot it one time, it about knocked me on my butt." Jeff laughed.

"What happened when you shot it?"

"What do you mean?"

"What happened to the lawn mower?"

"I didn't even hit it, I missed the lawn mower by a long shot." Jeff laughed, and so did Botich.

"So you're not a very good shot, is that what you're telling me?"

"No, not really!" Jeff laughed again.

Botich turned the conversation back to life at the parsonage.

"My dad kind of went through a personality change when he remarried," Jeff said. "He wasn't the same father I'd always grown up with. And he— He had a lot of changes. He got married less than a year [after Joy's death], he changed occupations, he became a pastor. And he just did a lot of changing, at once. And it kind of seemed like he was more partial to the girls at times. I guess a lot of it was, he didn't really know how to do it any other way, or something."

"Did you have any arguments with your dad on Saturday?"

"We had a real good day on Saturday . . . He said I'd been doing a pretty good job of shaping up."

"What did you really think of your father?"

"In terms of what?"

"In your relationship, in terms of how he treated you?"

"I knew he cared a lot about me. I know sometimes he didn't know exactly how to treat me, exactly how to talk to me. Because he didn't really understand some of the things that I do. But for the most part, we got along pretty well."

"You liked him better as a father before he met Dawn?"

"Yeah, I did," Jeff confirmed. "It wasn't like we had a bad relationship now. When I needed to talk to him, he was there for me."

"But your father changed a lot on you?"

"Yeah, he did."

"Did you think it was for the better or the worse, in your opinion?"

"I don't know, that's hard to say. Because spiritually and stuff, it was for the better. But I remember, I always knew how he used to be. You know, joke around, play games."

"Play ball with you?"

"Yeah, we'd do a lot of stuff together. I can't really say he's changed for the better. It's different now— It's just that he's changed." Again the present tense! "He didn't want us to use the name 'Dawn' with the girls. Wanted us to use 'your mom.' We have a conflict over that. Jacque did too." Back to the past tense. "They just didn't understand what it was to us, inside, to do that. That was just the way we felt. We couldn't really change it."

"Do you know who killed your mother and father?"

"No, I really don't. I don't know who would want to. I know my dad was checking up on some people, but I don't know what all he was doing. Mark Senter might be able to help, but I really have no idea."

"Did you have anything to do with this?"

Jeff didn't hesitate at Botich's suggestion that he might be involved in the murders. He looked the detective squarely in the eye.

"No, I didn't," he said.

CHAPTER 8

Botich wrapped up this interview just before six in the morning of May 1, 1989, but not before resolving how Jeff had gotten his car running again. According to Jeff, his father had replaced two critical fuses, just after returning to the house at 4 P.M., and given him back the previously hidden distributor cap. Jeff himself had replaced that—the restorations had taken only a few minutes. Then, after putting his tuxedo and his radio in the Mustang, just after Kim Oldenburg and her group had left, he'd driven east on Osborne to Maple, down Maple to State Route 4, then east to Highway 31.

South on 31, he'd stopped at Casey's, a gas station and convenience store on the highway, where he'd adjusted the idle on his car—he made a makeshift repair by inserting a piece of cardboard between the carburetor set-screw and the spring, reducing the idle rate. Then he'd gone on to Lynette's, he told Botich.

Botich wanted to see what Jeff would say about Darla's remark about Jeff's supposed "bad feeling" while at the amusement park.

"When you were up at the park, how did you feel when you were up there?"

"I don't know. At first I was happy, but sleepy. I was tired. I felt pretty good, though. Then, after a while, I started feeling like something was wrong. I talked to Darla about it. I told her I felt that something was wrong, I just had this feeling about it, that something was wrong."

"What kind of feeling was that? Can you explain it to me?"

"I don't know. It was just like something wasn't right. I could just feel something wasn't right."

He'd occasionally had such feelings in the past, Jeff told Botich—sort of like premonitions, especially around Darla. Botich could ask Darla if he didn't believe it, Jeff added.

That same morning, Jeff and his grandfather Jack Armstrong drove back to Lakeville. Jeff wanted to get into the house to retrieve a change of clothes, but Botich and Rutkowski wouldn't permit it—they were still working on the crime scene. A reporter for the *South Bend Tribune* tried to ask Jeff some questions, but Jeff wasn't talking.

Meanwhile, in South Bend, Dr. Rick Hoover was beginning the grisly task of documenting the gunshot wounds to the four dead Pelleys. All had been killed by shotgun blasts, deer slugs, he discovered, and except for the first shot at Bob Pelley, into their heads at very close range. Hoover also found two different shotgun waddings in the victims' wounds—one cardboard, one plastic, which meant the killer had used two different types of shells.

Or did it? Did two different types of shotgun slugs mean there were two different killers, each with different shotguns and shells? Two shotguns, each firing different types of ammunition? That raised another question. Just how many shots had been fired, anyway? Maybe six, if one counted the slug that had missed and wound up in the book. Then someone pointed out a gash in the drywall of the stairwell—was that evidence of a seventh shot, or a ricochet of one of the six? Since most pump-action shotguns held a total of four or five shots, depending on the length of the ammunition, a sixth or even a seventh shot either meant that the killer had reloaded, or there were two gunmen. The whole crime scene was a puzzle—some things just didn't add up.

"Lakeville Reacts to Shock of 4 in Family Slain," the *South Bend Tribune* headlined in that afternoon's newspaper.

"We have some evidence and we are following up on some leads that we are confident will lead us to someone,"

St. Joseph County Police spokesman Charles R. Feirrell told the newspaper. And in a companion story, also on the front page, headlined "Pastor's Absence No Prank," the paper recounted Bob's old gambit of reading the newspaper in church while wearing a T-shirt and blue jeans to get the members' undivided attention. But this time there was no message to the congregation—it was no joke, not even a homily.

Botich and Rutkowski knew—as did Krisor, Senter, and everyone else who'd been at the crime scene—that reconstructing the movements of everyone who had been in or near the parsonage on Saturday, April 29, was the key. They were convinced that the murders had taken place on Saturday afternoon, and as far as they could tell, that meant there was only one person with the opportunity, the means and the motive.

Jeff Pelley.

Who had been in the house at 4:45 P.M. on Saturday afternoon? By his own admission, Jeff.

Who had fired shotguns in the past, and who knew where a shotgun might be found in the house, assuming that Jeff was lying about his father having gotten rid of one—a 20-gauge—three weeks earlier? Jeff.

Who had been in dispute with his father, and his stepmother, Dawn, for several weeks before the murders? Jeff.

For Botich, Senter, Rutkowski, it was A-B-C.

And: who could possibly have locked all the doors and windows, and pulled all the curtains? Who had a key to the house? Who was most likely to have been at the bedroom end of the hallway where Bob had been found dead—someone with access to the more private areas of the house?

D-E-F—Jeff, Jeff and Jeff.

Who was cool and remote to the news that his father, stepmother and stepsisters had been found shot to death? Who had had "a bad feeling" on Sunday morning, about the same time police were swarming all over the parsonage in an effort to decipher just what the hell had happened? Whose car had supposedly been disabled, the insurance cancelled? Who had been grounded as a result of his criminal behavior, but whose car was missing from the crime scene? It was G, H, I, J and K—Jeff, Jeff, Jeff, Jeff and Jeff, on all counts. As far as John Botich could see, he *knew* who the killer was. From this point on, it was only a matter of finding the evidence to prove it.

As dawn emerged on the first day of May 1989, detectives from the St. Joseph County police continued interviewing, attempting to establish the precise times and movements of all other possible witnesses in the murders. Only when everyone who had seen or talked with the Pelleys on Saturday, April 29, was accounted for, could anyone begin to draw conclusions. The broad outline might have been clear to Botich, but the devil was always in the details.

As the interviewers soon discovered, the arguments between Jeff and his father were common knowledge among the church members, as well as in the broader community of Lakeville. Stories were recounted, their authenticity verified only by their repetition, not the most reliable indicator: supposedly, Bob had hit Jeff in the jaw, in a fistfight, on April 22, the Saturday before the murders. Maybe Bob had gone after Jeff again, this time with fatal results.

At one point, detectives interviewed Christina Keb, the 16-year-old daughter of Tom Keb, a member of the church and close friend of Bob's—the same man who had supposedly taken charge of some of the guns at Bob's request. Christina claimed to have seen Jeff the day before the murders were discovered, around noon, washing his car. In the back of the Mustang, she'd seen some "wine coolers"—probably a six-pack of Bartles & Jaymes, or something similar. She'd asked Jeff about the alcohol, she told police, but Jeff had told her to mind her own business. Then Bob had approached his son.

"Why are you washing your car?" Bob had demanded, according to Christina. The effort was a waste—he wasn't driving the Mustang to the prom, Bob had told his son. Christina said she watched as Bob and his son had gotten into a verbal argument.

And Christina remembered something else: at some point

while he was washing the Mustang, but before the argument with Bob, Janel and Jolene had approached. They wanted to spend the night sleeping over at the Keb house, and had asked her if it was all right.

"Go ask my mom," Christina told them. But when they returned, Christina's mother had said no—according to Christina, her mother had told the girls that the Keb family had too much to do. So Janel and Jolene stayed home that night.

A critical interview was with Kim Oldenburg. Botich and Rutkowski had already questioned her while still at Gurnee the night before. Yes, Kim confirmed, she'd been at the Pelley house late Saturday afternoon to show Bob and Dawn her prom dress; she knew Bob and Dawn well, and in the past had babysat the girls. She and her date, David Shoemaker, her mother, her brother and her brother's friend had arrived at the parsonage between 4:30 and 4:45 P.M. Matt Miller had stopped in, then rushed back to La Paz to retrieve the forgotten corsage.

According to Kim, she and her group were at the Pelleys' for about fifteen to twenty minutes, then left to go to Kris Holmgren's house, about a half-mile west on Osborne Road. They'd reached the Holmgren house at almost exactly five o'clock, Kim said. It took less than five minutes, maybe even one or two, to get to the Holmgrens' from the parsonage.

When she'd seen Jeff at the house that afternoon, he had been wearing blue jeans and a pink-and-blue shirt. In other words, he hadn't put on his tuxedo, even though he was supposed to pick up Darla in less than forty-five minutes. Jeff didn't seem very talkative, she said—she'd gotten the impression there was tension in the house. In fact, Jeff had seemed upset about something. When she and her date had driven back past the Pelley house around 5:30 P.M., Jeff's Mustang was gone.

By late that afternoon, Botich and Rutkowski were convinced that if pressed, Jeff would confess to the murders. Hey—he was just a kid, right? They asked if he would agree to take a polygraph test, a lie detector. This, in 1989, was standard police investigative procedure, generally seen as a means to incriminate a prime suspect—those who declined the test were hot; those who took the test and passed were eliminated. It wasn't the test that counted as much as the opportunity to use the test as a pretext for another interrogation, which very often led to clarifying statements that in turn led to new evidence. Eventually a person who was lying would find himself boxed in by his own deceptions.

In short, the lie detector was a sort of techno-scam designed to get a suspect to talk too much—there was no court in the United States that had agreed to admit its results as reliable. There were simply too many variables. But to police, they were still enormously useful in getting people to talk themselves into a confession.

Now the county police told Jeff they wanted him to take a "poly," as the police referred to the test. They could arrange to have an expert with the South Bend police, Lieutenant Brent Hemmerlein, administer the exam. If Jeff passed, they could dismiss him as a suspect and move on, and Jeff could go on with his life.

But in some police jurisdictions, the examiner wears two hats: not only is he the test administrator, he's also the "closer"—the investigator charged with sealing the deal, getting the confession, often using the same psychological techniques as a car salesman, with the lie detector machine in the background being the instrument of intimidation of the suspect.

Some might say the blurring of the roles between the polygraph examiner and the "closer" makes some "pre-polygraph" interviews suspect, such as the one Hemmerlein was to conduct of Jeff Pelley on the evening of May 1, 1989—there's a conflict of interest between evaluator and closer, so any such test has to be viewed with skepticism, because of its essentially coercive nature. The subject knows that refusing the test can make him a prime target, so he has to choose between answering the questions or putting himself into the crosshairs of any investigation.

Such critics would also say proper investigative procedure should separate the examiner from the "closer," if a polygraph test is to have any possible validity. The best procedure is to allow the examiner to conduct the polygraph, without accusation, then give the results to the "closer," so the closer can confront the suspect with the results of the test for the purpose of obtaining the confession. The critics say combining the two roles is sloppy investigative procedure.

Still, in South Bend, Hemmerlein was wearing both hats, at least on the evening of May 1, 1989. This would cause a number of problems later.

Just after seven that evening, Jeff Pelley and Jack Armstrong arrived at the South Bend police station. Later, there would be three versions of what happened: Jeff's, Jack's and Hemmerlein's. To say that they were all at variance with one another is a vast understatement.

In Jack Armstrong's version, Hemmerlein began by insisting that he meet with Jeff alone—to go over the questions to be asked on the polygraph. Jack agreed. Within a very short time though, according to Jack, Hemmerlein emerged and beckoned to him.

"He wants to talk to you," Hemmerlein told Jack.

Jack went into the room where Jeff was sitting. Jeff was crying.

"Grandpa," Jeff said, "he never asked me a question, he just came at me and chewed me out. I did not do it."

"I believe you," Jack said. "Come on, let's go."

Outside the room, Jack approached Hemmerlein and Krisor, the deputy district attorney.

"Did you actually accuse Jeff of doing this, without asking anything else?" Jack demanded. Hemmerlein nodded without saying anything, Jack recalled.

"You're stupid," Jack told him. He pulled Jeff toward the exit. "You don't talk to us anymore. We'll have a lawyer when you do." And with that, they left.

"We couldn't have been there more than fifteen minutes," Jack said later.

But that wasn't the way it happened, according to Hemmerlein. The encounter had lasted almost four hours, not fifteen minutes. And, Hemmerlein maintained, Jeff had eventually made statements that were at variance with what he'd told Botich earlier that morning. Not only that, Hemmerlein insisted, Jeff had actually asked him if he was likely to get the electric chair.

But the interview had not been recorded, and in fact, it appears that Hemmerlein's notes reflected as much of what Botich had already told him as to what Jeff had said in the early morning interview.

Hemmerlein later insisted that the interview with Jeff had actually begun at 8 P.M., although Jeff and his grandfather had arrived an hour earlier. Just what Jeff and Jack were doing in the police station for that unexplained hour was never made clear. But Jack later contended that that was false—that in fact, they'd only been in the police station for a short period of time, and had left when Hemmerlein immediately accused Jeff of being the killer.

For his part, Hemmerlein said that Jeff had quickly told him he wanted to speed things along—he had a 9 P.M. date with Darla.

Hemmerlein said he'd asked Jeff what issues he wanted to discuss during the polygraph, and Jeff had responded that he wanted to discuss the murders. At no time was Jeff actually connected to a polygraph machine. All this discussion was—ostensibly—to prepare Jeff for the promised lie detector test, although it never actually took place. At one point, Hemmerlein had confronted Jeff with a contradiction in his story: while he'd told Botich that morning that he'd stopped at Casey's service station on Highway 31 to fix his car, Darla had told police that Jeff had called her that afternoon from another service station—Amoco, at the south end of Lakeville, about a mile away from Casey's. So Jeff had to be lying, Hemmerlein said—for some reason, he didn't want the police to know that he'd stopped at the Amoco station.

At that point, Jeff had asked to talk to his grandfather, and after that, Jeff and Jack had walked out of the police station and begun to look for a lawyer. Or so Hemmerlein would later contend.

Whatever happened at this abortive pre-polygraph interview, one thing was clear: the St. Joseph County authorities had squandered their best and only chance to engage Jeff Pelley in subtle discussion of what had happened. The confrontational approach adopted by Hemmerlein was a miserable failure. Years later, Hemmerlein would testify as to his version of what had been said, which would be vehemently contradicted by Jack Armstrong.

But Hemmerlein said three things to Botich, Rutkowski and Krisor afterward—Jeff had lied to him about where he had been on Saturday afternoon after 5 P.M., Hemmerlein told them. Jeff had also asked if he would have to go to jail that very night, and was he likely to get the electric chair?

That definitely convinced Botich and Rutkowski—Jeff *had* to be the killer.

CHAPTER 9

The word that Jeff was the principal suspect in the murders spread quickly among the Olive Branch brethren, and soon seeped into the Lakeville community at large. All the old stories about Bob and his son—"the pastor's son," as some referred to him, with a slightly sardonic sneer animated by the incongruence of a minister of the Gospel who couldn't seem to get his own flesh and blood to obey the commandments—were circulated and re-circulated, sometimes gaining additional mileage in the retelling. The more people talked, the worse Jeff looked, at least in the popular view.

Jeff's forging of the check from the church ladies' fund was recalled, along with other supposed infractions and misdemeanors. Some recalled that Dawn had busted Jeff for parking his car in the afternoons at another church member's garage in Lakeville, where he was said to be "sleeping." The Pelleys' next-door neighbors, Harold "Irish" Saunders and his wife, Sheila, recalled that Jeff had been caught in his downstairs bedroom with a girl at one point, and that as a result, his room had been moved upstairs, just across the hall from Bob and Dawn's bedroom, to better keep an eye on him. Irish recalled coming home late one night to see Jeff in the new upstairs bedroom, gazing out at the darkness, with the vacant stare of the lost.

Hathaway remembered a conversation he'd had with Bob less than a month before the murders.

"Dave, do you think I'm a good father?" Bob asked. Hathaway tried to turn the question away with a joke. "Not as good as me," Hathaway said, "because then you'd be the best." But Bob was serious, Hathaway saw. He realized that there were strains in the Pelley household, partly the result of trying to merge two families, but exacerbated by the cramped quarters of the parsonage: seven people, one bathroom for five kids, and nowhere to escape. And Bob had a tendency to be firm, even dictatorial, when sometimes a deft touch was needed.

"You wouldn't treat Jacque the same way you'd treat Jolene, would you?" Hathaway asked. "No, you wouldn't, because they're different, they're different in age, have different ideas about things, different needs. What works for some won't work with others. You've got to find what works with each one."

Bob nodded—he saw what Dave was driving at. He'd recently been taking a course at Huntington University on "merged families." But it was one thing in the abstract, another thing entirely in practice. Bob allowed that maybe, just maybe, he'd been too hard on Jeff.

But Jeff hadn't made it easy. Some of his resentment of Dawn had seeped into his relationship with his father, as Jeff later admitted to Butich. And Jeff had been abruptly jerked away from his familiar haunts in Florida, away from his lifelong friends, thrust into a situation in which money was scarce, living space was cramped, and he had been made to adapt to circumstances he had no control over. He'd turned to petty crime to help escape his father's dominance—if he had a few dollars, he could stay away from the source of his unhappiness, the parsonage. And there was the Mustang—a passport to freedom, to independence, to near-adulthood, the means to absent oneself from the tensions of the merged household. Jeff sometimes drove the Mustang like a maniac, speeding up and down the back roads of Lakeville, recklessly endangering himself and others, so much so that some people on Osborne Road, at least, considered him a menace behind the wheel. Bob didn't exactly get it, but in a deeper sense, it seemed as though Jeff was deeply unhappy, angry, even, with a compulsion for self-destruction, as his threat to kill himself the previous year showed. The raw fact was, Jeff was only 17 years old, hormonally infused, wishing to be 25 overnight, desperate to separate himself from the paternal decisions that had removed him, against his will, from Florida to Lakeville, Indiana . . . the authority that told him, again and again, he was just a kid, powerless and of no account, whose entire life had been captured and held hostage by his father's paramour, Dawn. So Jeff resented Dawn—he couldn't help it, as he'd told Botich; as he put it, it wasn't her, it was the whole situation. It might have been "wrong thinking," but it was still how he really felt.

All things considered, it seemed quite likely that Bob Pelley had only the faintest understanding of the depth of confusion and disappointment in the heart of his eldest child.

Botich and other detectives kept trying to assemble the mosaic: who had been where on Saturday, and what did they recall?

From Matt Miller, they learned that when he'd raced back to the Holmgren house with the corsage, he'd passed the parsonage at about 5:10 P.M.; he'd seen Jeff's Mustang at the time, he said. But when he and Kris Holmgren and their group had passed the parsonage again at about 5:30 P.M., the Mustang was gone.

That made it definite, at least to Botich—Jeff was lying about leaving the parsonage at 4:50. A witness, Miller, had seen his car, still at the parsonage, at 5:10, which gave him at least twenty minutes after 4:50 to shoot everyone, tidy up, then drive away from the crime scene after 5:10.

Of course, if Kim Oldenburg was wrong—say, if she and her group had left the parsonage at 4:40 P.M.—that would be even better for the idea that Jeff was the killer, because in that case, Jeff would have had even more time.

Going against this notion was Kim Oldenburg's assertion that her group had arrived at the Holmgren house, a half-mile away, at 5 P.M. Surely it wouldn't have taken Kim Oldenburg's mother twenty minutes to drive just half a mile. But was Kim right when she'd said her group had arrived at the Holmgren house at 5 P.M.? Was it before that? Oldenburg's recollection, along with that of Matt Miller, was crucial evidence, and mostly equivocal. It was all a matter of minutes—ten minutes either way could make someone innocent, or a murderer.

So here was exposed the fallacy of Dame Christie's clocks—so much for the usefulness of the English murder mystery. The problem was, real people didn't usually pay much attention to the minute hand—not even real lords and ladies—and there weren't any dinner gongs whacked by servants as a reference point. In the real world, it was impossible to say with any precision, any certitude, exactly when Kim Oldenburg's group had last seen the Pelley family alive and well—it could have been any time between 4:45 and 5 P.M.

Given the way Jeff sometimes drove his Mustang, it was entirely possible he could have reached Lynette's house by 5:30 P.M. after killing everyone, cleaning up, then leaving the parsonage at 5:10, even with stops at two gas stations. But in his heart, Botich knew it would be cutting it very close. The clock—it was either Jeff's foremost accuser, or his best alibi witness. Without any reasonably accurate time of death, anything was possible. If the absence of one was the authorities' ace in the hole, it was also any defendant's reasonable doubt.

From Kim Oldenburg and the Easterdays, detectives learned that Bob, at least, had planned to drop in on the Easterday house later on Saturday afternoon to see Crystal Easterday's prom dress. When they hadn't arrived by 5:30 P.M., Crystal and her date went to the parsonage. They'd knocked on the doors around 5:45 P.M., but no one answered. All the curtains had been drawn. Jeff's car wasn't there, but Bob and Dawn's cars were. Mystified, Crystal and her date went on to the prom. Later, at the dance, she'd told Jeff that no one seemed to be home at the parsonage that evening. Jeff made no remark about this, Crystal told the detectives. Still later that evening, when someone told Jeff that they thought he'd been grounded for the prom, he had a terse reply: "That's all taken care of."

What did that mean? Again, it was something that could be heard two ways.

Detectives also interviewed the people Bob had been visiting on Saturday—Roger and Joyce Schafer in the morning, and John and Vera Howell in the afternoon. To both couples, Bob had been adamant that he was going to drive Jeff and Darla to the prom. That was as of at least 3 P.M. So what had happened between three, when Bob had insisted that he would drive Jeff and Darla to the dance, and two hours or so later, when Jeff had left in his own car? Was Bob saying one thing to the Schafers and the Howells, and another to Jeff?

And what about the dinner at the Emporium? No one recalled Bob telling them that he was also going to drive Jeff and Darla to South Bend for the dinner, then pick them up an hour or so later, drive them to the Elks Lodge, and then pick them up once more at midnight when the dance was over. That seemed like a lot of driving . . . Wasn't it more likely that Bob simply didn't know about the dinner at the Emporium, that Jeff had kept the gift certificate from Brenda Hale a secret from his father?

Brenda Hale said she'd talked to Bob at the church on Friday night—she was a member—and Bob had told her that he was going to drive Jeff and Darla to "the prom," but made no mention of the restaurant. True, Jeff had told Brenda Hale on the same night that he and Darla were going to attend the dinner (which was when Brenda had offered the gift certificate to Jeff on his promise to pay her back later), but Brenda might not have been troubled by the apparent contradiction—it was easy to assume that either Bob had misspoken, having meant to say he would drive Jeff and Darla to the restaurant, not the prom itself, and pick them up later after someone else had given them a ride to the dance, "the prom" being a generic reference to all the night's activities.

But what if? What if Bob had meant exactly what he'd said—no dinner, prom only, no after-prom, no Great America excursion?

Was it possible that Jeff's motive for the murders was simply that Bob wouldn't allow him to attend the dinner at the Emporium—that he saw no way to get there other than to commit wholesale slaughter, so he could drive his own car? That's what it seemed like, to Botich.

Was that why Jeff hadn't been wearing his tuxedo on Saturday afternoon when Kim Oldenburg dropped by—because Bob didn't know about the dinner plans, and Jeff hadn't told him, and didn't want to tip him off? That it was too soon to get dressed, as far as Bob understood?

From Lynette's mother, detectives established that Jeff had indeed arrived at the Greer house about five-thirty Saturday afternoon, and that he had called to say he would be a few minutes late. Mark Berger, Lynette's prom date, confirmed that Jeff had arrived at the house at five-thirty. It was at Lynette's house that Jeff had changed into the tuxedo.

When detectives interviewed Darla's mother, she told them of her mild astonishment at seeing Jeff early Sunday morning before the trek to Great America—she was surprised to see him driving the Mustang. She knew that Bob had taken the car away, and when she'd asked Jeff what was going on, he'd told her that he'd gotten "a day out of Pelley prison."

Someone tracked down the attendant at the Amoco station, Dennis Nicodemus, who knew Jeff from school. Jeff had come into the Amoco station just after 5:20 P.M., from—from the Quinn Road side, not Highway 31. He knew the approximate time, Nicodemus said, because his relief was late. Jeff borrowed a screwdriver, did something to the Mustang, and then pulled out about ten minutes later. When the trip from the parsonage to the Amoco station was timed using the route Jeff had claimed, it was no more than ten minutes. Using the Mulberry-to-Quinn route, though, it would be somewhat longer. Then Botich recalled what Jeff had said about stopping at Casey's. Maybe Jeff had made that up to account for some of the time between 4:50 and 5:10 P.M.—a phantom stop that had never taken place, in order to account for the time Jeff had spent ditching the shotgun and shell casings.

It all came back to the twenty minutes between 4:50 and 5:10 P.M. Jeff insisted that he'd left the parsonage just after Kim Oldenburg. But Matt Miller, the one with the forgotten corsage, was sure he'd seen Jeff's Mustang still parked at the parsonage at 5:10 P.M.. So either someone was gravely mistaken, or lying. For Botich, calculating—if Miller had arrived at the parsonage as early as 4:30 P.M., had then rushed out to retrieve the corsage, had driven all the way to La Paz, plucked the flowers out of his refrigerator, then rushed back to Lakeville and past the parsonage, it had to have taken at least thirty minutes, round trip.

If Miller had really seen Jeff's car around 5:10, that was evidence that Jeff was fabricating. And to Botich, if Jeff was lying, that was powerful evidence that he had to be the killer.

But of course, this all turned on the assumption that the murders had occurred on Saturday afternoon—if they'd taken place on Saturday evening or early Sunday morning, Jeff *couldn't* be the killer.

What if some person, or persons, had taken possession of the parsonage after Jeff left, locked the doors, drawn the curtains, and had killed or held the family incommunicado by the time Crystal and her date showed up? What was the significance of what appeared to be a cereal bowl in the living room and the supposed little girls' "church socks"? This was possible evidence that the murders had occurred Sunday morning, not Saturday afternoon.

If it wasn't an Agatha Christie mystery, it was close. The whole thing revolved around the clock—or minutes of the clock, anyway—and in this real-life case, the police had no meaningful, or at least provable, time of death. And without a time of death, or even a credible estimate, there would always be room for reasonable doubt.

CHAPTER 10

On Wednesday, May 3, 1989, the four dead Pelleys were mourned at a funeral ceremony at the Olive Branch church. The proceedings drew many from Lakeville, as well as the church members. Hathaway later recalled the television people aiming their cameras through the windows toward the altar—"the sanctuary," as Hathaway saw it. Hathaway felt the use—in his view, the commercial abuse—of the dead was beyond obscene. But those who pointed the cameras hadn't survived Okinawa, where the dead were far more numerous, much more than a mere commodity for the evening news. The only newsman on Iejima was Ernie Pyle, and he'd gotten killed.

After the funerals, several people approached Jeff to express their condolences for his loss. According to detectives assigned to watch the rites—a standard investigative technique—Jeff displayed no reaction: no weeping, certainly, or other discernible indications of grief. Knowing nothing of this family history, some at the funerals thought Jeff's unemotional behavior was proof positive that he had to be guilty. Where were the tears, the grief, the outrage? You couldn't see them on Jeff's face. Jacque later attributed her brother's stoicism to the early lessons from Bob—after their mother Joy Pelley's death, no crying was allowed.

In the aftermath of the funerals, the perception spread throughout the church memberships, and from there, throughout Lakeville—as Dave Hathaway later said, at least half the church members thought that Jeff had fired the shots, while another quarter believed that if he hadn't actually pulled the trigger, he knew who had. It was obvious to everyone that the St. Joseph County police believed Jeff was the killer. The police distributed a picture of Jeff—"One of three surviving Pelley children," as the *South Bend Tribune* put it the same day the four Pelleys were eulogized. The police denied that passing out the single photo of Jeff was in any way a suggestion that he was the killer. As to rumors that the police were only waiting for the funerals to be over to make an arrest, St. Joseph County Sheriff Joseph Nagy denied that, too.

"If we had a prime suspect and if we had enough evidence, we wouldn't wait one second," Nagy told the newspaper. "We would make an arrest right now."

Meanwhile, the detectives had uncovered even more equivocal evidence. On Saturday morning, before picking Jeff up at the McDonald's, Bob had spent some time in a Lakeville gun shop. He'd eyed the handguns that were for sale, dealer Steve Diller told the police, but had left without buying anything.

What, if anything, did this mean? Was Bob worried that someone might be gunning for him, and wanted to arm himself? But why? And when detectives prodded deeper, they discovered that Bob had done business with Diller before. In December 1987, he'd traded a .44-caliber Smith & Wesson magnum pistol—Dirty Harry's weapon of choice—to Diller for a Mossberg 500 pump-action shotgun. Diller claimed that Bob had paid the difference in cash, but that was weird: in 2008 a new Smith & Wesson .44 magnum retailed for $750, while the shotgun cost only $150—even assuming the prices were lower in 1989, why would Bob have paid Diller anything? It should have been the other way around.

Unless Bob wanted to get rid of the pistol, for some reason . . .

The Mossberg shotgun Bob had acquired in late 1987 came with two interchangeable barrels—one for shot, the other rifled for deer slugs. It was 20-gauge, exactly the type that had been used to shoot the Pelleys, or so the police experts surmised. The 500 had a pump action—slide the stock under the barrel to rack consecutive rounds, and fire with each pull of the trigger, boom-boom-boom, just like Steve McQueen in *The Getaway*. But this was the same weapon that Jeff said had disappeared just after his recent burglary trouble, and that he had no idea of what his father had done with it.

The shotgun—that was the key to the case, Botich and the rest of the investigators realized. Find the shotgun, find the shell casings—game over. But the police had searched all the roadsides off Osborne Road, off Maple, off Mulberry, and had found nothing. Given the short time frame between the departure of Kim Oldenburg from the Pelley house, and Jeff's arrival at Lynette Greer's, it seemed impossible that Jeff could have strayed very far off the roads to ditch the weapon—there just wasn't enough time. A search of the rubbish bins at the two gas stations was fruitless. A sheriff's posse of horsemen patrolled the two roadsides, and divers plunged into the many ponds and sloughs around Osborne Road, groping along the muddy bottoms. No one found anything.

The murder weapon had seemingly vanished.

By Wednesday or Thursday, a woman who lived with her husband and daughters in a small house about a quarter mile east of the parsonage realized, after reading the newspapers and hearing about the murders on television, that she might have pertinent information. This was Lois Stansbury, the daughter of a man who had another house just west of the parsonage at the northeast intersection of Osborne and Mulberry Roads.

She called Mark Senter and gave him evidence that Bob Pelley might have been alive and well as late as five o'clock on Saturday afternoon. Senter took the evidence—a receipt from a nearby K mart time-stamped at 4:03 P.M. Stansbury told Senter that after her expedition to K mart, she'd seen Bob Pelley in the parking lot of the church right around five o'clock, talking with a man she did not recognize. There was a black pick-up truck in the church parking lot, Stansbury said. Senter took the receipt into evidence, and told her that someone would talk to her later. But no one ever did, at least not until more than a decade later.

Almost from the time his grandfather Jack had checked him into the hotel room early Monday morning, Jeff had been under rather overt surveillance by the police. An officer had been posted to keep watch on the room, and there was always at least one officer who remained nearby, wherever Jeff went, over the following week. On Monday, May 1, after trying to retrieve clothes from the parsonage, Jeff attended a track meet at LaVille High School, where Darla and Lynette Greer were among those competing. He thought he was being shadowed by the police.

To Jeff, the idea that the police—or at least Botich—were convinced he was the killer was very obvious. He'd asserted his innocence to Botich, Rutkowski, Hemmerlein Darla Emmons, and his grandfather, Jack Armstrong, but the police clearly didn't believe him. Why else would they be watching him?

Still, while it was very clear that the police had Jeff as their "person of interest," if not prime suspect, in the days following the murders a number of rumors germinated in Lakeville. There was talk that devil worshippers had done the grisly deeds—it was an era when lurid tales of Satanism were a staple in the popular culture, and the death of a pastor only added fuel to that.

Others recalled seeing a limousine on Osborne Road around the time of the killings, which fueled speculation that the murders were the work of the Mafia, or the Colombians. Some said the limo they'd seen had Florida license plates—what would a Florida limo be doing in Lakeville, Indiana? There were also those who said the killings were payback for the Reverend Pelley's persistence in trying to expose the juvenile burglary ring he'd claimed had been operating around Lakeville—to shut him up.

"We had a lot of rumors going around," Botich said, years later. "Satanists, the Mafia, the Colombians, the limousine.

But I have to tell you, there were probably five or six limousines driving around the area that afternoon—it was prom night." The inescapable fact was, Botich said, there was simply no reliable evidence to suggest that anyone other than Jeff Pelley was involved in the murders.

Well, maybe. But at some point in the days after the killings, in an interview with both Botich and Senter, Jacque Pelley told them about the mysterious midnight summons to the Florida bank, the family's abrupt departure from Florida, the change of religious denomination, and the rumors about the stolen or laundered money in the Sunshine State. Still, to Botich and Senter, Jacque was 14 years old, and when those events had supposedly happened, she'd been only 12. And then Jacque's credibility was undercut: on the day the bodies had been found, after Jacque had been driven back to the parsonage from Huntington, a county police officer had asked her if she thought her brother was capable of committing four murders.

"Yes," Jacque had said—at least according to Hathaway, who was standing right next to her at the time. Years later Jacque would say she had no recollection of ever being asked that question by anyone, let alone a police officer. Of course, Jacque was in shock at the time—she might not have even understood what she was being asked.

But to the police in 1989, if Jacque believed that her brother was capable of the murders, then, a few weeks later, was sure that he wasn't, didn't that mean her stories about Florida were simply shadow-casting—an effort to drum up other possibilities, in part as a result of guilt stemming from her own original doubts about her brother?

As the spring of 1989 unfolded, the estate of Bob and Dawn Pelley was entered into the probate court of St. Joseph County. By late May 1989, Bob's older sister, Jon Boso of Ohio, had filed the requisite paperwork to be named personal representative of the estate, charged with fulfilling the terms of Bob's will. That document, signed in Fort Myers, Florida, on July 22, 1986, left all assets to Dawn Pelley, and in the event she died within ninety days of his death, to a trust to benefit Jeff, Jacque and the three Huber daughters—Jessica, Janel and Jolene.

In this probate filing, Bob's sister Jon agreed to act as her brother's personal representative, and thus gained initial control of whatever assets were in the estate. By the first of June, Jon Boso had established that her brother had a $100,000 life insurance policy with State Farm, along with another policy—possibly insuring Dawn separately—with American United Life Insurance Company. Together the two policies amounted to $129,000 in benefits. By the time the insurance paid off the following year, the total value of the estate was over $160,000, a fairly nice nest egg for the three survivors of the murders—Jeff, Jacque and Jessica.

On the other hand, it was also a possible motive.

CHAPTER 11

Bob's will was fairly standard, at least for a man with younger children. For one thing, it placed all assets in a trust, which in turn specified that each inheritor had to attain a certain age before gaining access to their share of the principal. There were two trustees named: Jon, Bob's sister; and Dawn's father, Edward Hayes, of Eaton Rapids, Michigan. But Jon Boso soon relinquished her position as trustee, and left decisions as to disbursements from the trust to Ed Hayes.

One of the most interesting aspects of this decision by Jon Boso centered around an encounter Jeff had with a prominent criminal defense lawyer in South Bend, Michael Dvorak. According to later claims filed with the St. Joseph County Court, Jeff, accompanied by his maternal grandfather, Jack Armstrong, consulted Dvorak sometime in the spring of 1989, not long after the murders. Explaining that he was at least a "person of interest" if not a prime suspect, Jeff discussed the case with Dvorak, with the eye of hiring him as his attorney. According to Dvorak's later statements, he'd named a fee for defending Jeff, if he was charged with murder. But then Jon Boso declined to release funds from the estate to pay Dvorak—she thought the fee was too much, at least according to Dvorak. According to other court records, Dvorak had in fact demanded a $5,000 retainer, a rather modest sum for a potential capital case.

Parsing this out, years later, is difficult. Clearly Bob's older sister was conflicted—on one hand, she wanted to defend her brother's eldest child, Jeff. But at the same time, her instinct was that Jeff had killed his father, her brother. Reconciling the two points of view was difficult, actually impossible. Whether the amount of the fee demanded by Dvorak was determinative to Jon Boso isn't clear—it's equally possible that she'd decided that Jeff had to be the killer, and simply couldn't bring herself to approve the money to defend him.

Certainly Botich came to believe the latter. In his contacts with Jon Boso, conducted over a number of years, Botich was certain that Bob's elder sister believed that Jeff was the killer. That this belief caused a split in the Pelley/Armstrong/Hayes family would later become painfully obvious, with Jon Boso, her mother, Maxine Pelley, and Ed Hayes becoming convinced of Jeff's guilt, while Jack and Mary Armstrong steadfastly defended him. Jacque was caught between two poles—Pelleys or Armstrongs—and in the end cast her lot with her older brother. It was a dilemma, a choice that no one should have to make.

In the days immediately following the murders, someone called the car insurance agency and had Jeff reinstated as a covered driver. Jeff took up temporary residence with the Schafers. Although he had finished his high school education early, in January, he wanted to attend the graduation ceremony for his high school class. Jessica, it appears, returned to Michigan with her maternal grandparents, Ed and Lara Hayes, and Jacque lived for a time with the Easterdays.

After the end of the school year, Jeff and Jacque stayed for a few weeks with the Armstrongs in Kentucky. Then Jeff returned to Lakeville for the rest of the summer, while Jacque went to live with an aunt in Colorado. On his return to Lakeville, Jeff stayed with another family, the Richardses. Jon Boso paid the family a modest sum from the Pelley estate for Jeff's room and board.

Throughout the summer, Jeff had periodic contact with both Botich and Senter, with Jeff actually seeking out the detectives. The conversations were always pleasant, Botich recalled—there was no anger or hostility from Jeff at their belief that he was the killer. It was almost as if he were fencing with them, dancing along the edge, genially probing to see if they had found any new evidence against him. To Botich, this seemed further confirmation that they were on the right track.

"Normally, if you have someone whose family has been murdered, they want to know whether there are any suspects, any new leads. But Jeff never asked any questions about any other suspects, and I found that strange," Botich said, years later.

Near the end of the summer, when Jeff was preparing to enroll at Manchester College, a Church of the Brethren school in North Manchester, Indiana, he dropped in on Senter. Always friendly, if just a bit smirky, at least in Senter's view, Jeff asked Senter a question: "Mark, do you think I did it?"

"Yes, Jeff, I do," Senter nodded. Jeff merely shook his head—there was no vehement denial, just a sort of sorrow at Senter's seeming obtuseness.

The trouble was, for St. Joseph County Prosecutor Mike Barnes, there just wasn't enough evidence. To Barnes, believing was far short of proving. Yes, the police might be sure Jeff was guilty; and it was even possible that one could assemble a timeline to show that only Jeff could have done it. But would it be unassailable? No.

What if Jeff were formally charged? Brought to court, made to stand trial, and was then found not guilty, based on the lack of beyond a-reasonable-doubt evidence? He would then be freed. What if, after all that, someone discovered incontrovertible evidence that Jeff *had* committed the murders, or even helped set them up—what then? If he'd been previously acquitted by a jury, there would be no way to charge him again—it would be double jeopardy, which held that no one could be tried twice for the same offense. So, as far as Barnes could see, the shrewd thing to do was—nothing. Maybe, he thought, at some time in the future, someone could get something that proved the case beyond a reasonable doubt. Like, maybe Jeff would talk to someone—Darla?—and confess. But so far, it just wasn't there—it was simply too thin, and too risky to take to court. Barnes' decision as to Jeff's possible guilt cleared the way—the insurance policies were paid to the estate of Robert Lee Pelley.

In attending Manchester College, Jeff was following Darla, who also enrolled there—or perhaps Darla was following Jeff. In any event, by the following year, the romance was over. Jeff dropped out. He decided to go to Florida, to Fort Myers, in fact, to resume the life that had been interrupted three years before by the strange sojourn to Indiana—the same place he had been, on his burglary-financed spring break, a little over a month before the murders. The place where his mother had died, his father had changed, and his own life had been altered forever.

In his father's 45-rpm-era parlance, Jeff had restarted the record. But in the language of his own generation, Jeff had rebooted.

II. FORT MYERS, FLORIDA

1976–2002

CHAPTER 12

Fort Myers lies about 130 miles south of Tampa on the Gulf Coast of Florida, about 120 miles west of Miami. There at the edge of the warmth of the Caribbean Sea, where the Lake Okeechobee–draining Caloosahatchee River meets San Carlos Bay and the silt-created barriers of Pine, Sanibel and Estero Islands, altogether about 600,000 people now reside.

This is flat scrubland, in its natural state dotted with swamps, cypress, oaks, pines and palmettos, interspersed with sawgrass. A traveler arriving from the east—from Miami—must traverse either the Tamiami Trail, the narrow highway that cuts through Big Cypress National Preserve, in which egrets, eagles, herons, owls, water moccasins, coral snakes, gators, skeeters and red necked swamp rats reside, or the slightly larger federal highway to the north—Alligator Alley, I-75. In either case, you don't want to wander very far off the road . . . this is Carl Hiaasen country, the original Florida.

In winter, the balmy shores of Fort Myers, and its principal suburb, Cape Coral, have long been a beacon to northerners. While Fort Myers was originally built as a military installation to keep at bay the ferocious Seminole Indians, adherents of a chief whom white settlers nicknamed "Billy Bowlegs," by early in the next century—that's 1900, to you twenty-first century whippersnappers—it was a destination of choice for new money: specifically, Thomas Alva Edison's light bulb money, and later Henry Ford's Model T money. The two tycoons—each the Bill Gates of his era— established winter estates at Fort Myers, just as they shared unshakeable faith in technology as the inevitable, virtuous future. Not unlike Bill, come to think of it.

As the twentieth century unfolded, Fort Myers grew from a sleepy gulf-side backwater to one of the largest commercial centers on Florida's west coast, eventually becoming the spring training home of the Philadelphia Athletics—and today, the Boston Red Sox and the Minnesota Twins.

Across the river, the city of Cape Coral was carved out of similar scrubland—originally cattle country, the peninsula that became Cape Coral stands as a bizarre amalgam of twentieth-century suburban kitsch pasted onto old-world Venice—a geometric maze of dredged channels form the back yards of drywalled, stucco-clad ranch houses, and even, lately, a few McMansions. A few years after the Pelleys departed in 1986, Veterans Memorial Highway was extended across the river from Fort Myers, almost all the way across the peninsula, wiping out the house that the Pelley family had lived in from 1983 to 1986.

The ideal of Florida, that sun-washed, balmy paradise, had always been a come-on, a sales gimmick, at least in Cape Coral. And by the time the highway extension obliterated the Pelley house on Southwest 25th Lane, one might as well have been living in East Irving, Texas, or even Levittown—it was all just one roadway, the same stop signs, the same traffic lights, the same strip malls, with all the same emporia—Colonel Sanders, True Value hardware, Burger King, McDonald's, Pizza Hut, Re/Max, again and again and again. Like the ubiquitous Southern weed, kudzu, the national brands had taken over.

And maybe, just maybe, that was what Bob Pelley had been trying to escape.

So many years later, it's difficult to get a grip on Bob Pelley's life in Florida, before his reincarnation as a pastor of the Olive Branch Brethren in Lakeville, Indiana. Who was he, really, before he and his merged family of seven moved into the cramped parsonage on Osborne Road? Did he have some sort of existence that he'd kept secret for many years—some sort of shadow side that he did not want his two wives, his five children, to know about?

Why was he so enamored of guns? Why such a large amount of life insurance? Was he only the honest pastor of the Olive Branch Brethren, dedicated to his rural flock, willing to accept a pittance for a chance to preach the Word? Or was he burying himself in a small Indiana town to separate himself from questionable bank transactions, or past sins, past associations, trying to reinvent himself as a man, as a soul, in accord with the precepts of the Nazarenes? To rid himself of sin, to perfect himself anew, by good works, in the tradition of his Nazarene faith?

For this we would have to know the caliber of Bob Pelley's soul, but so many years later, the footprints of his life are too indistinct to reach any useful conclusions. Even if such an assessment were possible, as human beings, we cannot judge those dimensions, because none of us can presume to know exactly how Bob Pelley saw reality—we can never walk in his shoes. This is the uniqueness of being human—we are all different, and all of us see things colored by our own experience, and our own necessities. We just don't know enough about others to condemn, which is why we should keep from casting stones. Or, as has so often been said, we shouldn't judge, lest we be . . .

Yet this truth should not prevent us from trying to assemble the facts, as best we can. We can judge not, because we cannot really know, but at the same time, we ought to face the truth squarely, as best as we can establish it. This is the distinction between faith, which is blind, and true charity, which is always informed, while accepting information's limitations.

There was an incident that took place in Florida in 1976 that is at most only faintly suggestive, and in the absence of harder evidence, one can only wonder.

On February 28 of that year, a car was found half-submerged in the shallow water of San Carlos Bay, south of Cape Coral and Fort Myers, just off the causeway that connects Sanibel Island to the mainland.

When the 1967 Mercury convertible was hauled from the water, there was no driver—or rather, no body. At first, that didn't mean much—there were fairly strong currents in the area. And then, too, there were sharks around . . .

But when no human remains floated to the surface within a week, and no one reported losing their car by veering off the causeway, things began to look peculiar. The car was registered to Harry William Stewart, with an address in Miami. The day after the car was found, a detective for the Sanibel Police Department, Sergeant Bill Trefny, received a telephone call from a man named Phillip E. Hawley, a Fort Myers private investigator, and owner of a local debt collection agency. Hawley told Trefny that he was Stewart's landlord at an apartment in Fort Myers. When Trefny met with Hawley, the latter produced a lease that had his own signature, but none by Stewart. When Hawley let Trefny into the apartment that Stewart had leased, Trefny found numerous magazines and bills, all addressed to Stewart, unopened, going back for many months. There were rat feces in the kitchen, and other signs that Stewart hadn't occupied the apartment for a very long time prior to his disappearance. In Trefny's mind, there was a real question as to whether the lost-at-sea Stewart had ever really lived in the apartment.

But without more leads, Trefny shrugged the whole thing off. Whoever Stewart had been, whatever he'd been doing out on the causeway, if he had ever actually been there, it seemed an insoluble mystery. Without a dead body, without an accident report, without evidence of a crime, Trefny had nothing to investigate.

Then, a year later, two insurance investigators showed up on Sanibel Island, each trying find out whether Harry William Stewart was a real person. It turned out that there were three life insurance policies covering him, one with a double indemnity clause that made the total payout for all three policies, in the event of Stewart's accidental demise, $86,000. The beneficiary on each policy was Phillip E. Hawley.

* * *

Soon, the insurance investigators and the Sanibel police were cooperating, joined by agents from the Florida Insurance Commission, as the state agency was then called. They began by trying to assemble a documentary record on Harry William Stewart. Almost immediately they hit pay dirt: a Harry William Stewart, born February 11, 1947, in West Palm Beach, had died eighteen days later, on March 1, 1947.

Yet a Florida driver's license issued to Harry William Stewart showed the same birth date. Then it turned out that on June 25, 1976—almost four months after the sunken Mercury had been found—a Harry W. Stewart, who listed the same address in Miami as found for the sunken car registration, had applied for a U.S. passport in Miami. This Harry W. Stewart listed his birth on February 11, 1947, also in West Palm Beach, and had posed for a passport photograph. The passport photo showed him smiling genially into the camera, apparently enjoying himself, at least four months after his car had gone into the drink, and his presumably dead body had floated away on the currents.

Given the March 1, 1947, death certificate for the infant Harry William Stewart, the fact that someone with the exact same birth date had applied for a passport in June 1976, a little more than three decades after baby Harry's death—someone who was seemingly the same person who owned a car found in San Carlos Bay near Sanibel Island four months earlier—it seemed pretty stinky.

The insurance companies declined to pay off.

A federal investigation into possible passport fraud was opened, and three months after that, an FBI agent in Miami obtained an arrest warrant for one Harry W. Stewart, whoever he was, to answer for the charge of possible passport violations. But as the years unfolded after 1976, no one could figure out the real identity of the man who claimed to be Harry W. Stewart.

First the local investigation faded out, then the state, and eventually, the federal. Years later, it would turn out that any surviving documents from the strange case of Harry William Stewart would be scarce—in our data-suffused society, our longer-term memory tends to suffer, and stuff gets tossed. Hey, it's old, who needs it? As information speeds up, time slows down; and as time decelerates and data proliferates, we survive by ignoring, if not forgetting, or even dumping, the past. In our own time, we tend to have too many facts, so we often incoherently jettison information we think we will never need, only to find out later that we do.

As it would turn out, a little over thirty years later, a number of people would say that Harry William Stewart was Bob Pelley.

"That's Bob," Mark Senter said, when shown the 1976 passport photograph of Harry William Stewart, in April 2008.

"It's Bob, all right," John Botich agreed. And Dave Hathaway—he thought the passport picture of Harry William Stewart was someone else, at least at first.

"It's Jeff," Hathaway said.

Well, of course, that couldn't be—in February 1976, when the Mercury was pulled out of the water, Jeff was only a little over 4 years old. But Hathaway had picked up on the outlines of family resemblance—the broad forehead, the jaw. To Hathaway, to Senter, to Botich, if Harry William Stewart wasn't Bob Pelley, he looked close enough in his features to make people think he might well have been.

Jacque, however, wasn't so sure. It might've been a picture of her father, she said in 2008, but maybe not. She couldn't say definitively; one of her mother's brothers assured her that the man in the passport photo *wasn't* Bob. But Jacque was very sure of one thing: Bob and Joy hadn't moved to Florida until 1979 or 1980—nearly three or four years after the events surrounding the sunken Mercury. In February 1976, when the Mercury went into San Carlos Bay, the Pelleys were still in Ohio. In Jacque's mind, her father certainly hadn't been gallivanting around Florida, buying cars, getting passports, renting apartments he never lived in—it was absurd.

But when the Pelleys arrived in Fort Myers about 1980, they became close friends with none other than Phillip E.

Hawley and his family, and indeed, the two families became closely intertwined over the next two decades, even after Bob and Dawn departed for Indiana—only to be murdered on the last weekend of April 1989. By the time he turned up in Florida in the early 1990s, Jeff Pelley would go to work for the Hawley family, have at least one real estate deal with them, and, in fact, eventually marry Phil's niece. In some ways, Jeff Pelley and the Hawleys *were* family, maybe even more than Jeff had ever been with his own father.

Like Bob Pelley, Phil Hawley is a complicated personality, someone with a rather colorful history in Lee County, where Fort Myers is the county seat. Phil's clipping file in the "morgue" of the Fort Myers newspaper, the *News-Press*, is fairly extensive. One of the articles, published in March 1978, recounts the saga of the mysteriously missing Harry William Stewart, and asserts that the insurance investigators first arrived in Sanibel after Phil had put in a written claim on one of the insurance policies.

Likewise, the article—an excellent piece of reporting by then *News-Press* staff writer Jim McGee, the same reporter who later exposed Gary Hart just prior to his *Monkey Business*—notes that one of the insurance policies was sold to Stewart by Robert Stintzi, who was a partner in Phil's private eye agency at the time, A & A Detective Recovery Corp., which seems to have been the auto repossession end of a debt collection business also owned by Phil.

Asked about Stewart at the time of his article, Phil told McGee he didn't want to discuss the matter. "I have nothing to say about that," McGee reported that Phil told him.

Looking back, it seems obvious the insurance investigators believed there was no such person as "Harry William Stewart"—at least an adult Harry William Stewart—that the crash into San Carlos Bay was a fake and that some sort of insurance scam was afoot. Just why "Stewart" would later have applied for a passport under the same apparently phony name is harder to understand, however—the passport wasn't needed to get the life insurance, and the application date, four months after he'd supposedly died in the crash, is odd. But the post-accident passport application might well have been an afterthought, "Stewart's" hedge against any future double-dealing by his confederates, since it would tend to prove that he hadn't died in any car wreck, and therefore, it might serve as leverage against anyone inclined to cheat him of his share of the insurance loot. The passport itself could have been a form of insurance, so to speak.

On the other hand, it's also fairly apparent that *News-Press* reporter Jim McGee had Phil Hawley in his sights. In an exposé published only a month earlier, McGee reported that Phil and some of his associates had formed a company to give immigration advice to undocumented aliens—for a fee.

"American Bureau of Citizenship"—"ABC"—with Phil Hawley as one of its principals, had organized a lucrative business advising undocumented aliens on how to get square with the federal immigration authorities, using a federally approved form each desperate immigrant filled out with their name and address. ABC had collected the official-looking forms and various fees, and then had done nothing, at least according to McGee. The implication of McGee's reporting was that Phil was running some sort of scam, victimizing illegals, a scam that promised safety from *La Migra*, for money. When people who paid were nevertheless rounded up and deported, complaints abounded.

McGee's reporting on ABC suggested, but did not definitely establish, that Phil's ABC enterprise, as it was called, had turned the addresses of the undocumented aliens over to the immigration authorities. However, it also reported that Phil had previously been deeply involved in Southwest Florida Republican Party politics, and thus, someone presumably sympathetic to the state's latent nativist sentiments. The suggestion was that Phil had been involved in a double scam: the first to take the immigrants' money, the second to cause their arrest and deportation.

But Phil had told McGee he didn't see it that way, at all—as far as he was concerned, he was only helping immigrants, mostly by providing a contact point in case the federal immigration authorities arrested them. He would then put them in touch with a Fort Myers lawyer. In effect, Phil, using his role as a "detective" associated with an attorney, was acting as a "capper," someone who touts lawyers for a piece of the action. The fact that most of those arrested never had a chance to call the number for legal assistance was the federal government's fault, Phil told McGee. But in the immediate aftermath of McGee's "ABC" reporting, experts from even the immigration service had condemned Phil's operation, and the Florida bar opened an investigation into the possibility that Phil was dispensing legal advice without a license.

So Phil wasn't at all eager to give McGee any comments the following month, when it turned out that he was the main beneficiary on life insurance issued to a man who had seemingly disappeared, who might not have really died, and in fact, might have never actually existed, at least as an adult. But the insurance investigators, even backed by the FBI, the state insurance enforcers, and the Sanibel police, were unable to assemble any criminal case against Phil, and eventually the whole thing went out with the tide.

Early the following year, 1979, Phil agreed to shut down "ABC." That was around the same time that Bob and Joy Pelley arrived in Florida from Ohio, at least according to Jacque Pelley.

Phil Hawley had been born in 1940, and with his wife, Linda, was the father of five boys: Pierre, born in 1958; Paul, born in 1959; Danny, born in 1963; David, born in 1964; and Martin, born in 1972. According to Phil, Jeff and Martin were the closest of friends in the Pelley family's Cape Coral days, attending school together, and often playing together, as the 1980s unfolded. Phil recalled Jeff frequently being around the Hawley family house on Winkler Road in Fort Myers, even though the Pelleys lived in Cape Coral.

Phil, it appears, was a patriarch of sorts, presiding over his extended family of five sons, their wives, and their children, as well as a few others. As he was to put it in the fall of 2006:

> I have raised five of my own sons, and I took in and helped raise three other boys when they were troubled as teens, and they had problems in their home, and their parents elected to either put them out or, for some reason, they were turned over to me by the court. Each one of them has grown into a good Christian man today, and I took them into my home. I raised them as Jeff [Pelley] was always raised, as a Christian teen, and I taught them, as his father taught him, to always work hard, to always do right and to always live a good Christian life.

A slightly rotund figure, seemingly jolly, Phil was an exceedingly sharp person—clever, someone who knew how to arrange things. By the early 2000s, Phil and his sons were officers and directors of quite a few corporations, around half of which would eventually become defunct. Some of those corporations would be taken over by the Hawleys under contentious circumstances, one of them involving a murder.

Based on Phil Hawley's later assertions, it appears that the Hawley family, like the Pelley family before the Olive Branch Brethren, were members of the Church of the Nazarene. In later years, Phil would refer to Bob as his "best friend." Exactly how the Hawley and Pelley families came to know one another wasn't clear, later, although it was probably through the Nazarene church, assuming there wasn't a connection dating back to 1976. Jacque, who recalled moving to Fort Myers in 1980, knew that her father had done some work for the Hawleys, apparently part-time and on weekends, throughout the early 1980s, although she couldn't recall what the nature of the job might have been. In her mind, her father had either helped the Hawleys set up a computer system, or had helped put up drywall, or maybe both.

In those days, Phil's main enterprise was tracking down delinquent debtors, and repossessing cars. The *News-Press* clipping file has at least two 1970s reports of employees of Phil's A & A Detective Recovery Corp. allegedly having improperly seized vehicles from people who had already paid off their auto loans. In one case, Robert Stintzi—he of the Stewart life insurance policy—was accused by the Lee County sheriff of posing as an official lawman, flashing a badge, contrary to law, in order to get the keys to a car that he claimed should be repossessed.

Having a man inside the telephone company might be very useful to a debt collector, and the same could be said for having someone inside a bank's data processing headquarters. In those very early days of VISA, knowing in a timely fashion where a delinquent debtor might be found could be very useful. But beyond those fundamental facts, there's no evidence to suggest that Bob provided any inside information to Phil's debt collection–private detective businesses—Jacque, for instance, was quite sure that her father hadn't helped Phil with debt collection.

By 1982 or early 1983, Bob's employment as a "tech" with United Telephone had ended, and he had moved on to Landmark Bank. His two children, Jeff, then 10, and Jacque, 7, soon adjusted to their new neighborhood in Cape Coral, and as noted, were close to the extended Hawley family, including Hawley cousins, one of whom Jeff would eventually marry.

But in 1986, the Pelleys abruptly pulled out of Cape Coral, and as Jacque recalled the story, it all had to do with something that had happened at the bank. Danny Hawley, Phil's third son, would later recall a similar circumstance—something had happened at the bank, a problem that "got more serious," as Danny put it, and which led to Bob's decision to quit and move his family to Indiana in November 1986. Danny claimed that Bob had then been working part-time for him, which was how he knew about the problem at the bank: Bob had talked to him about it.

Yet, if there *was* a problem at the bank, it seems to have been well-hidden. Although a proposed merger of Landmark with Citizens and Southern Bank of Georgia was held up for a time over some accounting issues, it eventually went through, about eight months before the Pelleys left Cape Coral. Likewise, there was nothing in the records of the federal Office of Thrift Supervision or the Comptroller of the Currency to indicate that the bank was sanctioned, or punished for illicit behavior. The only scandal publicly associated with the bank was the freelance money laundering undertaken by three bank employees for the Colombian in Fort Lauderdale, and that took place at least two years before Bob quit. So Jacque's recollection, even if perhaps supported by Danny Hawley, seems ephemeral—was Bob really feuding with pooh-bahs at the bank in 1985 to 1986 over missing money, or money-laundering? Or was there something else going on? At this point, twenty-five years later, so many records have been jettisoned, it's impossible to say.

On the other hand, many years later, a woman who had been the receptionist at the bank's data processing fortress in Fort Myers was asked what she recalled about the sudden departure of the Pelleys from Cape Coral. Nan Parrish remembered Bob Pelley very vividly, even fondly, as a gregarious, humorous man who sometimes took his children to work. It was part of Nan's job to screen the visitors to the fortress, to make sure the unauthorized didn't get inside, where all the mundane mechanics of banking, such as checks, deposits and balances, were processed and computed. She well remembered Joy Pelley's death, and the devastating impact it had had on Bob, despite his reluctance to show his emotions.

Then Bob had gotten married again, to Dawn, in November 1985. And then, a year after that, Bob had told Nan that he and his merged family were leaving Cape Coral. There was nothing in Nan Parrish's memory about any missing money, no midnight confrontation at the fortress, nothing about money-laundering, or drug cartels. "He just said they wanted to get a fresh start," Nan would recall, many years later.

And even Jacque, despite her recollections of the murky circumstances of the family's departure and her later suspicions, admitted that might have been true: "You have to understand that when they got married, Dawn came to live in my mom's home," Jacque said later. "The home that had been decorated by my mom."

It was difficult for Dawn, Jacque said, because of Joy's ghost, which seemed to hover over the rooms of the house in Cape Coral—indeed, everywhere the Pelleys went.

"They went to church where my mom had gone to church, and my dad's friends were my mom's friends . . ." And in fact, Dawn, a recent arrival in Cape Coral, was very far from her own friends and family, back in Michigan and Ohio. It was not at all surprising that Dawn, at least, wanted a "fresh start."

CHAPTER 13

By the late 1980s, Phil Hawley and his sons had begun to prosper. Besides the collection agency and its "detective" arm, the Florida Secretary of State's offices show a plethora of corporations formed by the Hawleys in the era, not least of which was the Hawley Construction Company. Other entities included a motorcycle dealership, a gun shop and a firing range, as well as numerous land development enterprises. Almost all of the dozen or so corporations formed by the Hawleys over the previous three decades included Phil, Phil's wife, Linda, and his sons Pierre, Paul, Danny, Dave and Martin as officers and directors. Clearly, the various Hawley businesses were a closely held family enterprise. On paper, Phil would assert in June 1989, he was worth a little over $12,000,000.

A little less than a year after the Pelley family had left Cape Coral for Indiana in late 1986, a debtor's account was referred to one of the three Hawley debt collection businesses, this one called Credit Bureau of Ft. Myers. Debt collection businesses often buy delinquent accounts from earlier creditors for cents on the dollar, in the hope that they will be more effective collecting and thus make a profit. In a way, it's a form of gambling.

This debtor was C. Eric Dawson, a 41-year-old promoter from Michigan with a rather checkered past. As a reporter for the Fort Myers *News-Press*, Peter Franceschina, later reconstructed the story, the Hawley debt collection business initially set out to recoup about $40,000 from Dawson—money he owed from various judgments against him in Michigan. But then things began to turn weird—as a local Lee County Sheriff's Office investigator, Tom Kontinos, would later tell Franceschina, it became a matter of who was trying to scam whom.

Based on Franceschina's reporting, along with Kontinos' own independent, corroborating recollection two decades later, it's hard to avoid the impression that Dawson was some sort of high-flying grifter, adept at keeping a lot of balls in the air at once, relying on balance sheet sleight of ink, tomorrow's blue skies, obscured by azure smoke and mirrors, all the better to borrow from Peter to pay the proverbial Paul. In other words, Dawson was a Ponzi artist, adept at gulling new investors to pay off, at least partially, the old.

Glib, an excellent salesman, a man with big ideas and bigger talk, Dawson had first run into trouble in Michigan selling stocks and bonds, eventually being fined $30,000 by the National Association of Securities Dealers and banned from the profession, according to Franceschina. While still in Michigan, in the early 1980s, he'd formed a Florida company with some associates to purchase a failing motel on Fort Myers' main drag, Cleveland Avenue. After paying $815,000 down, according to Franceschina, Dawson's group soon defaulted on a $4,000,000 mortgage. Dawson had to file for bankruptcy.

Undaunted, Dawson and his wife and three children moved permanently to Fort Myers in August 1983. He initially began by selling solar water heaters, but soon was involved in land development deals. Among his associates was a tax and estate planning expert, John C. Guise. Between 1983 and 1988, Dawson and Guise contrived to get control of nearly $1,000,000 in a trust fund benefiting two elderly women, Ella and Regina Riedl, twin sisters in their nineties, by posing as religious devotees, claiming that the Lord had sent them and that interest on the trust fund would go to pay for Christian missionary work. Eventually, the money would disappear, and in 1991 Guise would be indicted by the federal government on twenty-three counts of bank fraud, money-laundering and blackmail. Convicted in 1992, the then-55-year-old Guise would be paroled a few years later.

C. Eric Dawson would suffer a rather different fate.

By the mid-1980s—about the same time that Joy Pelley was dying, and Bob Pelley was remarrying, then leaving Fort Myers a year later—C. Eric Dawson had at least three land development projects in the works: first, seventy-one acres off Winkler Road, south of downtown Fort Myers, to be built as a high-quality master-planned residential community; second, an upscale condominium project at Fort Myers Beach, the "Bac-Bay Health and Racquet Club"; and third, a parcel of vacant land off Corkscrew Road, also south of Fort Myers, to be developed as a "Christian community," which Dawson called "Familyland." Dawson was juggling them all, using one to finance the other, enmeshing each in his Ponzi scam. As Franceschina later said, Dawson actually built nothing—all three projects were essentially illusory Hollywood sets. Each of the projects was heavily mortgaged, generally in small pieces to small investors at $30,000 to $40,000 each—in fact, Dawson seems to have anticipated today's collateralized mortgage crisis, which clearly marks him as a man ahead of his time.

Altogether, the multiple mortgages represented debts totaling about $5 million, to scores of investors, a good many of them retired and/or religiously devout. Dawson used the early money to gull later investors—that's how a Ponzi scheme works.

If he could have somehow actually brought off all three projects, Dawson's juggling act would have had its own reward, perhaps even permanent solvency. But as anyone experienced in using financial leverage knows, time is the enemy. As the clock ticked away, Dawson found it harder and harder to keep all his balls in the air. Inevitably, several balls fell, and Dawson came to the attention of the Hawley debt collection business, now on the trail of his bad old days in Michigan. A debt collector employed by the Hawleys, Barry Crowe, contacted Dawson and began pressing him for repayment of about $40,000 on various obligations. Dawson told Crowe he had no money, that everything was tied up in the land development projects, and that he was virtually judgment-proof.

Then, several weeks later, a tipster who worked in a local bank told Crowe he'd seen Dawson in the bank with a shoebox filled with cash—Dawson had flashed it preparatory to depositing it, probably to get a bank loan, but then thought better of it, since the bank was legally obligated to report any cash deposits of more than $10,000. At that point, according to Franceschina's story, Crowe called Dawson and threatened to expose him to the Internal Revenue Service if he didn't make arrangements to pay off the $40,000 in debts held by the Hawley collection agency.

Dawson made a few payments, according to Franceschina, while he tried to figure out how to handle this new juggling act. Then he called Phil Hawley for a meeting—to make him an offer he couldn't refuse: if Phil Hawley could borrow several million dollars from a bank and loan it to him, Dawson could complete the condo project. Once the project was finished, Dawson could pay Hawley back, with interest, and then make good on the debts. Dawson apparently agreed to sign over some of the condo units to the Hawleys to guarantee the loan. Whether he actually did this would later become a subject of great controversy; after all, Dawson's forte was in saying one thing but doing another.

"They were being scammed by a scammer," Lee County Sheriff's Detective Kontinos later told Franceschina, meaning the Hawleys were the scam victims. "And they were trying to *scam* a scammer. Trying to get the quick money is always a problem." In Kontinos' assessment, each side was trying to put one over on the other.

Eventually, Phil Hawley would claim that he put around $2,000,000 into Dawson's projects, money that apparently included advances on the construction costs of the condo project—Hawley Construction would be one of the contractors.

But by the summer of 1988, Dawson had pre-sold some of the condos to a Canadian investor, but apparently kept the sale proceeds from the Hawleys.

Then, on the afternoon of September 9, 1988, C. Eric Dawson vanished.

At first, some thought that Dawson had simply skipped out. His car was found at the Fort Myers airport, and rumors began to circulate: Dawson had gone to Brazil; Dawson was in Mexico; Dawson had joined Robert Vesco in the Bahamas—or was it Cuba? Or: Dawson had entered the witness protection program to hide out from the mob—or, alternatively, he was being protected from the government *by* the mob.

The next day, Phil and Dawson's wife, Susan, went to Dawson's office and searched it. Within a week, the Hawleys had control of the office and all of Dawson's paperwork on the various projects. Soon Phil and sons notified various mortgage holders of the projects that they had taken over.

Then, on November 20, 1988, two hunters stumbled on the remains of a dead man in a shallow grave in a wooded area southeast of the city. It was the body of C. Eric Dawson. Dawson had been shot in the back of the head by a bullet from a .22-caliber gun and dumped into the grave, which was then sealed with sacks of pre-mixed concrete. A recent rainstorm had weakened the concrete "tomb," as the media referred to it, and wild hogs had broken through and begun gnawing on the dead man's legs.

Two days later, documents deeding the Bac-Bay interests from Dawson to the Hawleys were filed with the Lee County recorder. Dawson had seemingly signed the documents three days before his September 9 disappearance. Eventually, other documents surfaced, asserting the Hawleys' control over the Winkler Road property, as well as the corporation controlling "Familyland."

Sheriff's Detective Kontinos and an investigator for the Florida State Attorney, James Fitzpatrick, were assigned to investigate Dawson's murder. Almost immediately they noticed the recent filing of the documents linking Dawson to the Hawleys. When they inspected the documents closely, they noticed that the signatures on some appeared to be identical. When they held the documents up to a window, one on top of the other, the signatures appeared to match exactly. Kontinos and Fitzpatrick concluded that the documents were forged.

Throughout the winter of 1988–1989, Kontinos and Fitzpatrick continued to investigate the tangled affairs of C. Eric Dawson, and his relationship to the Hawley enterprises, and soon became convinced that someone associated with the Hawleys had murdered Dawson, if for no other reason than to extricate the family businesses from Dawson's imminent financial collapse. By the early spring of 1989, Kontinos and Fitzpatrick had obtained search warrants for several of the Hawley family homes and offices.

Kontinos was later to recall the atmosphere in the days leading up to the searches. The fact that an investigation into Dawson's murder was under way was common knowledge in the community, as was the fact that the Hawleys were targets. Kontinos recalled rumors to the effect that all the Hawleys were packing guns, although the idea of an entire family preparing to engage in a shoot-out with lawmen as in *The Sons of Katie Elder* seems far-fetched. But perhaps it wasn't the police that the Hawleys were concerned about, but someone behind Dawson . . .

In the affidavits for the searches, Kontinos and Fitzpatrick laid out their case:

> Based on these facts and specifically that Phillip Hawley and Danny Hawley have lied under oath, have prepared and recorded forged, fabricated and altered documents which in effect have transferred major assets worth millions of dollars from the deceased to a corporation wholly controlled by Phillip Hawley and his family, and that Phillip Hawley immediately took control of the deceased's business records and accounts and closed the business office of the deceased within a week of the time of the deceased's unexplained disappearance, as if

> he knew Eric Dawson would not be returning, makes Phillip Hawley and his sons prime suspects in the murder of Eric Dawson.

These warrants were served on April 4, 1989, just three weeks before Bob Pelley, Dawn Pelley, Janel and Jolene were found shot to death in Lakeville, Indiana.

And then, in July 1989, even as Jeff Pelley was enduring the suspicions of friends, neighbors and police in Lakeville, Phil and Danny Hawley were arrested in Fort Myers and charged with multiple counts of fraud, theft, usury and forgery in connection with C. Eric Dawson's convoluted affairs. Prosecutors made it clear that they intended to prove the Hawleys were behind Dawson's murder, and that the murder was for the purpose of gaining control of Dawson's embattled projects.

CHAPTER 14

That members of two unrelated but intertwined families, the Pelleys and the Hawleys, should each be suspects in two apparently unconnected murders, committed hundreds of miles apart, yet both taking place within an eight-month time span, seems bizarre, but nevertheless, those are the facts.

It is another strange fact that at least some of the events surrounding C. Eric Dawson and his associate, John Guise, the tax-advising con artist who made a fat living gulling Christian believers, seems to echo some of the rumors recalled by Jacque Pelley—a missing million dollars, bank fraud, money-laundering. The fact that Dawson and Guise were using religion to inveigle their victims also stands out, although Dawson and Guise victimized Baptists, not Nazarenes. Given that Dawson and Guise were operating in Fort Myers between 1983 and 1989, and had significant dealings with local banks, one can only wonder what Bob Pelley, or even Harry William Stewart, knew about their activities.

In short, there are enough coincidences and overlaps to set an investigator's nose twitching over these events, coming as close together as they did, and emanating from the same locale. Yet the Lakeville authorities in 1989 knew nothing about the Hawleys' difficulties with the law in Florida, and the Florida investigators knew nothing about the Pelleys' murders, or Jeff Pelley, in Indiana.

It wasn't until the spring of 2008 that Detective Kontinos, by then retired from the Lee County Sheriff's Office, finally learned of the Pelley murders, that Phil Hawley's "best friend" Bob Pelley's son Jeff was a suspect in those murders and that Jeff had married Phil Hawley's niece, and in fact had gone to work for the Hawley enterprises after he moved to Florida in the early 1990s.

Mark Senter and John Botich in Indiana were familiar with the name Hawley, but only because of Jeff's later marriage. Neither knew, back in 1989, that Phil and his sons were "the prime suspects" in the 1988 murder of C. Eric Dawson. In fact, Senter and Botich knew nothing of Kontinos, and Kontinos knew nothing of Botich and Senter and their suspicions of Jeff Pelley, or the murder of Phil's former "best friend," Bob, who some thought so closely resembled Harry William Stewart.

But trying to connect dots, even if they're not actually related, has never been a strong suit in American law enforcement—just as with national intelligence agencies, cops like to keep the details of their investigations to themselves. Sometimes this is good, but just as often, it's bad.

By the fall of 1991, someone would put the two murder cases together—at least as a suspicious circumstance—but merely as background to yet another criminal case: one that eventually led to Jeff's arrest for attempting to defraud his own trust, to get some of the life insurance money left behind by his father after Bob's murder at the end of April 1989.

By the summer of 1991, the forgery-fraud-usury trial of the Hawleys—Phil and Danny had been joined as defendants by David and Paul—was finally imminent. Two years of pretrial maneuvering, including bankruptcies for some of the Hawleys, and Phil's effort to have himself declared indigent for the purpose of obtaining a publicly paid defense lawyer, had intervened and caused delay.

By that time, Jeff was living with Phil's sister and her daughter. Both worked at a local hospital's business office, while Jeff was employed at the Hawley debt collection firm.

Jeff was now 19 years old, still growing up too fast. Although the Pelley trust had specified that he be 26 years old before he could gain access to the trust principal, Jeff wanted the money sooner—like right now.

From Jeff's perspective, it was his money, after all, and the fact that he had to go through Dawn's father, Ed Hayes, to get anything from the trust galled him. He barely knew Ed Hayes. Jon Boso had long since declined any role as a trustee.

Late in July or August 1991, Jeff called Hayes in Michigan with a sad tale. He'd just undergone surgery for malignant melanoma—cancer—and the bill for the surgery was over $20,000, Jeff told Hayes. His future mother-in-law, Phil's sister, had paid the bill. Could he please have $20,000 from the trust to repay her?

Hayes, sensing that something wasn't right, asked Jeff to send him a copy of the hospital invoice and a cancelled check as proof. A week later, Hayes received a copy of a hospital bill, along with a cancelled check showing payment of $20,359.93 from his future mother-in-law's checking account to the hospital. Hayes looked over the bill and believed it legitimate. But he also thought there were some excessive charges on the bill. He noticed that a biopsy showed the supposed cancerous lesions were benign, not malignant. Hayes called the hospital, using the number listed on the bill. A woman answered the telephone, but wasn't able to answer any of Hayes' questions about the bill or the procedures involved.

Hayes hung up and dialed information for Fort Myers, and obtained a different telephone number for the hospital. This time he reached someone who could provide answers, and the information was disappointing, although not altogether surprising: the hospital had no record of any patient named Robert Jeffrey Pelley, or even Jeff Pelley. Intrigued by his questions, the hospital asked Hayes to send them a copy of the supposed bill. The hospital soon began an investigation.

A few days later, Jeff called Hayes to find out when he'd get the money. Hayes told Jeff he'd just found out the bill was fake. Confronted, Jeff admitted the deception, but then provided reasons as to why he needed the money from the trust, and why he'd felt he had to use trickery to get it. A few minutes after this call ended, Hayes received another call, this one from Jeff's future mother-in-law, Phil's sister, swearing she knew nothing of the ruse, and begging Hayes not to report it to the hospital—she feared for her job.

But by that time, the hospital administrators had already zeroed in on Jeff, his future wife, who also worked for the hospital, and the future mother-in-law, Phil's sister. In subsequent interviews with the hospital's security chief, Jeff took full responsibility for what had happened, saying that neither Phil's sister nor his fiancée had known what he was up to.

According to Jeff, he'd become familiar with the hospital's billing practices while working at the Hawleys' "Fort Myers Credit Bureau," which apparently had been hired to collect bad debts to the hospital. Since he knew what the real bills looked like, it was simple to make a fake. Then he'd kept a signed blank check his future mother-in-law had given him to buy groceries, filled in the bogus amount, and superimposed the cancellation marks on the check by use of a copy machine.

To set the scam in motion, he'd obtained a second telephone line, installed it in a closet, and call-forwarded it to a friend's number. Jeff steadfastly refused to identify the friend. By claiming that the call had been automatically forwarded to an unnamed friend, he was shifting any blame away from his future wife and mother-in-law, one of whom might possibly have been the female voice who had answered Hayes' call to the phony number a few weeks earlier. Despite having caught Jeff red-handed, and even having his confession, the hospital officials decided not to report Jeff to law enforcement authorities, and absolved Jeff's future mother-in-law and wife from any involvement.

There the matter rested for a week or so. Then someone—no one later admitted to it—sent an anonymous letter to the Florida State Attorney's Office, recounting the facts of the phone-in-the-closet scam. By this point, Botich and Senter back in Indiana had heard the tale from Ed Hayes, with whom they had remained in contact since the Pelley murders. Botich and Senter realized that this might be a break: if they could get someone in Florida to pull Jeff in and put him under arrest for wire fraud—the telephone call to Hayes—maybe they could spook Jeff into even more damaging admissions. Whether Botich or Senter, or Hayes, or someone at the hospital, was the author of the anonymous letter isn't known, but someone familiar with at least some of the details of the phone-in-the-closet scam had to be.

With an official if anonymous communication in hand, the Florida State Attorney had no choice but to launch a criminal investigation. This task was referred to a state insurance investigator, William "Biff" Lagan. Lagan began by interviewing the hospital people, who told him they hadn't reported the attempted scam to the police because they were afraid of Jeff Pelley—they knew that he was a suspect in the murders of his family back in Indiana.

By October 10, 1991, just as the Hawleys' trial on forgery charges in the C. Eric Dawson case was starting, Lagan had sworn affidavits from Ed and Lara Hayes, alleging that Jeff had committed wire fraud. Senter had driven up to Michigan from Indiana to collect the affidavits, and had forwarded them to Lagan in Florida.

In his report, eventually filed with the Florida State Attorney on February 12, 1992, Lagan included the following:

> Importance of this investigation heightened since the individuals accused in this letter of being accomplices in a crime are also direct family members of individuals under indictment in this judicial circuit for a multi-million dollar fraud scheme and possible involvement in the murder of C. Eric Dawson of Ft. Myers in 1988. . . .
>
> Investigation has revealed the following chain of events:
>
> On April 29, 1989, Robert (Jeff's father), Dawn (stepmother), Jolene and Janel (stepsisters) were brutally murdered by shotgun fire inside their Lakeville, Indiana, home. Jeffrey Pelley is a prime suspect in these murders.
>
> As a result of these deaths, Jeffrey is afforded ap-

> proximately $69,000 [sic] in estate trust funds. Edward Hayes is the sole executor [sic] of Pelley's estate. Stipulations of the estate and trust allow Jeffrey access to the funds only in the event of an emergency, mutual consent of the executor [sic], or until he is 23 years old.

Bob's trust document permitted Jeff to access half the amount due once he graduated from college, which he had not done, or turned 23, the rest when he was 26. In September 1991, Jeff was only 20. Ed Hayes wasn't the executor, he was the sole remaining trustee, after Jon Boso had opted out. Jeff's share of the trust, minus his college expenses, was actually less than $50,000, not $63,000.

This was the first and only time that anyone in either Indiana or Florida had even peripherally associated the four Lakeville murders with that of C. Eric Dawson eight months earlier. The hint of a possible connection was just that, a mere sniff of a suggestion, based solely on the interconnectedness of the suspect parties—Jeff in the first case, the Hawleys in the second. But without more evidence—say, a confession in one case or the other—there was simply no way to connect the two prospective ends of a putative tunnel. Both on paper and in a court of law, the two murder cases had no provable connection, outside of the wispiest of hunches.

What was more, there wasn't even any significant evidence to prove who had committed any of the murders, let alone tying even one to the Hawleys or Jeff Pelley. It was absolutely the sheerest of coincidence.

But it was an odd coincidence.

The trial of Phil Hawley and sons began the following day, October 11, 1991. Franceschina of the Fort Myers *News-Press* was there. He later recalled that the proceeding took six weeks, although, to Franceschina, it seemed more like six months.

In the run-up to the trial of Phil and his offspring, Lee County Judge Elmer O. Friday had limited the prosecution as to what it could tell the jury about Dawson's murder. After all, no murder weapon had ever been found, and it was only supposition, bolstered by cause and effect, that suggested the Hawleys had anything to do with Dawson's demise. A lawyer for Phil, Ed Couse, argued that the prosecutors had it backward: they had to first prove that the Hawleys committed the murder of Dawson—which could not be done—*then* charge the forgeries; to assert or even suggest or imply that the Hawleys were responsible for Dawson's demise, in the absence of evidence, was overwhelmingly prejudicial. A jury might convict Phil and his sons simply because the state had suggested they were really murderers. The murder charge would dwarf the theft, forgery and usury charges, which was what the trial was really all about.

Judge Friday agreed, and ruled that prosecutors could only show that Dawson had been murdered, not present any supposition or argument that the Hawleys had done the deed. There was also no need to go into who else might have done it, he said.

But Kontinos, for one, was convinced that if they hadn't done it themselves, they'd brought in some outside talent to do the job. Rumors abounded about some professional hit man from Tampa, but there was simply no meaningful evidence. Kontinos had hoped to find the murder weapon during the April 4, 1989, search at the Hawley house, but it wasn't there. In later years, Kontinos could still recall serving the search warrant: after gaining entrance to the Hawley house, Kontinos said he had found a large safe.

"Phil," Kontinos said—by this point, after six months' investigation, they were on a first-name basis—"either you can unlock that safe for us, or we'll blow it open."

Phil unlocked the safe, according to Kontinos. The detective searched through it, but found no .22 pistol. He did, however, find reams of stock certificates for the many companies the Hawleys had incorporated over the preceding decade, including Caribbean International Industries, the company which had taken over Dawson's interest in the Bac-Bay condo project. He also found a copy of the document signed by Dawson that matched the supposed forged signatures, or so Kontinos claimed. The original document, however, remained missing.

On the basis of this and other evidence, the trial of Phil Hawley and three of his five sons opened on October 11, 1991, even as some authorities in Florida and Indiana were thinking of ways to scare the bejeesus out of Phil's future nephew-in-law, Jeff Pelley.

CHAPTER 15

"Signature of Dead Man Key in Theft, Forgery Trial," the *News-Press* headlined as the Hawley trial opened. Franceschina summarized:

> Prosecutors have charged Phil Hawley and his sons Danny, David and Paul with multiple counts of grand theft, forgery, making a false notary and criminal usury, which is making a loan with an illegal interest rate of 45 percent or higher.
>
> Phil Hawley's attorney, E. G. Couse, told jurors Eric Dawson might have forged his own signature so he could later lay claim to the property if it was foreclosed upon . . .

"I would suggest to you," Crouse told the jury in his opening statement, "that a lot of what you're going to hear and a lot of what the state proposes is not evidence of guilt, but a lot of it is going to involve coincidence." Of course, there was also a lot of coincidence involving the Hawleys and the Pelleys.

Jim Long, a lawyer for Danny, Dave and Paul, contended that the three sons should never have been charged in the case.

"When father Phil Hawley did not admit to killing his best friend, C. Eric Dawson, when father Phil Hawley would not say that he did something he did not do—" But the prosecutors objected. If they weren't allowed to link Phil to the Dawson murder in front of the jury, neither could the sons' lawyer bring it up as a motive for the prosecution's decision to charge the Hawleys, they contended. This would just be the start of one of the most contentious trials in Florida's history.

"The state would have you believe," Long went on, despite the judge's admonition, "that 'Honor thy father' means 'Steal and forge.' " The judge verbally whacked Long again, and the case of *State* vs. *Hawley* was off and running, or actually, stumbling.

No one then observed that although Bob Pelley had been Phil's "best friend" in 1986, by his disappearance in 1988, C. Eric Dawson had been Phil's "best friend." But hey—what are friends for?

The struggle between the State of Florida and the Hawleys would last until late November 1991, while the two sides battled over the validity of Dawson's signature on various documents. An FBI specialist testified that there was no doubt in his mind that one signature, on a deed turning over the seventy-one-acre Winkler Road property to the Hawleys, had been forged. For their part, the Hawleys tried to rebut that testimony with an expert of their own, but ran into difficulties: their first expert, a former consultant to the CIA and the Secret Service, agreed with the FBI expert.

A second expert died of natural causes before he could testify. A third expert was murdered by her boyfriend in Arkansas before she could make it to the stand, and the testimony of a fourth was disallowed by the judge because the defense lawyers hadn't given the prosecutor enough time to prepare for her cross-examination. When the defense asked to put her testimony on the record anyway, outside the presence of the jury, in case of appeal, the expert said she agreed the signatures were tracings, but said only Dawson himself could have made such a perfect copy. But she also had to admit that she'd had no formal training in handwriting analysis.

A devastating blow to the Hawleys was delivered by Barry Crowe, by now a former employee of the Hawley debt collection business, and the one who had first contacted Dawson back in 1987 to get money that Dawson owed. He recalled being asked to witness Dawson's signature on some documents, although Dawson himself wasn't around at the time—in fact, Crowe said, he joked about the matter, asking the Hawleys if they were sure it was Dawson's signature. He'd been assured that it was Dawson's writing, Crowe testified.

After Kontinos and Fitzpatrick had served their search warrants in early April 1989, Crowe went on, he'd been pulled in by law enforcement, and then agreed to wear a "wire" to get evidence against the Hawleys. Crowe did it, and in a half-hour, profanity-laced recorded conversation between Crowe, Danny and Dave on April 12, 1989, Dave and Danny insisted that they had seen Dawson sign one of the documents just before he disappeared. The cops had nothing on them, Dave had insisted to Crowe.

As to some of the other documents, the defense kept trying to establish that Dawson himself had *wanted* his signature to seem to be a forgery. At one point, Dawson's widow, Susan, admitted that she had sworn in an unrelated civil case against Dawson that her signature had been forged, presumably by her husband. James Long, the defense lawyer for the Hawley sons, then attempted to question Susan about some $800,000 in life insurance Dawson supposedly had, but was precluded by Judge Friday—the trial wasn't going after alternative killers, Friday ruled, a decision that would foreshadow the thinking of a judge in Jeff Pelley's own murder case almost fifteen years later.

In 2008, Long would recall the Hawley trial as "surreal," not least because Judge Friday kept falling asleep on the bench.

"It was like something from *The Twilight Zone*," he remembered. "We'd come in and start at nine, he'd fall asleep by nine-thirty, we'd go out in the hallway to smoke cigarettes until he woke up again." The prosecutors kept insisting that Long should be the one to wake the judge up, but Long said *they* should do it. So the judge slumbered on.

The prosecutors kept trying to introduce evidence trying to tie the Hawleys to Dawson's murder—they wanted to show that the alleged forgery-theft was the motive for the killing.

But the defense said that if the prosecutors could claim murder as part of the forgery, they should be entitled to show that Dawson had plenty of other people mad at him besides the Hawleys—not to mention the supposed $800,000 in life insurance. Judge Friday didn't want to let any of the murder evidence in—it would only foul up the case, he said, with all sorts of extraneous, irrelevant evidence. Once that stuff came in, the jury would be in the box for years, given C. Eric Dawson's life and times.

Much of the wrangling over the Dawson murder took place with the jury penned up in the jury room, out of earshot and increasingly frustrated. That led Judge Friday to tell the lawyers, "If I were a juror, I'd be terrified and confused."

That was Franceschina's impression, too.

"In the courtroom, the lawyers can't agree on anything," he reported to the readers of the *News-Press*. "If one side isn't objecting, the other is. The issues sometimes take hours to resolve, only to crop up again in a few minutes after the jury has been ushered back into the courtroom." Franceschina thought the record for uninterrupted testimony was only thirteen minutes.

The Hawley trial straggled on into late November, with Danny and David both taking the stand to swear that Dawson had been in the Hawley office on the day one of the documents was signed. That was a slightly different story from what they'd maintained in the spring of 1989, when they'd said they'd actually seen Dawson provide his signature. Now Dave admitted that he hadn't actually witnessed Dawson sign, only that he knew he'd been in the office that day.

The case finally went to the beleaguered six-person jury on Friday, November 22, 1991.

"There is one thing for sure," prosecutor Dwight Brock told the jury in his closing argument. "When somebody put that .twenty-two in the back of his head, he [Dawson] wasn't going to be successful any longer. They had ceased his business operations, permanently." The Hawley lawyers immediately demanded a mistrial, claiming prosecutorial misconduct for Brock's implication that the Hawleys were responsible for Dawson's still-unsolved murder. The judge denied the motion.

"Hawleys Convicted of Forgery," the *News-Press* headlined the following day. After deliberating for six hours, the jury found Phil, Danny and Dave guilty of multiple counts of forgery, criminal usury, and grand theft. Paul was convicted of "forgery-related" counts, according to Franceschina's report. Judge Friday allowed father and sons to remain free on $25,000 bail pending sentencing, which was set for January 1992.

"Hawleys Could Get 30 Years in Prison," the newspaper reported on the eve of the sentencing in early January 1992. But that was only if the judge threw the book at them, Franceschina reported in the body of his story in the *News-Press*. State sentencing guidelines were substantially lower—3½ to 5 years.

But two days later, Judge Friday sentenced Phil alone to 120 days in jail—only 20 days to be served consecutively. Danny, Dave and Paul received probation. This happened even after State Attorney Investigator James Fitzpatrick—the same agent who had worked with Lagan on Jeff's phone-in-the-closet case that fall—testified that he'd received an anonymous telephone call the week before from a man who claimed that one of the Hawleys had tried to hire him to commit a murder. But Fitzpatrick admitted that he hadn't gotten the caller's name or telephone number, so Judge Friday said such unsubstantiated hearsay couldn't be considered in imposing a sentence.

Judge Friday said he was mystified as to how Phil could have gotten so encumbered with Dawson to begin with.

"This, of course, brings up a deep contrast, the black and white of human conduct," Friday said. "How did it happen, especially with the values Phil Hawley demonstrated over the years?" It was so out-of-character, Friday said, he was going to withhold a formal finding of guilt on the most serious charge against Phil, the grand theft count. That was how Phil avoided time in the state pen.

The *News-Press* editorial page was puzzled, too.

"Strange Punishment," the paper opined on January 10, 1992:

> In the Hawley case, the punishment does not fit the crime . . . [the judge was] apparently in deep sympathy with the convicted Hawleys . . .
>
> The Hawleys' conduct isn't hard to understand, Judge. The father and his boys did it for money—a lot of money—the oldest reason in the book . . . what is really hard to understand about this case is why such behavior didn't draw more punishment than a slap on the wrist.

Franceschina had a rather more cynical take on the denouement of *State* vs. *Hawley*: noting, years later, that he thought Judge Friday, a veteran of Florida's political wars, and a man who was well-connected, had taken a dive. Kontinos and Fitzpatrick believed the same thing.

But even as the Hawleys were essentially walking away from the Dawson wreckage—except for their financial losses on Dawson's projects—Lagan was zeroing in on Jeff.

CHAPTER 16

In his 1992 report, filed with the Florida Department of Insurance, Division of Insurance Fraud—Lagan's agency—Lagan asserted that Jeff had been caught fair-and-square, trying to con money out of the trust from Edward Hayes. After summarizing the allegations and the evidence, Lagan asserted that the fraud division was "obliged to forward its investigative findings to the Michigan State Police," especially since Jeff was still a suspect in the Pelley family murders.

But Lagan soon discovered that no one in the Michigan State Police was interested in prosecuting Jeff, or even arresting him, especially since Jeff had never obtained any actual money from Hayes. Lagan took his report to the Florida State Attorney, and found yawns there, too. The Indiana people might be willing to prosecute, but they had no jurisdiction—none of the acts had taken place in Indiana.

But Lagan didn't give up—Botich and Senter were egging him on, they admitted later. Eventually, Lagan took his report to the United States Attorney's office for the central district of Florida. There he finally found a willing prosecutor, and on February 15, 1994, almost two years after he'd filed his initial report with his insurance supervisors, Jeff was arrested by the FBI, accompanied by Lagan, Botich, Senter and Cape Coral police.

And a SWAT team.

The two Indiana detectives arrived in Fort Myers accompanied by an assistant prosecuting attorney from St. Joseph County, Jane Becker. After meeting with the FBI, Lagan and the Cape Coral cops, the group went to the dwelling Jeff shared with his recently wed bride and new mother-in-law, Phil's sister, and took him into custody. The SWAT team was definitely over the top, but as Lagan recalled it later, "We wanted to scare the snot out of the kid."

In fact, that's what happened, according to Botich and Senter. As soon as Jeff saw the police, they recalled, he turned pale.

"He just assumed we were there to arrest him for the murders," Senter recalled. "He didn't even have to ask why we were there."

But when he discovered that Botich and Senter had no charges against him, and that the arrest was on a federal wire fraud charge—the telephone call to Hayes—Jeff relaxed. He now realized that Botich and Senter were only using the arrest to intimidate him into confessing to the murders. Again, Jeff steadfastly denied any involvement. Soon his bride, Phil's niece—they'd been married two weeks before—arrived and posted a $50,000 bond for his release.

Back in South Bend, Jeff's arrest was front-page news. A reporter for the *South Bend Tribune* tracked down Ed Hayes in Michigan.

"He never gave me any trouble before," Hayes told the reporter. Still, Hayes said, he wasn't surprised that Jeff had tried to finagle his way into the trust. "In fact, I would've been surprised if he hadn't . . ."

Botich, for his part, refused to say that Jeff was a suspect in the family murders. He was only a source of information, Botich told the newspaper.

But two weeks later, St. Joseph County Prosecutor Michael Barnes said that Jeff *was* a suspect—the prime suspect. "Although Michael P. Barnes considers Robert J. 'Jeff' Pelley a prime suspect in the 1989 slayings of his family," the *Tribune's* Marti Goodlad Heline reported, "the St. Joseph County prosecutor has no immediate plans to attempt to bring Pelley to Indiana for questioning or prosecution." There still wasn't enough evidence against Jeff to insure a conviction, Barnes insisted.

But casting a shadow south, Barnes claimed that Jeff had refused to answer any questions from Botich, Senter and Becker about the murders, after his wire fraud pinch.

That wasn't the way Botich saw it, though. In another newspaper story, published in late April to mark the fifth anniversary of the killings, "Botich describe[d] his relationship to Jeff Pelley as good, noting that Pelley has never refused to talk to him," the *Tribune's* Kevin Boughal reported.

"He's my suspect, everybody knows that," Botich told Boughal.

For his part, in the same article, Barnes defended his lack of action in the case: there just wasn't enough evidence to arrest Jeff, let alone bring him to trial for the murders, Barnes insisted. And when some in the community, not least Dave Hathaway, criticized Barnes for his failure to act, Barnes retorted that some people just didn't understand how the system worked. To suggestions that he convene a grand jury to consider an indictment, Barnes pointed out that the law in Indiana forbade him to call a second grand jury if an original grand jury refused to bring charges, unless there was new evidence; it was definitely double jeopardy—as Yogi Berra had said, it would be déjà vu all over again. Barnes wanted to keep the first grand jury option unused as long as he could.

Even if an original grand jury indicted Jeff, that would start the clock running—he'd have to go to trial within a year, if not sooner, based on the state's speedy trial rules, and the inescapable fact was, there simply wasn't enough evidence, so far. Maybe the public demanded action, but in Barnes' view, charging a defendant without sufficient evidence was foolhardy—or maybe even dishonest.

That spring in 1994, Jeff pled guilty to attempted wire fraud for the phone-in-the-closet scam, and in late July was sentenced to 6 months' home detention, probably a reasonable outcome, given that he hadn't actually received any money from Hayes, and that the money was actually his to begin with. But it had been a rough five years for Jeff, who was now 22.

First had come the awful murders, followed by his becoming the prime suspect, then the embarrassment over the telephone scam, then the Hawley trial; then had come a series of small-claims actions against him, filed after a computer business he'd tried to start ran aground. The business reversal was probably why he'd tried to get the trust money from Hayes—he was desperate for cash.

Then had come an even worse disaster: while driving south on Cleveland Avenue in Fort Myers in March 1993, in a newly leased Honda, Jeff had broadsided another car, killing the driver, Janet Ady, and injuring her passenger husband, David.

David Ady soon sued Jeff, the Honda dealership and the lease finance company that had actually owned Jeff's car. A witness to the crash said Jeff claimed that he'd fallen asleep, but in a later deposition, Jeff claimed that the cruise control on the car had malfunctioned. Exactly why Jeff would be using the cruise control on a street with stoplights every few hundred feet wasn't clear—if he had, maybe it had suddenly cut in—who knew? But still, in some ways Jeff was just a kid—it was possible he was actually using the cruise control on a heavily traveled city street.

Worse, it turned out that Jeff had no insurance. Jeff said he'd thought the insurance was the responsibility of the leasing company—he thought it was part of the lease price. The case went all the way to the Florida Supreme Court, which held that leasing companies were liable for any uninsured drivers of their leased vehicles. The Florida legislature soon after passed a law making insurance mandatory for leases. David Ady eventually settled his lawsuit with Honda and its Fort Myers dealership for $1.7 million. From the Lee County Court records, there's no indication that Jeff was assessed any liability for Janet Ady's death.

"The car accident was really rough on Jeff," Jacque would recall. It wasn't that Jacque was as insensitive to the Adys as the remark suggests—after all, the Adys had it far rougher than Jeff: Janet Ady had died and David Ady was sorely injured but by the time she made that observation, Jacque was totally focused on defending her brother. Everything else seemed to be reduced to the simple test: how could it help Jeff?

Perhaps because of the financial strains of the failed computer business, or because of the looming liability to David Ady, Jeff and his wife divorced in April 1997. But a little over two years later, a week after his twenty-eighth birthday, they remarried. Soon they would have a child together, and life finally began to brighten for Jeff.

Moving away from the debt collection business of the Hawleys, Jeff began taking advanced courses in computer database programming, then network systems. By the end of the 1990s, he'd obtained work as a consultant to IBM, working with businesses to upgrade their networks—the sort of work Bob himself would likely have embraced, had he not felt the call to the pastorate. Jeff seems to have been very successful in this field—according to some accounts, by early 2002, he was in line to earn as much as $100,000 a year as an IBM/Microsoft network consultant, and was traveling widely.

As far as Jeff was concerned, the past was past—after a very rough start in life, he had much to look forward to.

But the past has a way of reemerging, usually when least expected.

Although almost a decade had gone by since the awful events in the parsonage, the murder of the four Pelleys was hardly forgotten in St. Joseph County. While Prosecutor Michael P. Barnes acknowledged that Jeff was the prime suspect, he steadfastly insisted that there simply wasn't enough evidence to charge him. Barnes' posture, while legally defensible, didn't sit well with a number of his constituents, including, among others, Dave Hathaway of Lakeville.

In early 1994, in fact, after learning of Jeff's arrest in the Florida wire fraud case, Hathaway had written a letter to the *South Bend Tribune*, criticizing Barnes for his reluctance to bring charges, or at least failing to convene a grand jury to investigate the murders, which remained so vivid in his memory. The bloody evidence of the shootings, with the little girls, one of them clutching her mother, haunted Hathaway—in his mind, if God was just, the savage violator of decency should be punished, and in this world.

"Since I was the one who discovered their bodies, I am writing to inform the people of the community that we are still very much in prayer that this hideous crime will be solved, and that someone will step forward to help bring this about," Hathaway informed the newspaper. Hathaway was hardly alone—there were many in Lakeville who believed that Barnes was far too timid when it came to charging Jeff. They wanted something done—they wanted resolution, or, as the news media would later call it, "closure," which was really just another way of giving everyone else a chance to say, *Hey, it's over, let's go on*. This is always the choice of the undead and the uninvolved, who choose not to dwell on something no one could now do anything about—usually the people who care most about "closure."

Actual survivors never have "closure"—they never forget.

Still, the reality was, the murders had seeped into the community as some sort of secret shame, and almost everyone wanted the cloud banished, and their bucolic ideal restored. If the authorities could say that Jeff had done it, that it had nothing to do with *them*, everything would go back to normal.

But Barnes was adamant—no evidence, no charges. So the murder of the four Pelleys festered, and eventually became a poison in the body politic of St. Joseph County.

By 1998, dissatisfaction with Barnes' performance as prosecutor seemed widespread. That year he was challenged for reelection by a young South Bend lawyer, Christopher Toth, a Republican ideologically opposed to Barnes' middle-of-the-road, Democratic Party moderation, at least when it came to issues of crime and punishment.

Toth was 37, a Navy veteran, with experience in the Naval Criminal Investigative Service, and apparently, the Office of Naval Intelligence, the largely mysterious ONI. He wanted to invigorate the investigation of unsolved murder cases, in part by increasing the involvement of deputy prosecutors with police, sending them out to crime scenes as on-the-spot advisors. Previously Barnes had formed a "Special Crimes Unit," composed of detectives from South Bend, the county police, and the nearby city of Mishawaka, which responded directly to the prosecutor's office. Toth wanted to beef up that unit with more personnel, and use the additional resources to look into old, still-unsolved murders, like the Pelley case.

When the ballots were counted late on the night of November 3, 1998, Toth had crushed Barnes with 56 percent of the total, a margin of almost 10,000 votes. As soon as he took office in 1999, Toth swept the old Barnes loyalists from the prosecutor's office and brought in his own team. One was Mike Swanson of the South Bend police, who had been an evidence technician at the parsonage ten years earlier. Swanson was appointed commander of the Special Crimes Unit shortly after Toth took office. He began reviewing the old investigative files on the Pelley case, and by early 2000, told Toth that he believed a case against Jeff could be made.

On the eleventh anniversary of the Pelley murders, April 29, 2000, Toth held a news conference to announce that the Pelley case was being "reopened."

CHAPTER 17

Later, Toth was criticized by his opponents, some of them police officers, for his penchant for drama—grandstanding, some called it. He was never one to put out a simple news release when a full-dress media circus might lead the evening local news broadcast. But then, Toth was a politician as well as a prosecutor, and doubtless felt it was important to let the public know he was on the job.

"Obviously, this case left an indelible mark on the psyche of the community," Toth told reporters, as he made his announcement. "It was a horrible, tragic case. Any time there's a quadruple murder, you can't leave the case on the shelf forever." Toth claimed that the Special Crimes Unit had developed some new leads, but in retrospect, this seems to have been an overstatement: the only new development was a decision to send some of the clothing found in the parsonage to the Federal Bureau of Investigation for DNA analysis, along with some of the shotgun-shell wadding collected from the victims' bodies. The hope was that the FBI could develop more information on the make of the shotgun, which was still missing after a decade, or possibly some DNA from the unknown shooter.

Four days after Toth's "stunning" announcement, as the *Tribune* called it, the newspaper's editorialist noted that Toth was "putting his political future at considerable risk" by reopening the Pelley case:

> If he is successful, Toth will have solved puzzles that have intrigued county residents for more than a decade

> and will rightfully earn accolades for having done so. But, if he fails, Toth will inevitably be judged at least partially at fault by his critics, despite the uphill nature of his quest. Make no mistake, what Toth is doing takes political courage.

Thus, almost from the outset of the "reopening," the Pelley case acquired a political tinge, and as the investigation went forward into the year 2002—and as Toth's campaign got under way that year, the perception began to grow in some circles that he was using the murders for his own ends, that is, to insure his reelection: where Barnes had been loath, Toth was ready to rock and roll, as far as Jeff and the four dead Pelleys were concerned.

In fact, there was little new evidence to be found. Detectives from the Special Crimes Unit fanned out and reinterviewed many of the witnesses from 1989—including Kim Oldenburg, the Easterdays, the Schafers, the Howells, Brenda Hale, Matt Miller and of course, Jon Boso and Ed Hayes. But the investigators persisted, contacting other witnesses who tended to corroborate the information already in hand. That, in Toth's view, made the case against Jeff stronger.

"Essentially, what we did is, we took the evidence, we reinterviewed people that had not been interviewed as thoroughly as they should have been the first time," Toth said later. "Many of the new interviews confirmed some of the information we had already received, which made that evidence stronger."

The case was like a jigsaw puzzle, Toth said.

"Some people would look at a puzzle and say, 'All the pieces aren't there,' or 'The pieces don't fit.' Somebody with a little bit more commitment and dedication may say, 'Yes, the pieces *do* fit.' "

This could be interpreted as a swipe at Barnes, and by extension, Botich and Senter . . . if only they had worked with a little more "commitment and dedication" . . . Naturally, this made some of the older police officers resentful, and suspicious of Toth's motives.

By April 2002, Toth had been successful in expanding the Special Crimes Unit, and with the extra resources formed a "cold case" team. The first project of the new unit was the Pelley case. Once again many of the primary witnesses were interviewed, including, this time, Jacque. Two investigators traveled to see her at her home in a Midwestern state, she recalled.

"My husband called me at work one day and said two guys just showed up in our back yard looking for me. They wanted to know if I would talk with them. They were staying at a local motel. Honestly, I did not want to talk to them, because I was so tired of my words being twisted. So I said no. My husband told them that, and they said either I needed to talk to them there or they would make it so that I would have to go back to Indiana and speak with them [there]."

Jacque didn't want to go back to Indiana, so she arranged to meet the two detectives at a local lawyer's office—so she would have a witness. She also taped the conversation. By this point, of course, Jacque was convinced that the Indiana authorities were out to get her brother, and that they were incompetent, or worse—even crooks.

"They were typical of South Bend cops, narrow-minded jerks. Even the lawyer picked up on that." Once again Jacque brought up the rumors that had attended the family's abrupt departure from Florida—the midnight meeting at the bank, the suggestion about money-laundering or a missing million dollars. By now Jacque had done some research, clipping articles from Florida newspapers having to do with banks, drugs and money-laundering. She'd unearthed the Colombian laundering story involving Bob's bank, and another incident involving a notorious Fort Myers cocaine dealer who'd blown up the federal Drug Enforcement Administration office in Fort Myers.

It was ludicrous to believe Jeff was the killer, Jacque told the detectives—the real killer was someone from Florida intent on eliminating her father as a possible witness. The detectives assured her they would check out the rumors.

"But that never happened," she said. "That was not the

first time that I told the cops about it, but it was the first time that I actually had papers in my hand to show them."

Then, on August 7, 2002, Toth's office obtained criminal information that named Jeff Pelley as the murderer of his father, stepmother and two stepsisters. The prosecutors asked that the information be sealed by the court, pending Jeff's arrest.

As it happened, Jeff was in Australia on a computer network consultancy job when the charges were filed, and so didn't learn about them until Saturday morning, August 10, 2002. That was when he was going through customs at the Los Angeles International Airport on his way back from Australia. An agent checked Jeff's passport against a computer database and learned that Jeff was the subject of a fugitive warrant from South Bend, Indiana, issued three days earlier. The agent put Jeff under arrest, and asked officers from the Los Angeles Police Department to pick him up and hold him for transport back to Indiana. By noon the same day, Jeff was being booked into jail in Los Angeles.

Although the information, arrest warrant and affidavit of probable cause—the facts to support an arrest—had been ordered sealed by the Indiana court, somehow the word leaked. A *Tribune* reporter, Linda Mullen, tracked down Toth on Sunday to see if the story was true. Toth told her he wasn't "at liberty to discuss it until tomorrow," thereby essentially confirming the story.

"Pelley Arrested," the *South Bend Tribune* headlined the following day. "Son Held in 1989 Slaying of Family."

Although Toth was technically adhering to the court's sealing order, Mullen quickly found confirmation of the arrest from Ed Hayes in Michigan, Bob's mother, Maxine Pelley, in Ohio, and Mary Armstrong in Kentucky. But at once the split in the family was plain. Hayes made it obvious that he believed Jeff was involved in the murders, and so did Maxine Pelley.

"We knew that they would come [to a conclusion] and it would somehow be unraveled," Maxine told the newspaper.

"Bad? Sure we feel bad; that's our grandson . . . It's a mystery to us . . . All we know is that our son is gone and they said that Jeff had been in on it."

But at the same time, Mary Armstrong in Kentucky strongly denied that her daughter Joy's son, her grandson, could have killed anyone. Like Jacque, she accused the Indiana investigators of "tunnel vision," and the failure to look elsewhere for the killer or killers. Jeff simply wasn't capable of murder, Mary said.

Even as South Benders were reading Mullen's account of the arrest on Monday, Toth was holding another news conference. With Jeff now in custody in Los Angeles, a judge vacated the sealing order and released the affidavit of probable cause to the media. Such an affidavit was used in a number of states to justify a criminal charge and an arrest—an "information," as it was termed. The whole procedure was almost always ex parte—that is, there was no opportunity for the accused to dispute the alleged facts. It was all done in secret, before a judge, very much the same as a grand jury, only without the jury.

This gave prosecutors a significant advantage over the defense—once the accused were charged, then arrested, then in the slammer, they would have far less freedom to marshal resources to defend themselves.

Toth, flanked by lead prosecutor Ellen Corcella, admitted that the police had no new evidence from what had been available in 1989. But they suggested that the new "cold case" team had reviewed the old evidence and found enough to warrant a prosecution—a slam at Barnes, Botich and Senter, if anyone thought about it. If Toth's boys and girls could be so perspicacious, why hadn't Barnes, his old opponent from 1998?

But most of all, this seemed to be Toth's political justification—his team had done what Barnes' group had not, because they had more "commitment and dedication," or as Toth later put it, "sweat on the brow."

Botich and Senter, no fans of Toth, were chagrined, to say the least. They'd worked hard on the Pelley murder case, and to hear Toth suggest that they hadn't was very offensive. Like others in St. Joseph County, they guessed that Toth had only charged Jeff to improve his chances at the polls.

At the press conference on August 12, 2002, Corcella acknowledged that there was no physical evidence tying Jeff to the murders but said the circumstances indicated that only Jeff could have pulled the trigger. Because it was a circumstantial case, she said, that meant eliminating any alternative theory of the crimes. Corcella said the prosecutors were confident they could do that.

In retrospect, that seems to have been a rather bold overstatement by Corcella, especially given the Indiana authorities' failure to consider the Florida past of Bob Pelley, his involvement with the Hawleys, the Hawleys' involvement with Dawson, Dawson's involvement with Guise, Dawson's murder eight months before the Pelley murders, and the troubles in the Landmark Bank—not to mention the 1976 disappearance of Harry William Stewart. These were all factors that could have generated potentially "alternative theories of the crime" in 1989. As 12-year-old Jacque had sensed back then, even if she hadn't known any details, there might be others out to get Bob, or even Dawn.

At no point over the next four years would anyone from the St. Joseph County Prosecutor's Office or Police Department attempt to sort out these "alternative" theories of the murders, which had emanated from Florida, Michigan or Ohio—where Dawn's first husband, Ed Huber, as Senter later acknowledged, was said to have committed suicide . . .

In fact, there was virtually nothing in the Toth—subsequently Dvorak—investigation that came to bear on any of these out-of-state possibilities: in St. Joseph County, all politics were local, and apparently, so was justice.

So much for Corcella's assertion that Toth's "cold case" squad had eliminated "alternative" theories of the crime—the evidence seemed to show that Jeff had been targeted as the best way to prove to the voters that Toth was the best man for the job as prosecutor.

This shortcoming—the failure to look around for other,

out-of-state possibilities—would eventually become an important issue, as the Pelley case unfolded. It would bear directly on the question of whether Toth's office had rushed to judgment, whether they had ignored contradictory evidence for political purposes, and whether later, for similarly venial political purposes, Dvorak's group had also tried to slam a square peg into a round hole.

Like all such formal assertions, the prosecutors in August 2002 wanted to put the most incriminating face on the facts against Jeff Pelley in their affidavit of probable cause. After all, the purpose of the document was to convince a judge that it was "more probable than not" to believe that Jeff Pelley and no one else was the killer. That meant emphasizing facts that suggested Jeff was guilty, and ignoring facts that might mean he was not.

Thus, Corcella, Toth's chief deputy, who wrote the probable cause document, asserted that Jeff:

> was angry at his father for remarrying after the defendant's biological mother died; that the defendant was very resentful of his step-mother and her children; and that the defendant was prepared to defy his father's effort to punish him by limiting the defendant's ability to attend his high school prom dance and certain other prom night activities . . . Jeff harbored a strong dislike of his step-mother and resentment toward his father.

An unnamed witness whom Corcella identified as a "friend of the family" was quoted as telling investigators that Jeff "hated" Dawn, and that she'd seen him "display fits of anger including screaming and hollering, and that Dawn had informed [her] that she was really afraid of Jeff . . ."

Whether a witness who was not identified could be a significant part of a threshold document in a capital case, sufficient to arrest someone on a murder charge, was subject to considerable doubt—any person charged with a crime has a right to confront his accusers, to know who they are, and to test their truthfulness and bias. While it is true that "confidential informants" are often cited in drug cases, a multiple murder case is of an order of magnitude greater, and demands far greater scrutiny, especially when the alleged perpetrator is already in custody. A defendant has a right to test the reliability of the evidence.

After trying to establish Jeff's animus toward the victims in her affidavit, Corcella addressed the clock issues, noting that Kim Oldenburg had left the Pelley house "about 4:45, but certainly no later than 5:00 p.m.," pointing out that Jeff's claim that he left the house about 4:50 was contradicted by the corsage-forgetting Matt Miller; and noting the Amoco gas station attendant's observation of Jeff at 5:20 P.M. An investigator, Corcella said, had driven the route between the parsonage and the Amoco station, and reached the station in five minutes, while driving between 50 and 60 miles an hour most of the way. That suggested that Jeff might still have been at the parsonage as late as 5:15, Corcella asserted—he could have murdered everyone, cleaned up, taken a shower, and still arrived at the gas station by 5:20.

Examination of the parsonage, Corcella went on, showed that all the doors and windows had been locked, that the curtains had been drawn, and that there were no signs of forced entry or burglary. A total of six shots had been fired from a shotgun: two upstairs at Bob, a third from the top of the basement stairs that ricocheted off the lower stairwell, and three more at Dawn, Janel and Jolene, huddled on the basement floor. And Corcella added the capper: Bob had cancelled Jeff's car insurance more than two weeks before the murders, yet Jeff had still driven his Mustang to the prom.

"Based upon the above-described facts, there is probable cause to believe that Jeff Pelley murdered Robert, Dawn, Jolene and Janel Pelley on April 29, 1989 . . ." Corcella concluded.

> On the day of the prom, Jeff set in motion his murder plot after Kim Oldenburg and her date left the home.

The evidence provides reasonable cause to believe that after the Oldenburg visit, Jeff went to the bedroom area of the home where he had access to a shotgun, that when his father went towards the bedroom area, Jeff shot him in the upper chest, knocking his father to the ground, and then shot the father a second time, blowing off portions of his face.

Jeff then went to shoot his step-mother. It appears that he chased her into the basement because a shot was fired from the top landing of the basement stairs towards the bottom of the basement stairs. The evidence shows that Dawn Pelley must have been running to protect the little girls who were in the basement. Dawn Pelley was then killed with a shotgun blast and fell near the couch. Janel was also killed by a shot to the head. Jolene, Dawn's six-year-old daughter, was crouched behind her mother's body when she was shot in the head at close range.

The defendant then went into the unfinished portion of the basement and removed his clothes—the pink and blue checkered shirt, jeans and a pair of socks, placed them in the washer and began the wash cycle. The defendant did this in great haste, forgetting to remove the paper money and coins from his pocket or a store receipt he had received earlier that day.

The defendant then returned upstairs and took a shower, washed his hands and changed into new casual clothes, leaving a trace of blood evidence [in the bathroom]. The defendant locked the doors and windows and pulled down the blinds so that persons could not see into the residence. The defendant took his tuxedo with him, got into his car and drove to the Lakeville Amoco gas station. The defendant needed to explain his late departure to Darla and plainly did not want to use the phone in the Pelley residence, because telephone records would place him in the home at a specific time. The defendant arrived at the station at or

> about 5:20 p.m. The defendant rushed into the station to use the phone and informed Darla that he was running late because of car troubles, even though the only problem identified by the station attendant was a fast idle.
>
> The defendant then arrived at the Greer home where he changed into his tuxedo and attended all the prom events.

Even as the news of Jeff's arrest was unfolding in South Bend, his wife in Florida was scrambling to find a lawyer for him and raise the money for his defense. She got on the computer, searching online for a lawyer in Los Angeles experienced in criminal defense. Eventually she settled on Alan Baum, a Los Angeles–area attorney with a national reputation. Baum soon hustled down to see Jeff in the Los Angeles jail, and after talking with him, emerged convinced of Jeff's innocence. The very fact that charges had been filed thirteen years—*thirteen years!*—after the crimes made Baum believe that the case was very weak. And when he learned that even Toth had admitted there was no new evidence, after more than a decade, Baum was sure of it. He suspected that something else was going on—that Toth, facing a tough reelection fight in the fall, had just made Jeff Pelley a poster boy for the electoral proposition that the incumbent prosecutor was tough on crime. In other words, for purposes of his own political ambition.

That was pretty much what Baum told the South Bend news media two days later, when he said Jeff would not contest extradition to South Bend from California, but that Jeff was not guilty. Something else was afoot, Baum contended.

"Why now? Why Jeff? There may be political overtones. It seems to be certainly a question worth asking," Baum told the *Tribune's* Linda Mullen. The long delay between the crimes and investigation of 1989, Baum said, and the formal charges thirteen years later, raised profound issues of fairness.

"If there's no better evidence than what they had in 1989,

it's bound to affect his ability to get a fair trial . . . some judge is going to be given the opportunity to rule on a motion to dismiss in violation of the right to fair and speedy trial."

As it turned out, Baum would see to it that a great many judges in Indiana would have that opportunity over the next four years.

CHAPTER 18

The notion that Toth and his team had charged Jeff Pelley with mass murder for blatant political gain was somewhat unfair—those associated with Toth's Special Crimes "cold case" unit, including Swanson and Corcella, believed they had an obligation to the dead, especially the little girls found slaughtered, their brains blown out, in the basement of the parsonage. Nevertheless, the suggestion that the charges against Jeff were all about St. Joseph County politics soon became part of the election campaign, in which Toth's opponent was none other than Michael Dvorak, the same man Jeff and his grandfather Jack Armstrong had consulted as a potential defense lawyer in the summer of 1989.

But this was only a coincidence: Dvorak never dreamed that some erstwhile client he'd talked to in 1989 would more than a decade later be charged by his political opponent, when he'd first decided to run against Toth in 2002—who knew? That certainly wasn't why he'd run for the prosecutor's job. In fact, for Dvorak, it was decidedly inconvenient.

In his campaign against Toth in the summer of 2002, Dvorak made no claim that the charges against Jeff Pelley were merely the incumbent's attempt to wave the bloody shirts of two dead little girls to curry favor with the voters. Dvorak, having been a politician in the Indiana state legislature for several terms, knew there was no electoral advantage in overtly claiming that his opponent wanted to use gruesome murder to further his own ambitions. As an experienced politician, Dvorak knew it was much better for someone else to throw that sort of mud.

Toth himself gingerly skirted around the topic, insisting that it was his duty to enforce the law, politics be damned. Like Barnes, Toth was politically astute enough to understand that even denying such an unseemly allegation could only give it credibility, and thereby cost him votes.

Others were not so averse to linking the charges against Jeff to the forthcoming election, however.

One who did, surprisingly enough, was former South Bend police lieutenant Brent Hemmerlein, the same man who'd confronted Jeff in the evening interview of May 1, 1989—who'd claimed that Jeff had asked during that disputed evening about his chances for the electric chair.

As it happened, Hemmerlein had a strong dislike of Chris Toth, from a dispute that had taken place several years earlier. Toth had accused Hemmerlein of covering up for the South Bend police chief, who had been in a car accident allegedly involving the consumption of alcohol. Toth had subsequently charged Hemmerlein with a crime of obstruction.

This had infuriated Hemmerlein, who saw it as Toth's attempt to wrest control of the South Bend Police Department away from the professionals for his own purposes. Eventually the cover-up case was dismissed by Toth, but not before Hemmerlein resigned from the department. Hemmerlein therefore despised Toth—he blamed him for the end of his police career. He was angry—bitter, even.

As far as he could see, Toth all too often went off half-cocked, flying away into fantasies based on flimsy evidence, Hemmerlein's own experience being Exhibit A. To Hemmerlein, Toth habitually put politics ahead of ethics. As the election neared, Hemmerlein dispatched a letter to the *Tribune* endorsing Dvorak.

> Three years have passed but the memories are vivid for my family and me . . . We had to endure so much, as my career unraveled at the hands of St. Joseph County Prosecutor Chris Toth. Unfortunately, I am not alone.

> Others have suffered the same fate. Now, as the election approaches, I can no longer remain silent and must detail what I experienced from the self-serving, politically motivated Chris Toth . . .
>
> Chris Toth continues to operate the prosecutor's office [for] his own personal agenda . . . while the politically motivated arrest of Jeff Pelley takes center stage. And the list continues, with [other] homicide cases that were dismissed due to constitutional violations by Special Crimes investigators. But Special Crimes continues to investigate homicides without refresher courses on the Constitution or Criminal Investigations 101 . . .
>
> We must take action now. St. Joseph County residents need to take note and listen to the hundreds of voices who know what is happening in the prosecutor's office at present. There is a solution to the problem. The solution is Mike Dvorak. He is a man of integrity, common sense, understanding and experience, who isn't afraid of the courtroom. Let's vote for a man who will work with the community rather than against it. Now is not the time for silence!

Hurrah! Or such was the import of a high-ranking former South Bend police official's public jeremiad against the incumbent prosecutor. But Hemmerlein's letter referencing the prosecution of Jeff as "politically motivated" tore the scab off the wound.

A few days later, the *Tribune's* Linda Mullen explored the situation in a story headlined "Hot Debate over Cold Cases." The investigators assigned to the Special Crimes Unit and its "cold case" component were furious at Hemmerlein's assault—or insult, as they saw it.

"Do we give Jeff Pelley another day of freedom because there's an election?" the commander of the "cold case" unit, Jim Clark, demanded. And his superior, Mike Swanson, in charge of the Special Crimes Unit, said he was appalled. "Should we stop working in January because it's an election year?"

Politics had nothing to do with Jeff's arrest, Clark insisted. Instead it was the awful details of the murders that had driven the investigators forward. In fact, he said, Toth had had nothing to do with the decision to arrest Jeff, but had been on naval reserve duty when the arrest had been decided—the prosecutor had been out of the loop, Clark insisted.

"Politically motivated? Here's *our* motivation," Clark said, and with that, he produced a full-color, glossy photograph of Dawn and the girls lying dead on the basement floor. He threw it down on the table for Mullen to see.

"This case transcends politics," Swanson agreed. "We're talking six- and eight-year-old girls." But since Swanson, Clark and Corcetta's continued tenure in their jobs depended on Toth's reelection, the use of the graphic crime-scene photograph had to be seen as a last-ditch, political statement by the incumbent, an effort to use emotion to convince Mullen that Jeff Pelley was evil—that accusing him of the mass murder of his family was a matter of duty, not politics. The blood and the brains were mute evidence.

On election day, November 5, 2002, Democrat Dvorak swamped Toth, getting almost 61 percent of the vote to Toth's 34 percent. Dvorak's majority of a little over 47,000 votes was almost 17,000 votes over Toth's total of less than 31,000. In political terms, it was a wipe-out—in short, Toth had been thoroughly rejected by the St. Joseph County electorate.

Whether the vote could be seen as a public condemnation of Toth's charges against Jeff Pelley was another matter, however. Literally, the jury was still out on that question—in fact, it hadn't even been convened yet.

Dvorak, once Jeff's potential defense lawyer, kept his cards close to his chest. Until he was actually in office, Dvorak could see no useful purpose in getting involved in the Pelley case. As far as he could tell, he'd be damned if he promised to dismiss it—hey, he was once almost Jeff's lawyer—and damned if he agreed to the prosecution of his almost-client.

In that case, he might be condemned as the sycophantic tool of the detectives' Special Crimes Unit, a prosecutorial noodle in thrall to the Hemmerlein-condemned police, throwing his ethical obligations overboard to curry favor with the cops, who carried substantial political clout in South Bend. The truth was, Dvorak needed the political approval of the police to get elected. The cops might have hated Toth, but they weren't about to jump into bed with Dvorak without some promises. That's politics—or as someone once said, even before Tip O'Neill: "All politics is local."

Well, it was an almost impossible situation: the politics dictated, at least to Dvorak, that there was no way to emerge unscathed. But Dvorak was no political neophyte, after several terms in the legislature. Even before swearing the oath, he knew his best course was to keep his lips zipped, at least until he formally took office. Then he could let the process play out.

If the charges failed from lack of evidence, Dvorak would be off the hook. If a judge upheld them, Dvorak would do his duty. There was no political usefulness in getting involved in the squabble—Toth had charged Jeff, Toth had been defeated at the polls, and now Dvorak could hardly dismiss the charges—someone was sure to assert that Dvorak was in Jeff Pelley's pocket. Which Dvorak wanted to avoid in the worst way.

As far as Dvorak could see, he had no dog in the fight . . . but Dvorak had already decided to get rid of Swanson, Clark and Corcella, the retainers from the old regime. Who needed key personnel who were in Toth's inner circle? Was dumping Toth's pals evidence that he was on Pelley's side? Dvorak didn't think so.

Two days after the election, Jeff and his lawyers, Alan Baum and Andre Gammage of South Bend, were in court trying to arrange bail for Jeff. Toth and Corcella, still in office until January 1, 2003, resisted vehemently. They thought Jeff would bolt—get out of town, go to another country, anything to evade prosecution for mass murder. They wanted him in jail, day after day, until the final verdict and sentence.

* * *

The Pelley case had been assigned to Judge Roland W. Chamblee, Jr.—a lean, balding, rather colorfully spoken jurist who had a penchant for salty, often colloquial talk, especially when lawyers were up close at his bench, out of earshot of almost everyone except the court reporter.

"Just one hot second," was one of his favorite phrases, or "Fire away," along with rare bursts of scatological profanity. Chamblee ran his courtroom with an iron fist—lawyers argued with him at their peril, as well as that of their clients. Attorneys like Baum—from *Hollywood*, as Senter and Botich later sneered—were particularly susceptible to Judge Chamblee's derision.

Of course, Studio City wasn't Hollywood—it was a long way away, through the Cahuenga Pass into the San Fernando Valley—but the folks in South Bend didn't know that. To them, Baum was "Hollywood"—neon lights, Mulholland Drive, bad behavior, drugs, the ragged edge of the moral abyss, the aftereffect of rock and roll, in fact. If a man from "Hollywood" was representing Jeff, he had to be hiding something. Jeff had a disadvantage going in: folks in St. Joseph County weren't about to let a California city slicker—*from Hollywood!*—put one over on them!

Likewise, Chamblee had solicitous regard for jurors in his court—voters all, as he well knew. The transcript of the proceedings against Jeff Pelley would be replete with instances of Judge Chamblee playing to the affection of the jury, sometimes to the detriment of the litigants, whether prosecutors or defenders: laughter or grins from jurors, to Chamblee, were worth far more than any agonized groan from counsel.

On November 7, 2002, Baum and Gammage accompanied Jeff in an appearance before the judge. Since his unexpected arrest at Los Angeles International Airport on August 10, 2002, Jeff had been continuously in stir, first in Los Angeles for 10 days, later in custody in South Bend—almost 90 days, so far. For someone who had never been locked up for any extended period, for someone who'd thought he'd be back in the bosom of his family by the middle of August at the latest, after seventeen hours of trans-Pacific flight, spending almost 3 months behind bars, hundreds of miles away from kith and kin for crimes that had occurred thirteen years earlier, without a kiss, without a chance to say goodbye, without giving the hair of his toddler son a single tousle—*Go directly to jail, do not pass Go*—the shock was enormous.

Driven by Jeff's family, Baum and Gammage wanted to get him out, ASAP. The Hawleys of Fort Myers stood behind Jeff, steadfastly. Baum, in a written motion pleading for Jeff's release on bail, claimed there were numerous holes in Corcella's August 7 affidavit asserting that Jeff had committed the murders. The law, Baum contended, only allowed the court to deny bail to someone arrested on murder charges if the evidence was overwhelmingly "presumptive"—in Baum's view, that meant there had to be significant, palpable evidence that Jeff had committed the murders.

Merely alleging possibilities, "reasonable" beliefs, unsupported by hard facts, was insufficient to keep Jeff in the slammer—it was far less than "presumptive." Baum found Corcella's affidavit weak, because of information Corcella had omitted, or had chosen to interpret solely in the prosecution's favor.

In asking Chamblee to release Jeff on bail in late October 2002, Baum took direct aim at the weakest part of the state's case—the clock. Crucial to Baum's argument was his assertion that Kim Oldenburg had left the parsonage just before 5 P.M.

Where Corcella had pegged this time at "about 4:45," Baum shoved it ahead—after all, Kim had said her group had left between 4:45 and 5. If Corcella could interpret the fifteen-minute difference in the state's favor, Baum could do the same for his client. Four-forty-five was bad for Jeff, but five o'clock was good. As the Los Angeles lawyer put it:

> By selecting only those portions . . . that best suit its conclusion that Jeff Pelley committed these crimes, the state proposes a "time-line" for the events of late

afternoon/early evening of April 29. A more thorough review . . . paints a far different picture than presented in the Affidavit [Corcella's Probable Cause document in support of the information of August 7]. This more accurate view of the evidence leads to the conclusion that, if Jeff Pelley committed these crimes, he would have had approximately 9 minutes to:

1. Secure the weapon (which may or may not have been in the house) and at least 6 shotgun shells;
2. Kill his father upstairs and his step-mother and two step-sisters downstairs, reloading three times if the weapon was a double-barrel, or one time if it was a typical five load pump-action;
3. Gather up the six spent cartridges;
4. Wash his clothes so thoroughly that no evidence of blood (according to lab reports) could be found;
5. Shower and change clothes and put his tuxedo in his car;
6. Dispose of the weapon and the spent cartridges so cleverly that, despite the efforts of dozens of police officers, some using trained canines, searching a wide area for many days after the murders, they have never been found; and
7. Leave for the drive to the gas station.

It was impossible, Baum contended—there just wasn't enough time for Jeff to have done all these things and still get to the Greer house by 5:30 P.M. The clock was Jeff's best witness. If he'd left the parsonage five minutes after Kim and her group, just before 5, and arrived just after 5:20 P.M. at the gas station, that meant he would have had just over ten minutes to commit the murders and clean up. The only way the prosecution could even suggest that Jeff was the culprit was to shove Kim Oldenburg's departure from the parsonage back to 4:45 P.M., and even then, there wasn't enough time. And where was any evidence that the Oldenburg group had actually left at quarter to five, rather than ten minutes later? It didn't exist—not even Kim Oldenburg could establish that.

There were other problems with Corcella's affidavit, Baum asserted—for one thing, she'd failed to include the statements of Jacque and Jessica, who'd both told the police that the supposed conflict between Jeff and his father and stepmother didn't amount to much; Jessica, in fact, had told the police that she thought *Bob* murdered her mother and two sisters because Dawn was planning to divorce him, and had then killed himself. That was obviously impossible, since Bob had been shot twice, and there was no gun found next to his body, but to Baum it showed that Corcella was making a mountain out of a small speed bump, at least as far as Jeff's supposed motive was concerned—the fact that even Jessica had no suspicion of her stepbrother put the lie to Corcella's conception of the father-son dispute, and what had really happened.

There were still more holes in the prosecution's theory, according to Baum. Corcella had omitted the information from Lois Stansbury—her claimed encounter with Bob around 5 P.M. on Saturday afternoon, in which Stansbury had told Senter that she'd seen Bob holding a shovel, talking to the mystery man, as well as the black pickup truck. Stansbury's account had been included in the discovery sent to the defense by the prosecutors, but left out of the charging affidavit by Corcella, even though it suggested that Bob was alive and well at 5 P.M.—after the Oldenburg group, and possibly Jeff, had departed.

It also raised the possibility of another killer. The fact that police had never identified the man talking to Bob, or the black pickup truck, suggested that police had rushed to judgment in blaming Jeff Pelley: having decided that Jeff was the killer, right from the start, they weren't interested in anything that complicated that picture.

But then, in the early 1990s, the previous prosecutor, Michael Barnes, had told detectives Botich and Senter that they didn't have enough. And on that assessment, things had rested for more than a dozen years—at least until Toth had unseated Barnes as a "do-nothing" prosecutor in 1998. After that, to get reelected, Toth had charged the case against Jeff anyway, in an attempt to show the voters he was tough on crime. At least, that was how Baum saw the situation.

By the time of the bail hearing on November 7, 2002, Baum was confident that Judge Chamblee would recognize a weak case when he saw one, and release Jeff on bail. The Hawleys had come through with letters in support of Jeff, Phil's prominent among them:

> I have known Jeff for over 20 years. I was a close personal friend of his father, mother, and the entire family . . . Jeff also worked for me for several years and was an outstanding employee and very dedicated to his work . . . Jeff will without a doubt show up for his court dates, and keep every promise he makes to you and the court.

And, from Paul Hawley:

> My wife and I have known Jeff since he was a child, having been very close friends with his mother and father for many years as part of our church family. When his mother died at an early age, Jeff and his sister looked up to my wife as a confidant [sic] in her absence . . . Jeff is not a threat to society . . . we love and admire Jeff for the mature man he has become as a result of the way his late father raised him.

Jeff's wife, his mother-in-law, and several others from Florida chimed in: Jeff Pelley was an upstanding citizen, successful, utterly responsible, and hardly likely to flee Chamblee's jurisdiction, and certainly not capable of killing anyone.

CHAPTER 19

Because the defense had the burden of showing that the case against Jeff was weak—in order to convince Judge Chamblee to grant bail—Baum called the November 7 hearing's only witness, Craig Whitfield, a detective who had been assigned to the cold case unit when the investigation had been reopened in 2000. Baum believed he could use Whitfield to open a new theory of the murders. If he could do that, Baum thought, he could give Chamblee political cover to release Jeff on bail—if the case was demonstrably weak, Chamblee could justify his bail decision. Or so Baum reasoned.

Showing Whitfield a sheaf of police teletypes from Ohio, Baum asked him to identify them. The teletypes were inquiring about a possible murder case in South Bend, Whitfield acknowledged. Baum asked him to clarify.

"The department in Ohio is inquiring about any department having information of four people being killed in 1989 by a twelve-gauge shotgun," Whitfield summarized. "It indicates that a man, a wife and two little girls were murdered, were killed or being killed in the basement, and one child had on a white nightgown. 'Any department having knowledge to contact the Harrison County Sheriff's Office in Cincinnati, Ohio,' " Whitfield read from the teletypes.

The inquiry, Whitfield continued, had come from the Ohio department as a result of a claim by an Ohio prison inmate, one James Chapman, asserting that a fellow inmate he knew only as "Dave" had confessed murdering four people in South Bend in April 1989. "Dave" had told him one of the girls had been wearing a white nightgown, that he'd shot the two girls first while in the basement, that the woman had come running down the stairs, that he'd shot her, and then ascended the stairs to shoot a man, twice.

"Based on your investigation . . . and review of the crime-scene information, the location of where the bodies were found . . . is the location as reflected in Mr. Chapman's letter consistent with the crime scene in this case?"

"The locations, yes," Whitfield said.

This was shadow-casting by Baum, letting in just enough testimony from Chapman's claim to put the case against Jeff in doubt, but not so much as to undercut the claim's credibility. Still, there was ample reason to doubt Chapman's accuracy, if not his motive, and Corcella took advantage of it when it was her turn to cross-examine Whitfield. She established that Whitfield doubted Chapman's veracity.

Why? Corcella asked.

For one thing, neither child had been wearing a nightgown, let alone one that was white, Whitfield told Corcella. Not only that, from the way the bodies were lying on the basement floor, there was no way that Dawn had been shot after the two girls. Finally, the shots that had killed Bob had come from the bedroom end of the hallway, which indicated *he'd* been shot first. What—the killer had shot the three in the basement, then raced upstairs to the bedroom area for some unknown reason, emerging from that part of the house to shoot a late-arriving Bob? Why was the killer in the bedroom area, anyway? It was hard to fathom—in fact, the idea that the two girls had been shot first was ridiculous. That was Whitfield's assessment of Chapman's version of the murder scene.

Moreover, tests by the FBI had shown that the shotgun used was 20-gauge, not 12-gauge, Whitfield added. And the capper: Special Crimes detectives, including Clark, had gone to Ohio to try to talk with Chapman, who had been paroled from prison, but could not find him: the address he'd given to the parole authorities turned out to be bogus, according to Whitfield.

Taken together, these shortcomings in Chapman's tale

suggested that it was nothing more than a cellblock scam, cobbled together by Chapman based on news accounts of Jeff's arrest, and backdated to 1989, in some sort of feeble effort to trade information for parole or special privileges in prison, and passed on through well-meaning but ignorant police in Cincinnati, who clearly knew nothing about the Pelley murders, which had taken place more than a decade earlier.

So effectively did Corcella negate Baum's effort to shift Chamblee's attention away from Jeff and onto "Dave," it probably would have been better for Baum to have avoided the subject altogether. All it did was undercut Baum's own credibility, at least with Chamblee: it seemed as though Baum was flailing at shadows, that he was desperate. To some, Chamblee didn't appear willing to let some Hollywood lawyer make him the fool . . . if Baum wanted Chamblee to believe such silliness, he obviously had no respect for Chamblee . . . Whether that was true or not, the relationship between judge and defense counsel thereafter shifted into low gear.

But Corcella wasn't finished.

"Now," she asked, "have you done some additional interviews of individuals who were at a party with Jeff Pelley in August, after the murders of that same year, 1989?"

He had, Whitfield said. "We were looking through the old tip sheet that came in, and we ran down a couple of names that were on that. And we located a softball team that had a kegger party thrown by a person named Kurt Schafer." This, of course, was one of Jeff's closest friends, who lived just east on Osborne Road with his parents, Roger and Joyce Schafer.

At the kegger, Whitfield said, Jeff had been surrounded by other young people who had verbally, then physically assaulted him, demanding to know whether he had killed his family.

"And Jeff became very angry," Whitfield recounted. "And he said, 'I fucking killed them. I killed them all, and I will kill you.' "

When one of the partygoers taunted him further, saying he couldn't kill them because he didn't have a gun, Jeff had allegedly replied that he'd hidden the shotgun in a tree, that he knew just where it was, and that he could go get it, and come back and kill his tormentors.

And when someone demanded to know how he could have killed his own sisters, Jeff had supposedly responded, "They weren't my sisters."

But Baum had guessed this was coming, and he induced Whitfield to admit that there was at least one other participant at the kegger who'd sworn he'd heard Jeff say nothing of the sort. And further, the tale of the kegger hadn't come to the telephone tip line until several years after the murders, about the time Jeff had been arrested on the phone-in-the-closet scam, which had been front-page news in South Bend. The question was why the partygoers hadn't reported the alleged exchange when it had supposedly occurred in August 1989, but only later, in 1994.

Whitfield responded that the partygoers were afraid of Jeff, but it sounded pretty lame—the idea was that 17-year-old, 5 foot 7 inch Jeff Pelley, at 140 pounds, could intimidate people who were verbally and physically assaulting him, seemed unlikely. He couldn't kill all of them, could he? The implication was that those who claimed Jeff had made the statements either had some sort of beef with him, or were simply trying to get attention for themselves in light of the publicity over the Florida wire fraud. Or, banking on interest from the publicity stirred up by Jeff's phone-in-the-closet arrest, simply wanted to collect the telephone tipsters' crime stoppers reward. The entire kegger tale had the legs of a small caterpillar—very, very short.

Baum had one more arrow in his quiver. He asked Whitfield whether any work had been done by anyone to determine the time of death of any of the Pelleys. He'd asked Whitfield if he'd seen any reports on body temperature, lividity, rigor mortis—the various biological indicators of time of death.

He hadn't found anything in the files, Whitfield admitted.

"I did read the reports," he said. "And I still have a standing call in to Dr. Hoover to discuss it with him, and I haven't heard back from him yet."

But, of course, Hoover would later acknowledge that such biological evaluations had never been made the day the bodies were discovered. It wasn't his job at the time, and the county coroner—a close friend of the St. Joseph County police hierarchy—hadn't done them either.

"What I have attempted to do," Baum told Chamblee, ". . . is cast doubt upon the weight of the evidence. Not that there is no evidence at all, as the court heard today. There are certainly some suspicious circumstances. Now, if this were a bench trial, and both sides were to rest now, I think the decision would be clear—I don't think there's proof beyond a reasonable doubt, or anything close to it."

The law required the prosecutors to present "presumptive" evidence to justify no bail, Baum contended. But all they had was "reasonable," he said. The facts asserted by Corcella weren't even close to "probable."

"Reasonable" was less than "probable," and "probable" was well short of "presumptive." "Presumptive" implied much more likely than not. The St. Joseph County Prosecutor's Office couldn't come close to "presumptive" with their claims against Jeff Pelley, Baum said.

In advancing their case against Jeff, the prosecutors wanted to have it both ways, Baum continued: on one hand they were claiming Jeff had been in a maddened rush to commit mass murder, then to get to the Greer house by 5:30 P.M., so he could join Darla for the dinner at the Emporium. But at the same time, Jeff had been so deliberate, so calculating, so careful, so cool, that he'd left virtually no evidence behind.

It made no sense, especially for a boy who'd only been 17 at the time, Baum argued—it was crazy, it was nonsense, it had nothing to do with how murders happened in the real world. In the real world, people lost control of their emotions and killed loved ones—they didn't plot out mass murder two or three weeks in advance, then leave it to the last possible minute, when any number of things could go wrong.

Then there was the contradictory evidence about the guns. Some people claimed that Bob had told them he'd gotten rid of all the guns in the house, while others—9-year-old Jessica, primarily—had insisted that there was still one long gun in the house at the time of the murders. It was inconclusive, Baum argued. There was no clear evidence that any shotgun had been in the house on the day, evening or following morning when the Pelleys had been found dead. No one could put such a weapon into Jeff Pelley's hands in the days or hours before or after the murders.

Baum pointed out that Jessica had claimed that the whole thing had been murder-suicide, which couldn't possibly have been the case—but if Jessica was wrong about that, wasn't it possible that she was wrong about the availability of the gun?

Besides this, Baum went on, there was the matter of motive.

"First of all, it's almost absurd to attribute [Jeff's] not being able to go to the prom, if that were true, as a motive to kill his family, unless . . . he was a homicidal maniac. To attribute to him a premeditated plan to kill them all, so he could go to the prom, is absurd."

But by far the most important weakness of the state's case, Baum added, was still the clock—Jeff simply hadn't had enough time to commit the murders. And here the evidence as to the time of death was crucial, not for what it showed, but for what it did not, Baum contended.

If Jeff had left the parsonage at 4:50 P.M., as he had claimed, there was simply not enough time—there was no way he could have found the shotgun, loaded it, shot four people, picked up the five or six shell casings, put his clothes in the washing machine, taken a shower, put on new clothes, locked all the windows, closed all the drapes, put his tuxedo in the Mustang (and fixed it, if it was still undriveable, as the prosecution contended), ditched the shotgun and casings and any bloody clothes all in the five minutes after Kim Oldenburg's entourage had left, at the earliest, at 4:45. It was humanly impossible.

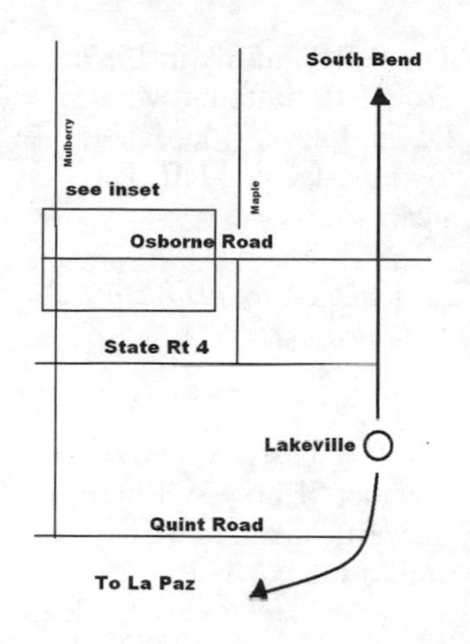

Vicinity of Lakeville, Indiana (not to scale). The major roads involved in the Pelley murder case.

Map by Carlton Smith

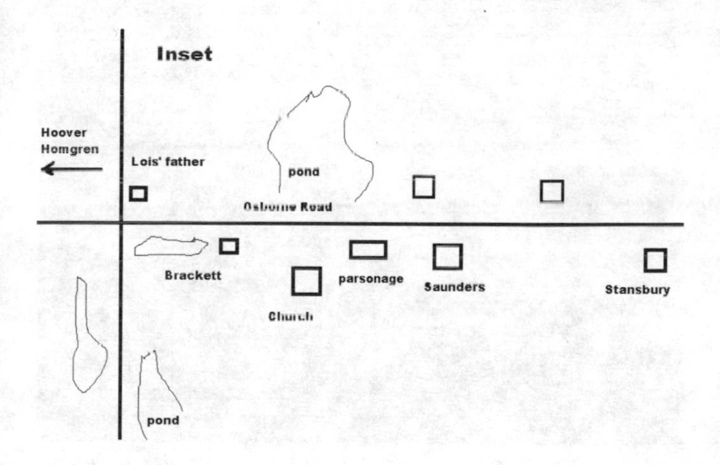

The relationship between the dwellings on Osborne Road, Lakeville, Indiana, in 1989.

Map by Carlton Smith

The Pelley family in 1987. From left, bottom row: Dawn, Jolene, Bob, Janel; top row: Jacque, Jeff, Jessica.

Lifetouch Church Directories and Portraits

The U.S. passport photograph of "Harry William Stewart," taken in Miami in June of 1976.

U.S. Passport Agency

The Olive Branch Church of United Brethren in Christ on Osborne Road, Lake-ville, Indiana.

Carlton Smith

The rear of the parsonage, showing the garage door, and the south-facing side door tried by Stephanie Fagan on the morning of April 29, 1989. All the doors and windows of the parsonage were locked, and the curtains drawn that morning.

Carlton Smith

Olive Branch United Brethren Sunday School superintendent David Hathaway. Hathaway, a World War II veteran of the Battle of Okinawa, discovered the bodies of the four murdered Pelleys on the morning of April 29, 1989.

Carlton Smith

Former Indiana State Police investigator Mark Senter, and St. Joseph County Police Deputy Chief John Botich in 2007. Senter was familiar with the Pelley family, and Botich became the lead investigator in the Pelley murder case.

Carlton Smith

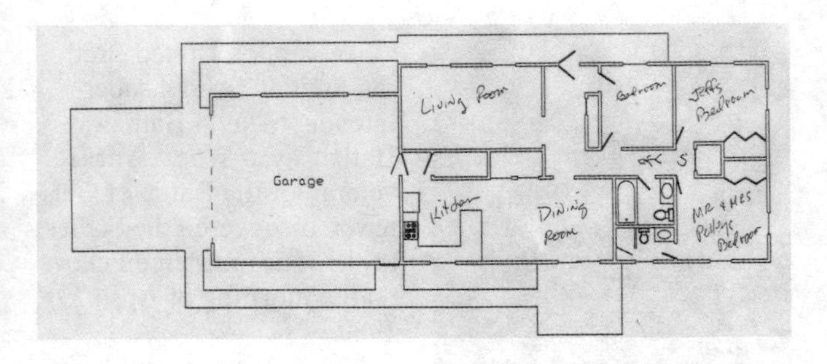

The ground floor diagram of the parsonage crime scene, compiled by St. Joseph County police shortly after April 29, 1989. St. Joseph County police, exhibit in Indiana vs. Robert Jeffrey Pelley.

St. Joseph County Police, 1989

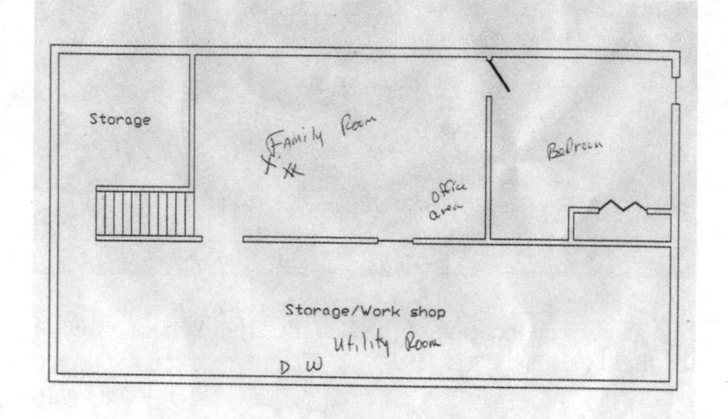

A police diagram of the basement floor of the parsonage, compiled by St. Joseph County Police shortly after April 29, 1989. St. Joseph County Police, exhibit in *Indiana vs. Robert Jeffrey Pelley.* *St. Joseph County Police, 1989*

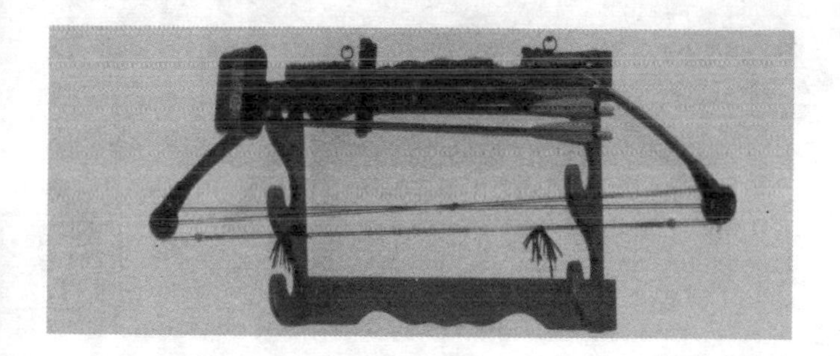

The gunrack in the bedroom of Robert and Dawn Pelley. Jessica Pelley testified that she'd seen a long gun in the rack before the murders, while her stepsister Jacque said there was no gun. *St. Joseph County Police*

Elks Club: The location of the LaVille High School prom on the night of April 28, 1989.

Carlton Smith

Jeff Pelley, at the time seventeen years old, during his videotaped interview by then-Detective John Botich on the morning of May 1, 1989. Jeff's grandmother Mary Armstrong is to Jeff's right, his grandfather Jack Armstrong is to his left.

Still photo captured by Carlton Smith from St. Joseph County Police videotape of interrogation

Defense investigator Scott Campbell, Jeff Pelley, and his sister Jacque arrive at the St. Joseph County Courthouse for the Pelley murder trial in July, 2006.

Photo by Santiago Flores, South Bend Tribune

Alan Baum of Studio City, California, Jeff's lead defense lawyer.

Carlton Smith

Michael Dvorak, St. Joseph County Prosecuting Attorney, once almost Jeff Pelley's defense lawyer. Questions were initially raised about Dvorak's possible conflict of interest in the case.

St. Joseph County Prosecutor's Office

Frank Schaffer, the lead St. Joseph County prosecutor in the Pelley case, with his wife after Jeff Pelley was convicted in July of 2006.

Photo by Santiago Flores, South Bend Tribune

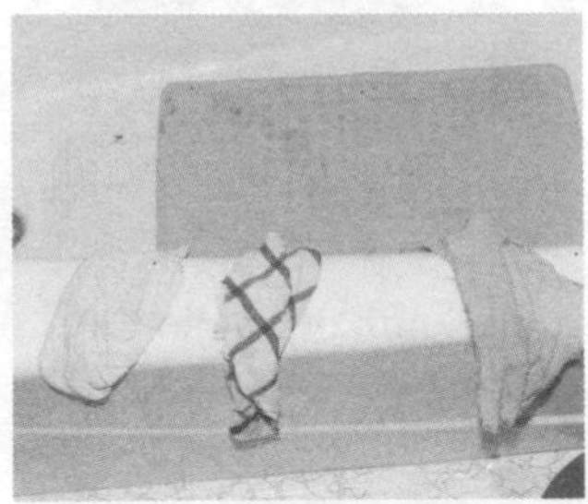

The bathtub at the parsonage, April 29, 1989. Jeff Pelley's defense claimed that the moisture on the washcloths and the bathmat proved that the murders of the Pelleys had to have taken place long after he left the house.
St. Joseph County Police

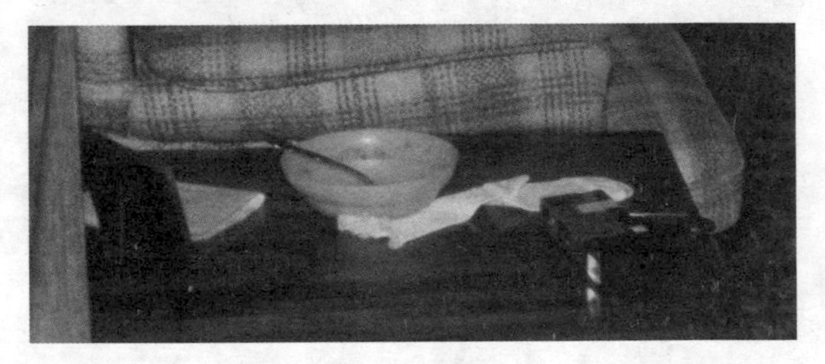

The living room on the morning the Pelley murders were discovered. The bowl and apparent church sock on the end table might suggest that the murders occurred on Sunday morning, rather than Saturday evening.

blow-up by Carlton Smith of St. Joseph Police photo

If Jeff actually left the parsonage at 4:50 P.M., he could not possibly have been the killer.

On the other hand, even if Jeff had actually left at 5:10 P.M.—twenty minutes later, as the prosecutors contended—that would only have given him a maximum twenty-five minutes for the murders and the clean-up. That is, if Kim's group had in fact left, at the earliest of her estimates, at 4:45. But Kim had said that it had taken less than five minutes for her group, including her mother, brother and date, as well as two others, to get the Holmgren house a mile or so west on Osborne Road, which suggested that Kim, et al., had left at some time *after* 4:45—maybe even at 4:55.

In fact, Kim had said that her group had arrived at the Holmgrens' "on time," by 5 P.M., and had then waited for Matt Miller to show up with the forgotten corsage.

In his argument for bail, Baum skipped over Miller's assertion that he'd driven by the parsonage at 5:10 or 5:15, and had seen Jeff's Mustang still there, which suggested that Jeff was still at the parsonage at least ten minutes after five. But this also calls Miller's assertions into question—did he *really* see Jeff's Mustang, or was he confused from prior days' observations, or some other influence? Was there enmity between Matt and Jeff?

As Miller's testimony was crucial to both sides, it's surprising that he was not called as a witness at that point—it's likely that neither side was as yet entirely sure of what Miller might say under cross-examination.

But if one accepts that Miller's sighting was accurate, it suggests that Jeff was lying as to the time he'd left the parsonage. In murder cases, especially those dependent on extremely short timelines, lying is *not* good—in fact, it's usually highly incriminating, as even Dame Christie would testify. Matt Miller's claimed observation of Jeff's Mustang at 5:10 or 5:15 on Saturday evening was the key evidence against Jeff.

For what it's worth, the supposed later departure from the parsonage by the Oldenburg group—after 4:45 P.M.—seems contradicted by Lois Stansbury's own supposed sighting of Bob with the shovel, the mystery man and the pickup truck just before 5—she'd seen nothing of Kim's six-person group clambering into Kim's mother's car at supposedly five minutes to 5, and she should have, if she'd really been there at the time—unless Kim's group had left some minutes before. Exactly why Bob would have been holding a shovel, after seeing off the Oldenburg group, and minutes before he and Dawn were supposed to be going to the Easterday house, seems fairly odd.

In review, it seems possible that Loïs Stansbury might have confused the day she'd been to Kmart with another day—it's impossible to say for sure. Except—that Lois' Kmart receipt seemed to surely indicate the date and time she'd left the store.

Arggh! Where is Agatha Christie when we need her? Where are the church bells tolling, to tell us when people were where? In real life, murder is not so simple.

Still, either way—4:50 or 5:10—in Baum's opinion, there simply wasn't enough time for Jeff to have killed everyone. He would have to have been busier than someone on the old television show *Beat the Clock* to accomplish all necessary clean-up and auto repair within the maximum of twenty minutes, or the minimum of five. The single most important flaw in the prosecution's case was the lack of any clear time of death, Baum argued.

"We have to recognize the fact, either by reason of oversight or lack of recognition of the significance, we have no evidence as to what the time of death was. Even had these matters been looked into . . . when the bodies were found, it would have been medically impossible to fix the time of death as between four-fifty-five and five-ten."

That meant there was just as much likelihood that the murders had been committed *after* 5:30, at a time when Jeff Pelley was arriving at the Greer house, attending the prom, or even on the way to Great America. No time of death meant there was no way to implicate a prime suspect.

But by insisting that the murders and clean-up had taken

place in less than twenty-five minutes, the prosecution had effectively eliminated all other possibilities, in an effort to pin the crimes on Jeff.

"Should you set bail?" Baum concluded. "Yes, you *should* set bail. Jeff Pelley is not a flight risk. He has family that he would sooner cut off his arm, or worse, than abandon. He has a wife and six-year-old child." Baum said Chamblee should set bail at $25,000, cash.

No, no, no, Corcella insisted, when it was her turn. Bail should not be granted, or if it was, it should be substantial—say, $750,000.

"When you look at this case," she told Chamblee, "at what did not, or could not, be in this case, all the evidence points directly to Jeff Pelley as the perpetrator of this crime . . . we know it's not murder-suicide . . . we know it's not an intruder, the house is completely locked up. In order to believe it's an intruder, you have to believe that some time after Mr. [Jeff] Pelley left the house, an intruder came in. And the most meticulous burglar on this earth, who didn't move anything—nothing, obviously, was missing—and that he was so compulsive that, as he left the house, he locked the door behind him? Now, that's burglary for you . . ."

But with this, Corcella skipped over the possibility that the murders might have been for something other than burglary—say, a professional hit, in which there might well have been no evidence of burglary, with the doors locked to prevent premature discovery of the bodies, to allow the killers to get far away. But then, she had no evidence for or against this concept, so in her mind, it did not arise. She focused on what the evidence did say: the killer had to be someone who had intimate familiarity with the house, as the shots from the bedroom area indicated.

As for the gun confusion: who was to say that Jeff hadn't planted a shotgun in the house hours or even days earlier? Could anyone say for sure that Bob had really gotten all the weapons out of the house? Wasn't it possible that the 20-gauge pump shotgun had remained, lying on the rack in the bedroom, below the bow and arrows?

"And he [Baum] says, 'He'd have to be a homicidal maniac.' We don't dispute that—that's our position. Any look at those photographs [of the victims] shows it's a homicidal maniac who killed that family."

Bob's cancellation of the car insurance, and the lack of reinstatement by Saturday, showed conclusively that he'd had no intention of allowing Jeff to drive the gray-silver Mustang to the prom, she said. That was solid evidence that Jeff was lying when he'd told Botich that his father had relented on his "grounding."

It could not be true.

As to the time of death—while it was true that there was no scientifically established time of death, there was still powerful circumstantial evidence that indicated the murders had to have occurred late Saturday afternoon, before Jeff had driven off to the prom. For one, the girls were not dressed for bed; besides that, Crystal Easterday and her date had arrived at the parsonage between 5:30 and 6 P.M., and no one answered the door. Jeff's car was gone, but the two other Pelley cars were in the driveway, demonstrating that the family had to have been in the house, dead, when Crystal and her date had arrived.

As to the clock: even if one accepted the short time frame between 5 and 5:10 for the narrowest window, there was still enough time for Jeff to have murdered everyone. "That is ample time to have committed these murders, changed clothes, got in the car, and get to the gas station," she told Chamblee.

As to bail, Jeff had "ample resources," Corcella contended—clearly an overstatement of his financial condition—and with substantial cash behind him, he was a flight risk, given that he was possibly facing life in prison. For that reason alone, she argued, Chamblee should deny bail.

One week later, Chamblee did exactly that—no bail for Jeff. In his ruling, Chamblee cited the determining factor—the disputed kegger party.

"While this court could not and would not weigh the credibility of these or any other potential witnesses, the court finds that such evidence, if believed by a jury, could be sufficient to support a finding of guilt," Chamblee asserted.

Just why Chamblee couldn't weigh the credibility of Whitfield's characterization of witnesses who weren't actually called to testify under oath wasn't obvious. Significantly, however, none of the witnesses who supposedly heard Jeff make incriminating statements at the kegger eventually testified at his trial—as Senter and Botich later recalled, their credibility had come into question in the early 1990s, and the entire issue of the kegger party and Jeff's supposed statements was never addressed by any jury. Toth's reliance on the unverified statements of witnesses never called to withstand cross-examination subjected the charges against Jeff to significant doubt.

In fact, at least three of the supposed witnesses had died by the time the Pelley case finally came to trial, years later—two from natural causes, and one in a car wreck. Nevertheless, the supposed hearsay from the kegger party was enough to keep Jeff in jail, at least in the fall of 2002.

A little over a month after bail was denied by Chamblee, Jeff's lawyers made a new attack on the case against their client: they wanted the charges dismissed on grounds that Jeff had been denied a speedy trial, a violation of his rights under the Fifth and Sixth Amendments to the Constitution, as well as the Indiana state constitution. In fact, Baum and Gammage contended, the state was too late to charge Jeff—thirteen years too late.

But even before that cloud floated onto the horizon, a rather different sort of storm blew up, one which soon led Dvorak to accuse Corcella of attempting to sabotage the case against Jeff, perhaps to further her own ambition.

CHAPTER 20

Even before the election and the bail hearing, some of the investigators had been hard at work trying to assemble more details of Jeff's history over the previous dozen years. At some point in October, detectives had contacted Bob's sister—Jeff's aunt—Jon Boso, in Ohio. As the executor of the Pelley estate, Jon possessed financial records dating back to the 1980s for Bob and Dawn, including old bills, bank statements, check registers and the like. Among these papers, Jon found a pad with notes related to the meeting Jeff and Jack Armstrong had had with Mike Dvorak back in the summer of 1989.

The notes indicated that Jeff and Jack had discussed the case, at least in generalities, with Dvorak, and possibly others in his private law office, some of whom were now slated to join the prosecutor's staff after January 1, 2003. Jon also told the detectives that after the meeting with Dvorak, Jeff had called her to say that Dvorak was willing to represent him in the case, but wanted a retainer of $5,000. Jon had told Jeff the fee was too high—she wouldn't approve it as an expense of the estate.

For some reason, this information did not come out before the election—possibly Toth thought it was too hot to handle, that it would only underscore the claims that he was using the Pelley case for political ends. Accusing his opponent of being potentially sympathetic to Jeff because of their long-ago conversation could only add fuel to the Pelley-as-politics pyre.

But once the election was over, Corcella passed the information about Dvorak on to Andre Gammage, Jeff's second-chair defense lawyer, and later, to a reporter for the *Tribune*. Corcetta believed Dvorak's contact with Jeff back in 1989, in which the case had undoubtedly been discussed, meant Dvorak had at least the appearance, if not the actuality, of a conflict-of-interest: he could not now be responsible for prosecuting the man who had potentially confided in him, as a defense lawyer, thirteen years before.

A week before Christmas in 2002, Corcella went public with her concerns about Dvorak, and said the incoming prosecutor should recuse himself and turn the case over to a special prosecutor.

"He can't do Pelley," Corcella told reporters Gwen O'Brien and Matthew S. Galbraith of the *Tribune*, "and he knew this during the campaign. He hid it from the public." In essence, Corcella was accusing Dvorak of bad faith with voters prior to the election. Baum and Gammage said they agreed with Corcella.

"If there's any suggestion of anyone in his [soon-to-be-former private practice] office having had any personal contact with Jeffrey and his family about the case, it is incumbent upon Mike to recuse himself and his [soon-to-be-assumed public] office," Baum told the reporters. "Recusal is his ethical duty, and he needs to bring it to the court's attention."

Dvorak didn't want to talk about recusal, or even acknowledge that he'd been consulted by Jeff thirteen years before.

"I cannot even answer the question without jeopardizing the case," he said. Then he took a shot at Corcella—it was Toth's chief deputy who'd put the case in trouble by telling the news media about the old consultation, Dvorak said.

"When a prosecutor mouths off in public, the defense can use it to their advantage, and that can make a difference on whether there is a guilty or not guilty verdict," Dvorak said. "The election is over. Maybe Miss Corcella has a problem dealing with that."

This was a suggestion that Corcella was retaliating because Dvorak had fired her a day or so after the election.

Corcella rejected that—she said she'd gone public because Dvorak was ignoring the issue of the potential conflict, thereby exposing any eventual conviction of Jeff to a later reversal by a higher court.

Even if Dvorak brought in a special prosecutor at that late date—say, someone from the Office of the Indiana Attorney General—there might not be enough time for the new lawyer to prepare for the trial, which was scheduled to start in early February, Corcella maintained. A delay for more preparation could violate Jeff's speedy trial rights, and could possibly result in the dismissal of charges against him—in fact, such a dismissal might even make it impossible to ever charge Jeff again for the four murders, because of constitutional prohibitions against double jeopardy. Of course, in November and December 2002, Dvorak had no legal authority to bring in a special prosecutor—he wasn't due to take office until January 1, 2003—which suggests that Corcella had been hoping that the new prosecutor would appoint *her* special prosecutor, and when rebuffed, had then spilled the beans.

For his part, Baum assured the two reporters that delay was the last thing Jeff wanted. Jeff had been in jail for more than four months, Baum said, and he wanted the case resolved as soon as possible—Jeff knew he hadn't committed the crimes, and just wanted to get back to his wife and son in Florida.

But Baum was already beginning to suspect that Dvorak and those who were due to come into office with him wanted to drag things out, if they could—Baum thought the case was so thin that Dvorak and his entourage, faced with the political necessity of convicting someone they hadn't charged, were desperate for more time. Whether Baum was correct in his suspicion isn't known, but as things would turn out, the case would drag out for far longer than anyone could then imagine.

III. STILL MORE CLOCKS

January 2003–July 2006

CHAPTER 21

The late December 2002 demand for the case's outright dismissal on constitutional grounds would be, for both sides, just the first whiff of what would turn out to be an enormously stinky container of writhing annelids—in plain English, a large can of squirming, slimy, legal worms. In various permutations, this and similar claims would infest the case of *State of Indiana* v. *Robert Jeffrey Pelley* for the next three-and-a-half years. But even then, it would not be over. The question of what was or was not a "speedy trial," and who was responsible if it wasn't, would make *Indiana* v. *Pelley* a significant legal landmark.

As the Sixth Amendment to the United States Constitution has it,

> IN ALL CRIMINAL PROSECUTIONS, THE ACCUSED SHALL ENJOY THE RIGHT TO A SPEEDY AND PUBLIC TRIAL . . .

Criminal defense lawyers like Baum usually like to split the words "speedy" and "public," as the conjunction suggests that the pairing of the two adjectives comprises the very definition of justice. But as Baum had told the *Tribune* after Jeff's arrest, his client was entitled to a "*fair* and speedy trial," an elision of the Constitution favored by many defense lawyers, most of whom aren't particularly enamored of the "public" part of the constitutional equation.

"Fair," to Baum, meant "due process," which essentially

means following the rules of the law. In Baum's view, the rules required putting the rights of the defendant ahead of those of the public, at least, to observe justice in action—the "public" part of the Constitution. In Baum's opinion, a defendant's right to a fair trial under the Fifth Amendment superseded the right of the body politic to observe it under the First and Sixth Amendments.

As the Fifth Amendment puts it:

> NO PERSON SHALL . . . BE DEPRIVED OF LIFE, LIBERTY, OR PROPERTY, WITHOUT DUE PROCESS OF LAW . . .

The Pelley case was an example of prejudicial publicity, a violation of due process, Baum believed, and the publicity from so many years of frustration over the authorities' failure to solve the case suggested to him that it would be difficult, perhaps impossible, to find a jury willing to consider the issues on the merits, rather than the politics. That Toth, et al., had been so public, so loquacious, in the run-up to the election, was itself a violation of due process. To Baum, Toth and his group had simply been using Jeff Pelley's arrest as a campaign poster for Toth's reelection.

There was more: when the authorities took thirteen years to charge Jeff Pelley, that was also a violation of due process, at least in Baum's universe, because it had deprived Jeff of the opportunity to discover information that might have helped him defend himself, had the charges been filed much sooner. In short, there was nothing "due" at all about the process, to Baum. In fact, he believed it was highly "un-due," and extremely cynical, to say the least.

The decade-plus delay between the original investigation in 1989 and Toth's decision to charge Jeff so many years later—just before an election—made a fair trial impossible, Baum and Gammage contended. Some critical witnesses were dead, others were missing, and still others readily admitted that the events had happened so many years earlier, they could no longer trust their memories.

Even Toth had admitted that there was no new evidence—

and that was just rubbing salt into the constitutional wound, according to Baum. If the same evidence to charge Jeff in 1989 was sufficient to accuse him thirteen years later, why hadn't he been charged thirteen years before, when he could have best defended himself?

It was bad faith in the extreme, Baum argued—new evidence could at least be investigated, but old evidence, now musty from years of being ignored, simply compounded the injury to the defendant. It was worse than unfair—it violated every precept of due process. The only fair thing to do—and there was precedent for it in both federal and Indiana law—was to dismiss the charges outright as too stale and impossible to prove, and let everyone go home.

In addition to these overarching constitutional claims, Baum and Gammage would rely on an Indiana court rule that established strict limits for how soon a defendant had to have his trial after being charged. Indiana Criminal Procedure Rule 4, had six sections.

The first, 4(A), required a defendant to be released on his own recognizance—that is, without posting bail—if not brought to trial within six months. That rule was automatic—it applied whether the defense demanded it or not. The clock started running the day a person was arrested or charged, whichever was later, which, in Jeff's case, was August 10, 2002, when he'd been nabbed going through Customs at Los Angeles International Airport. The clock could be temporarily stopped if the defendant asked for a continuance, or did something to prevent the timely trial, or if a prosecutor asked for a continuance, which could not exceed ninety days.

But once the continuance was up, the clock started running again. In the absence of a continuance, that meant Jeff had to be let out of jail on his own recognizance by February 10, 2003, unless his trial had started. Chamblee had scheduled the trial to begin February 3.

The second section, 4(B), was rather more draconian. It permitted a defendant to demand a trial within seventy days. If a trial didn't start before the seventy days elapsed, a judge was required to "discharge" the defendant, that is, let him go free forever on the charges, unless the delay was caused by the defendant. The only exception to this rule was if the prosecutor certified to the court that court congestion, or an undefined "emergency," made a trial within seventy days impossible. If a defendant asked to be "discharged" once the seventy days were up, the prosecutor could try to prove to the judge that more time was needed to assemble evidence.

If the judge was satisfied that was the case, the clock could be extended for another ninety days.

But after that, the defendant had to be tried, or freed. This clock only started once the defendant demanded a speedy trial under Rule 4(B). Baum and Gammage had made this demand on November 26, 2002, which meant that Jeff's trial had to start by February 5, 2003, or else.

The third section, 4(C), was much the same as 4(B), but had a time limit of one year from the date of the original charge. Like 4(A), it was automatic—it didn't require a demand from the defense to set the clock running—and this clock could be suspended by continuances sought by the defense or prosecution; but in the case of the prosecution, the suspension could not exceed ninety days. If the defendant, however, didn't get his trial within one year of arrest—plus any delays caused by the defendant—he had to be freed forever, unless a prosecutor could demonstrate court congestion, or the ninety-day extension to collect new evidence.

All three of these speedy-trial clocks were therefore clicking away as Toth's regime vacated the premises of the St. Joseph County Prosecutor's Office on December 31, 2002, and as Michael Dvorak moved in, on January 1, 2003.

Then, in early January, having already set the seventy-day clock ticking, and knowing that the other two clocks were running as well, the defense asked Chamblee to appoint a special prosecutor to replace Dvorak. Thus, Baum and Gammage were attempting a squeeze play of sorts: on one hand, demanding a trial within the seventy-day limit, but at the same time, filing a motion that might make meeting that deadline impossible for the prosecution.

An appointment of a special prosecutor would almost certainly require a significant delay, as Corcella had prophesied in late November. If Chamblee held that the prosecution had known that Dvorak would have to be replaced, but had failed to act, any delay beyond the seventy days should be on their heads, Baum and Gammage contended, and should result in the dismissal of the murder charges, because the case hadn't come to trial within seventy days.

The special prosecutor issue was to be heard by Judge Chamblee on January 7, 2003, five days after Dvorak had been sworn in.

As this hearing opened, Baum asked that his petition demanding Dvorak's replacement by a special prosecutor be filed under seal, and that any testimony be heard in a closed courtroom, or at least, in the judge's chambers—that is, out of the public eye.

This upset the South Bend news media: television, radio and the *Tribune*, representatives of which had packed the courtroom. As soon as Baum made it clear to Chamblee that he wanted everything done in secret, the media representatives raised the alarm, and their bosses made calls to bring in their own legal talent in an effort to head this off. Jeff Pelley was very big news in South Bend, and the media people weren't about to let the story go behind closed doors without making a fight.

Chamblee had known this was going to happen. All those reporters eyeballing him and Jeff Pelley were enough to convince him, if he hadn't already realized it, that he was in the eye of a news media blizzard, at least one of local proportions. He told Baum that if he could cite any case or statute that permitted him to seal the petition or close the courtroom, he'd consider doing it.

Baum was momentarily flummoxed—he couldn't think of any, offhand. Chamblee said he'd give him a few hours to dig up some precedent or statute that authorized a secret proceeding, and adjourned the hearing.

* * *

Baum needed to establish that Jeff had given Dvorak confidential information in the 1989 consultation—that was the only way Baum could justify kicking Dvorak off the case. But he didn't want the media to know or report any details of what Jeff might have told Dvorak back then—that might give some people, i.e., prospective jurors, the notion that Jeff had confided guilty secrets to Dvorak.

It was possible, for instance, that Jeff had told Dvorak that he and his father hadn't been getting along, or that he didn't like Dawn. That wasn't inculpatory—it wasn't like Jeff telling Dvorak he'd pulled the trigger—but it wouldn't do Jeff any good to have prospective jurors ruminating about this before what appeared to be an imminent trial. Holding the hearing behind closed doors, Baum felt, could establish exactly what Jeff had told Dvorak, while protecting Jeff's right to a fair trial. This was at the crux of the Sixth versus Fifth versus First Amendment issue, for Baum: Jeff's rights to defend himself under "due process" should take precedence.

When court reconvened in the afternoon, Baum pointed out that Indiana court rules only required all "trials" to be held in open court, but "all other acts or proceedings may be done or conducted by a judge in chambers." In other words, Chamblee could bring all the parties, but not the news media, into his chambers and thrash out the disqualification issue there—because they weren't actually in "trial" yet. He suggested that the collective media's lawyer, Gerald Lutkus of South Bend—retained only that morning—join them behind closed doors, if Lutkus would agree to keep his clients in the dark about what was said.

The judge invited Lutkus to say what he thought of Baum's idea. Nothing doing, Lutkus said. There was no way he was going to go into a closed-door proceeding, then keep his mouth shut—he had his own clients, who were paying him big money to object to any closure. As for Baum's proposal to do everything secretly, Lutkus said, there was ample precedent from the United States Supreme Court that required all court hearings to be open: that was the way justice was done in the United States of America. He cited *Richmond Newspapers,*

Inc. v. *Virginia*, a 1980 bellwether case on public access to court proceedings, which stood for the proposition that justice should be done in public, so that all the parties could be held accountable to public opinion. Hey—it's democracy.

Chamblee agreed with Lutkus. The fact that he'd already read the gist of Baum's recusal petition demanding Dvorak's removal in the newspaper the week before had pretty much wiped out any need for secrecy, he told Baum.

This ruling effectively kept Jeff off the witness stand. There was no way Baum was going to allow his client to tell the court and the world at large what he'd told Dvorak all those years before, which was what was needed to establish that the newly elected prosecutor had a potential conflict of interest.

If Jeff couldn't say what he'd told Dvorak—chapter and verse—Baum could only rely on Jeff's simple affidavit asserting that he'd met with Dvorak in 1989 and had discussed the case with him. But Dvorak had already countered that with his own declaration, saying that, while he'd met with Jeff, he couldn't recall any details of the discussion. It was a stand-off.

The specifics of what the two had talked about didn't matter, Baum protested—it was the "appearance of a conflict" that counted. Chamblee said he couldn't act on appearances, he had to have evidence of an actual conflict, under the Indiana recusal statute for prosecutors.

Well, Baum said, he wanted to make one other thing clear.

"I think it is important to observe . . . that it might seem as though by petitioning for the appointment of a special prosecutor, that what Mr. Pelley is saying is that he made incriminating statements [to Dvorak]. But what I want to hasten to point out, it is not only a guilty person who has the right to petition for a special prosecutor to avoid a conflict of interest, it is an innocent person as well."

"Well, I trust you assume that I know that," Chamblee told him, "and this tidbit is given for the benefit of others than myself."

"The press might not know that," Baum agreed.

Chamblee now asked Scott Duerring, Dvorak's newly appointed chief deputy prosecutor, to respond to Baum's effort to get his boss thrown off the case.

There was no way that Jeff could show that any confidential information had passed between Jeff and Dvorak, Duerring said. There had to be "clear and convincing" evidence that Jeff had told Dvorak anything different from what he'd told police, which, of course, wasn't confidential, because the police had it on videotape.

Baum objected.

"It's not fair to put the burden on the defendant to take the risk that Mr. Dvorak, although he claims now not to have any present recollection—we've got a lengthy trial coming up. And I don't think that it's appropriate for my client to bear the risk that Mr. Dvorak isn't at some point going to remember something. It's just impossible for us to prove, but we've made enough of a showing to show an actual conflict does exist."

Chamblee said he was doubtful that an actual conflict existed. In any case, it was up to him to decide, by Indiana law, and if all he had to go on was Jeff's bare-bones affidavit and Dvorak's I-don't-remember declaration, he didn't believe the defense had met the required burden to justify dumping Dvorak or his office.

The next day, Chamblee formally denied the petition for the appointment of a special prosecutor. The squeeze play had failed, although a seed was planted for a possible later appeal.

Ten days later, on January 17, 2003, Chamblee held more pre-trial hearings. With the opening of the trial set for February 3, to keep up with the seventy-day clock, the judge wanted to get the Fifth and Sixth Amendment speedy-trial dismissal motion out of the way. In addition, the defense had filed a motion seeking the suppression of all of Jeff's statements to Hemmerlein on May 1, 1989, in which Jeff had supposedly asked about his chances of getting "the electric chair."

In this suppression motion, Baum contended that Jack

Armstrong had no authority to waive Jeff's Miranda rights back in 1989, since he wasn't a legal guardian at the time—the law required such a de facto legal guardian to have been a caregiver for at least one year, Baum asserted, and Jack wasn't even close to qualifying. The only legal representative for Jeff as of May 1, 1989, was Bob's sister, Jon Boso, because of the will, and no one had bothered to consult with her—to Baum, the police were in such a sweat to accuse Jeff Pelley that they hadn't bothered to figure out what was legal.

Baum wanted the disputed conversation with Hemmerlein suppressed, because if the jury believed Hemmerlein, it hardly helped Jeff look innocent. Getting Hemmerlein's story out of the trial might make it possible to call Jeff as a witness on his own behalf; but if Hemmerlein's story was told to the jury, it would be much harder to put Jeff on the stand.

Chamblee decided to deal with the suppression of the "electric chair" conversation first. The prosecution had the burden of proving that the testimony was admissible, so Duerring called the first witnesses, Botich and Hemmerlein—and introduced the two Miranda waivers Jeff and Jack Armstrong had signed on May 1, 1989. Botich said he believed the procedure was correct because of former prosecutor Jack Krisor's advice. Jeff was never in custody, he said, and had been free to leave at any time. On cross-examination, Baum established that Botich had no independent way of knowing whether Krisor's advice was correct, or who Jeff's legal guardian had been at the time.

Botich admitted that although Jeff was not in custody, he still considered Jeff "a suspect." With this, Baum hoped to convince Chamblee that Jeff had been under the control of the police at the time, a necessary condition to proving that the interview with Hemmerlein, more than fourteen hours later, required an "in custody" waiver from a responsible party, who Baum contended could not be Jack Armstrong..

This was a technical objection on Baum's part, but the art of being a defense lawyer is to dot every *i* and cross every *t*. Baum pointed to case law that suggested a guardian had to have had physical custody of a minor for more than a year to be qualified to approve such a waiver. Jack didn't meet the requirements, Baum contended.

But Baum's main interest was Hemmerlein, who had just returned to law enforcement after the years of exile under Toth. In fact, Dvorak—perhaps grateful for Hemmerlein's pre-election public blast of Toth in the pages of the *Tribune*—had appointed Hemmerlein commander of the prosecutor's Family Violence and Special Victims Unit on January 2, the same day Dvorak had taken the oath of office.

However, Baum wanted to make sure before Hemmerlein took the witness stand, that he said nothing about any "lie detector" test, which, after all, had been the main purpose of the May 1 evening interview, although it never came off. The last thing Baum wanted was for the news media to report that Jeff had refused a lie detector test.

But this was ridiculous: Baum's own moving papers had already revealed that the purpose of the interview was to prepare for the polygraph test, and the media had already read the briefs—that horse had already left the barn. Nevertheless, Duerring agreed to tell Hemmerlein to simply refer to the evening discussion as "an interview" without mentioning the words "polygraph" or "lie detector."

In Hemmerlein's testimony, Duerring once again established that Jeff and Jack had voluntarily signed the waivers, and that Jeff had been free to leave at any time, and had in fact done so, terminating the interview on the evening of May 1, 1989, around 11 P.M. In fact, even while in Gurnee, Jeff had demanded to speak to Jack Armstrong, and no one else—not his aunt, Jon Boso, or a lawyer. So Jack Armstrong was Jeff's own choice as an adult representative, Duerring contended.

He definitely believed Jeff was "a suspect," Hemmerlein told Baum on cross-examination, because of what had been said by Botich, Rutkowski and Krisor. Baum established that Hemmerlein had no idea if the waivers were valid, or whether Jack Armstrong could legally waive his grandson's

Miranda rights. He was only following directions given him by Krisor, Hemmerlein admitted.

That concluded the state's evidence in favor of letting Jeff's statement about the "electric chair" come into evidence. Now Baum called his own witness: Jeff Pelley.

CHAPTER 22

Now 31 years old, a husband and father, Jeff was several inches shorter than his father's six feet, and probably 30 pounds lighter. His hair was rather long, in the style of the times, but otherwise one could look at him—or photograph him, as the *Tribune* did—and hardly see a "homicidal maniac," as Corcella had called him a few months earlier. Looking at Jeff Pelley, he seemed only a young dad, handsome, well-groomed, perhaps slightly yuppified, but hardly the sort of person capable of shotgunning four people to death, including two little girls.

But this was grown-up Jeff. How he might have been back in late April 1989, at 17, was another matter. Reporters in the courtroom leaned forward—this would be their first chance to hear Jeff Pelley, the accused mass murderer, speak for himself.

Baum's purpose in putting his client on the witness stand was quite limited: he wanted to establish that Jeff had been, for all practical purposes, "in custody" at the time of the two interviews and that therefore a Miranda violation had occurred, based on the technical premise that Jack wasn't qualified to approve the questioning, since he couldn't be Jeff's legal guardian. That way, he hoped to get the "electric chair" statement thrown out. There was probably a secondary objective, however—for the first time in almost fourteen years, the public, through the assembled news media, would be able to see that Jeff was polite, well-spoken, not some sort of monster—certainly not some sort of drooling version of Jack Nicholson in *The Shining.*

Well, defense lawyers weren't above using the "public" part of the Constitution if it helped defend their clients. There was nothing hypocritical about this: in the adversarial system of American justice, a defense lawyer's ethical duty is to advocate for his or her client as zealously as possible—that's the lawyer's role, the lawyer's part of the justice system, although it's only when an individual has been falsely accused that it's most appreciated. One can only recall the defense attorneys of the last days of the Soviet Union, toadies for the state, to appreciate the distinction.

By putting Jeff on the stand, Baum was also playing to the future jury pool, in case a trial actually came off. Politics aren't always conducted in the voting booth—planting doubt in the minds of those who might have to decide Jeff's fate was a matter of guerilla campaigning, as Baum well knew.

Baum focused on what Hemmerlein had said to Jeff when he wanted to leave the pre-polygraph interview to make his date with Darla.

"[He said], basically, that we were not through," Jeff testified. The implication was that Hemmerlein had intimidated Jeff into answering still more questions, even when he'd wanted to leave. Police lieutenants could have that effect on 17-year-olds.

To make the point about the "in custody" issue even more clearly, Baum asked Jeff if it was true that a police officer had been stationed outside the Armstrongs' hotel room door on May 1, 1989—as if Jeff were under police guard.

Yes, Jeff replied, he and his grandparents had been told an officer would be stationed outside the room when they left after the morning questioning.

And was it true that Jeff had been under police surveillance at the high school track meet that afternoon?

"We were accompanied throughout the first few days of that week," Jeff answered.

Duerring's cross-examination of Jeff was limited only to the areas that Baum had asked about.

He couldn't, for instance, simply ask, *Did you do it?* That isn't the way the law works in the United States. Because the essential issue of the murders hadn't been raised by Baum, Duerring had no right to ask such questions.

The only question at this point was whether Jeff had felt coerced during the two May 1 police interviews, and whether he had knowingly or even legally waived his rights under *Miranda*, which, as every viewer of television cop shows in America knows by now, requires a suspect to be advised of his right to an attorney, or to silence, before speaking to detectives—"otherwise it may be used against you in a court of law."

Duerring first tried to establish that Jeff was very bright—implying that he was smart enough to know his *Miranda* rights—by asking if it wasn't true that he'd completed all his high school course work six months early. Jeff admitted that, and said he'd recorded mostly A's and B's while in LaVille High School. Answering, he was so soft-spoken, so diffident as to seem almost naïve. Chamblee had to tell him to speak up.

Because Baum had already established that Jon Boso, Bob's sister, was, by terms of Bob's will, Jeff's legal guardian after his death, Duerring asked why Jeff hadn't lived with her after the murders.

"She had no desire for me to live with her," Jeff said.

Duerring knew he couldn't get away with asking the obvious follow-up—wasn't Jon's lack of "desire" to live with her nephew because she thought he was guilty?

While this might have played well in the media, it wasn't useful to get slapped down by Chamblee after an outraged objection from Baum—Duerring knew full well that the judge had already absorbed the point.

Was he really claiming that the police had been watching him in the days right after the murders? Duerring asked.

He thought so, Jeff replied, although he admitted that his memory of the events of the days after the murders was hazy.

Well, had anyone from the police ever restricted his movements? Duerring continued.

No, Jeff said.

"Is it possible that this person—if, in fact, this person was there—was posted to protect your safety?"

"It's entirely possible," Jeff said.

Wasn't it true that Hemmerlein had told Jeff he could leave anytime he wanted? And hadn't Jeff in fact done exactly that?

Yes, Jeff admitted. But there might have been more to it.

"And I think that I made a request for an attorney or something at that point. And that might have changed things, too."

Duerring thought Jeff's response had opened the door—he could now ask about the lie detector test. But before he barged into this swamp, he wanted to get a green light from Chamblee. He asked to approach the bench, where a conversation could be held out of earshot of the news media's eager ears.

"In my opinion, the defendant is dancing around the issue," Duerring whispered to Chamblee. "He was brought there to perform a polygraph examination. He decided he didn't want to go through with it . . ."

The fact was, Duerring went on, Jeff's decision not to take the lie detector test proved he was not "in custody." After all, the police could have taken the refusal as evidence of guilt, and possibly arrested him on the spot. And even Jeff had asked Hemmerlein if he was going to go to jail that evening. The fact that he'd walked away from the police station with his grandfather surely demonstrated that Jeff was not "in custody" by any stretch of the imagination.

"I'm going to ask him," Duerring continued, " 'Well, isn't it true you were unwilling to take a polygraph? You said you wouldn't take it.' And [then] they [Jeff and Jack] got up and left." Which proved there was no "in custody" issue—no one had coerced Jeff Pelley. He'd declined and simply walked away, Duerring said.

But Chamblee said talking about the polygraph would be going too far—it didn't add anything to the "in custody" issue—it was pure speculation on Duerring's part to assume that Jeff had terminated the interview with Hemmerlein simply because he didn't want to take the lie detector test.

While Chamblee didn't say so, there were all sorts of reasons why Jeff might have declined to take the test—maybe he just didn't trust Hemmerlein, which was hardly evidence of guilt. If one believed Jeff's side of the story, in fact, Hemmerlein had accused him from the beginning of being the murderer. Maybe Jeff simply didn't want to take a polygraph from a man who seemed so obviously biased, and if so, who could blame him?

But this was what Baum should have cross-examined Hemmerlein about, even before calling Jeff to the stand—Hemmerlein's bias. For instance, Baum might have confronted Hemmerlein with the evidence that he'd written a letter to the *Tribune* in late October that decried the "political prosecution" of Jeff Pelley. Did Hemmerlein still believe the prosecution of Jeff was "political"?

Was he lying then, or was he lying now, in any lawyer's classic pincer?

But apparently Baum didn't know about the letter, or understand much about St. Joseph County politics—or grasp the possible significance of the fact that Dvorak had hired Hemmerlein for a top job in his new regime on his first day in office, or any possible reason as to why Hemmerlein was now testifying in a way that appeared to contradict his earlier letter to the editor, published only a week or so before the crucial election.

As an airline commuter from Studio City, California, to South Bend, flying in from time to time for Jeff Pelley hearings, Baum had no feel for who was who, or what was what, when it came to local politics and vulnerabilities: that's why it's always best for defendants to engage local attorneys as their lead lawyers, people who know what's really going on. Baum could have significantly undercut Hemmerlein's credibility about the second interview of May 1 at this early juncture, if he'd only known what to ask. It would later come back to haunt him, and Jeff Pelley.

* * *

After Jeff stepped down, Duerring tried to soften the "in custody" claim of Baum by recalling John Botich.

Was it true Botich had assigned someone to keep Jeff under surveillance on May 1, 1989, or thereafter?

"I don't recall that," Botich said. "I don't know what the reason would have been."

In fact, since he'd been the lead investigator in the murders, Botich added, if that had actually been done, someone would have told him about it, and no one ever did.

For the news media, that seemed to indicate three possibilities—Jeff was paranoid, Botich was out of the loop, or Jeff was lying.

Having taken the testimony on the "electric chair" issue, Chamblee now did a rather odd thing, albeit with the agreement of the prosecution and defense. Rather than hear argument from the two sides on the "electric chair" suppression question and render an immediate decision, he decided to take new testimony—this on the defense's Fifth and Sixth Amendments motion to dismiss the case because of the time lag between 1989 and 2002.

As Chamblee explained, he only wanted to minimize inconvenience to the witnesses by getting them on and off the witness stand as quickly as possible. The lawyers could always sort out the various finer legal points later, he said. But in consideration of real people's lives, of real people's time and money, the best thing to do was get all the witnesses on and off the stand, on all issues, without interrupting things for any long-winded, legalistic disputations from the lawyers.

So now the ball was in Baum's court—he had to bring on witnesses to demonstrate that the failure to file charges back in 1989, even though the evidence hadn't changed one whit by August 2002, was deleterious to Jeff's ability to defend himself.

Baum's first witness in this regard was Chris Toth, the electorally repudiated former prosecuting attorney.

* * *

If Baum was secretly hoping that, *Perry Mason*–style, he could induce Toth to abjectly confess that he'd only charged Jeff with mass murder to get reelected, he was dreaming. There was no way Toth was going to say any such thing—in fact, according to the defiant Toth, he could barely remember the Pelley case from his tenure as prosecuting attorney. Baum had the wrong witness, Toth repeatedly advised him—he should have called Corcella.

It was Corcella who knew what was what, and why the case had been charged more than thirteen years after the crimes.

Well, said Baum, what did Toth mean when, at a press conference held on the day of Jeff's arrest, he'd admitted that there was no new evidence?

Baum was distorting the context, Toth said. It wasn't that there was no new evidence, it was just that the old evidence was being looked at in a new way. Corcella had made that clear, at the same press conference, he added.

"It was not so much that we went out and found a smoking gun," Toth said, "as [much as] we simply put some sweat on our brow and hit the pavement and tried to bring some justice to those victims, no differently than prosecutors who are bringing prosecutions, even now, against Nazi death camp guards."

Baum was taken aback by this analogy, and was momentarily speechless. Chamblee intervened.

"Mr. Toth, will you answer his question as best you can without giving a speech? I'm serious."

Admonished, Toth tried to explain what he meant by looking at the old evidence in a new way.

"When we brought all the pieces together, we were able to find that all the pieces fit very, very well, and that this homicide was committed by Jeffrey Pelley. And there was evidence to not only support bringing a charge . . . but we had a good faith basis that we could prove the case beyond a reasonable doubt."

When it was his turn, Duerring asked Toth whether he believed any delay that had occurred in charging Jeff during his term of office had inconvenienced the defense.

"I think, actually, quite the contrary," Toth said. "The passing of time makes it more difficult to prosecute any case."

Chamblee had apparently heard enough.

"The issue isn't what he thinks about it . . . the question is whether *I* think that there's been some undue delay." He asked Baum if he had any other witnesses for the proposition that the case should be dismissed because of the delay under the Fifth and Sixth Amendments.

No, Baum said—at least, not at that time.

After a break for lunch, both sides argued the "electric chair" suppression motion, and Chamblee took it under advisement. Then the judge asked Baum if he was ready to argue the motion to dismiss the case under the federal constitutional claims of the Fifth and Sixth Amendments.

No, Baum said—he wanted to adjourn the hearing on the dismissal motion until another day. He might have some new witnesses later, he said.

But then a new problem arose. The state wanted a continuance—there was new evidence, after all, and it wasn't from the supposed softball kegger of the summer of 1989, used to keep Jeff in jail in November 2002. In fact, it was a gun—maybe not smoking, but still a gun, and left where Jeff Pelley could have put it that fateful day on April 29, 1989.

CHAPTER 23

On the day after the election of November 8, 2002, even as Dvorak was basking in the glow of his overwhelming victory, a man contacted the police to tell them of an old shotgun he'd once found wedged in a tree in the woods along Highway 4, the same route Jeff had said he'd taken to the gas stations in 1989. The man told police he'd found the weapon perhaps eight or nine years before, while looking for mushrooms—he hadn't thought it was important until he'd read all the recent publicity about the Pelley case. Craig Whitfield took possession of the gun, which was 20-gauge, albeit a single-shot model. There appeared to be a small smear of old blood on the gun.

Perhaps because of the transition between the Toth and Dvorak administrations after November 8, 2002, nothing was done to test the weapon for any scientific linkage to the wadding and slugs found at the crime scene, or the apparent blood to see if it matched any of the Pelley victims. Finally, sometime in December 2002, the shotgun was sent to the FBI Lab for analysis. Then it turned out that the FBI couldn't do any work on the gun—at least, not right away. The bureau was moving its firearms laboratory to a new location, and it needed at least a month before it could offer any help.

So Duerring asked Chamblee to grant a sixty-day continuance from the February 3 trial date.

Chamblee asked Baum if he'd agree to a delay.

Baum was torn. He wanted the FBI to do the ballistic examination, because he was convinced it would show that the newly disclosed gun could not possibly have been the murder weapon. He was sure it couldn't be a single-shot weapon, which would have required reloading after every shot—there simply wouldn't have been, in Baum's view, enough time to fire six or seven shots if the killer had had to load a new deer slug before each firing.

Wouldn't the victims have tried to run away? Wouldn't Dawn have attacked the single-shot-firing killer to protect her children? Would she simply lie down in the basement to be murdered, along with her two youngest daughters? No. In Baum's mind, the murder weapon had to be a multi-shell shotgun, capable of firing multiple shots within a second or two for each. It was the only explanation for such carnage, unless there was more than one shooter.

But markings on the recovered slugs might show whether the barrel of the murder gun had been rifled, that is, grooved, as the Mossberg 500 slug barrel was. If the shotgun found by the mushroom hunter *wasn't* rifled, if in fact it wasn't even a slug barrel, but a smooth-bore for bird or buckshot, the chances were excellent that the old shotgun had had nothing to do with the murders, and Baum would be able to prove it. Baum also wanted time to hire his own gun expert to make an independent examination.

On the other hand, Baum didn't want Jeff's speedy trial claims to be voided by any agreement to a continuance. The expiration of the seventy-day clock was only days away.

Baum told the judge he wanted the testing but didn't want Jeff's speedy trial demands to suffer for it. It wasn't the fault of the defense that no one had thought to send the gun to the lab until it was too late. Baum said he'd agree to the delay if the judge granted bail for Jeff.

This was probably a tactical error on Baum's part. The reality was, if the newly disclosed shotgun couldn't be matched to the murder scene, the chances were very high that the state wouldn't introduce it as evidence anyway. So that meant, possibly, that there was no need for tests. Baum could have said, in effect—Let the prosecution have their tests, we don't care. We know it's not the murder weapon. But in the meantime, we insist on our seventy-day trial rights.

But there must have been some sliver of doubt in Baum's mind—he wanted the tests before trial.

"I think he's saying he'd like to have his cake, and eat it, too," Chamblee told Duerring at the hearing.

Duerring didn't want Jeff out on bail, but he *did* want the continuance. He also wanted the defense to *agree* to the continuance. That way it wouldn't count against the state in terms of the seventy-day, six-month and one-year speedy-trial clocks Baum was pressing so vigorously. He pointed out that the defense had been told about the gun as early as mid- to late November 2002.

If they'd wanted it tested by their own expert, they could have done it then, Duerring said. Making the state pay for the foul-up would be unfair, he added—it wasn't the prosecution's fault that the FBI had decided to move its laboratory.

Baum now said he would "acquiesce" in the motion for continuance, which was well short of agreeing, or even joining in. It was a distinction without a real difference, Chamblee pointed out, as far as the seventy-day speedy-trial rule was concerned, although it might make a difference with the six-month or one-year rules.

Well, it was confusing for nearly everyone, the judge as well as the lawyers—what was the difference between objecting, not objecting, "acquiescing," or agreeing? Was it "joining," or not? Why would one clock stop while the others kept on turning? The case law on Indiana rules was contradictory, the definitions tended to be sorted out on a case-by-case basis, and as far as Chamblee could see, there were no cases on Rule 4(A), the six-month clock, or 4(C), the one-year clock. The issue had never come up before.

The point was, Chamblee noted, the defense wasn't actually objecting to the prosecution's demand for a continuance, which meant at least the seventy-day clock could be stopped, without forcing the court to "discharge" Jeff. If Baum wanted the new evidence, he had to drop his insistence on the seventy-day rule.

But that didn't mean the judge couldn't reconsider bail on his own, Baum persisted, irrespective of any of the speedy-trial clocks.

Chamblee said he'd think it over.

"As much as I'm sure you all would like to get all the evidence and get this matter resolved," Chamblee told Baum, "as would the community and the family, I'm not sure, [just] because it may take a month or longer, that I have the authority to simply say, 'It ain't fair that he stays in jail anymore,' if the evidence . . . was such to deny the bond in the first place." He noted that there were other people, arrested before Jeff, who were also in jail, who hadn't yet had their day in court. He couldn't grant Jeff bail merely on the basis of sympathy—it wouldn't be fair.

Still, while he was mulling over this renewed request for bail, Chamblee added, just what did Baum want to do about the adjourned hearing on the motion to dismiss because of the time lag between 1989 and 2002, the overarching Fifth and Sixth Amendment constitutional claims? It was one thing to haggle over Indiana court rules, but the claim stemming from the thirteen-year delay could make everything else moot. Chamblee wanted to get that one out of the way ASAP.

Well, Baum replied, as long as they were going to delay the trial for sixty days because of the new-old shotgun, he'd like that put off, too—he had an idea that the examination of the gun might affect this, as well.

Okay, Chamblee said. But he noted, now that the defense had "acquiesced" to the sixty-day gun-testing continuance, that meant the first seventy-day speedy-trial clock under Indiana Rule 4(B)—the one the defense had demanded in late November—was no longer ticking. In not objecting to the prosecution's request for a sixty-day continuance, it was like going back to 12:01 A.M. of Day One, at least on the seventy-day clock—if they wanted that clock to start up again, the defense now had to make a *new* demand for a trial under 4(B).

If the defense made it that same day, that would mean Jeff's trial had to start in late March.

But Baum had another trial, scheduled to begin in Tampa, Florida, on March 27. Sighing, he agreed to an April 21 trial date, eschewing a new seventy-day speedy-trial demand. That meant Jeff would have to stay in jail until then, unless Chamblee agreed to let him out on bail on other grounds, which sounded unlikely, given what Chamblee had just said.

Meanwhile, Baum believed the six-month speedy-trial rule still applied—that clock, he thought, was still ticking, as was the one-year clock, maybe. Acquiescing, in his mind, was different from agreeing. But already, the two remaining Indiana speedy-trial clocks under 4(A) and 4 (C) were beginning to twirl at different rates, depending on who was calculating them.

The following week, Chamblee denied the defense request to suppress the "electric chair" statement, and rejected the renewed request for bail for Jeff. And in a formal order granting the state's request for a sixty-day continuance to complete the gun tests, Chamblee charged the state for the delay, which meant it counted against the six-month and one-year speedy-trial clocks. Or so Chamblee said at the time.

Then another problem came up, which would blow away the mainsprings of all the clocks, maybe even irreparably. Legally, it was a bit like throwing the Pelley case into a black hole, where even time ceased to exist, as some theories suggested. Albert Einstein had once said that such things could not rationally exist. But of course, Albert had been a patent clerk, not a lawyer.

On August 22, 2002, ten days after the arrest, and about the time Jeff was arriving in South Bend from Los Angeles, Toth's ultimately dis-elected prosecutorial crew had served a subpoena *duces tecum* on the Family & Children's Center (FCC), a South Bend mental health counseling service. The subpoena demanded "any and all counseling records from 'the Rev. Robert J. Pelley family from 1986–1989.' "

Of course, the Reverend Bob was actually Robert *L.* Pelley, not Robert *J.* Pelley—which meant Jeff, who wasn't a reverend. Technically, the subpoena was invalid on its face, having specified the wrong Pelley—but attention to detail wasn't, apparently, Toth's strong suit.

The Family & Children's Center was the place where Bob, Dawn and Jeff had gone for counseling assistance in 1988 and 1989, beginning at about the time Jeff had threatened to kill himself after the grounding due to the shoplifting situation in the spring of 1988.

The subpoena did not include a return date, that is, a deadline for production of the records. In what appeared to be another casualty of the hand-off between Toth and Dvorak, no one from the new prosecutor's office followed through on the subpoena.

In fact, it seems likely that no one in Dvorak's incoming group even knew about it, and that Toth's outgoing loyalists never bothered to tell anyone about the counseling records. Or perhaps they had simply forgotten about it.

Now, at the end of February 2003, the Family & Children's Center moved to quash this subpoena—that is, to ask Judge Chamblee to rule it out of order. Lawyers for the FCC, as it was called, said that Indiana law required their clients to keep such records secret. The FCC demanded a hearing from Chamblee. It wasn't about Jeff Pelley, as far as the FCC was concerned—it was about keeping its counseling records confidential. Once law enforcement could barge in and seize that sort of material, the FCC might as well close up shop—no one would trust them, ever again.

Dvorak's prosecutors, finally catching up with what their predecessors had done, now said they indeed wanted the FCC's Pelley family counseling records. Dvorak's outfit suspected that the records might be a trove of potentially incriminating information about Jeff—possibly even an expressed intent of murder, prior to the killings. That evidence might prove the case, in that it could strengthen the alleged motive considerably. The stage was set for a three-cornered legal squabble.

By the time it was over, the carefully laid scheduling plans of Chamblee would be in ruins, and the prosecution of Jeff Pelley would be in serious legal jeopardy.

There is a relatively important sidelight to what was about to unfold with regard to these counseling records—a factor that later came into play in Indiana's higher courts. As it happened, a law that made counseling records by social workers confidential hadn't been approved by the Indiana legislature until a year after the Pelley murders. Some thought that meant counseling records assembled before then were fair game for review by law enforcement, while others were sure the new statute had to be retroactive—after all, what good was it to keep secret therapeutic conversations held after 1990, but allow authorities to paw through medical/psychological/social histories that took place *before* 1990? The intent of the 1990 law was clearly to let communicants and their social workers speak freely with one another, the same as priests, ministers, doctors and lawyers. There couldn't be some sort of arbitrary cut-off—that these conversations can be used as evidence, while these others are sacrosanct. It made no sense.

But Botich had known about these records almost from the start, and had told Barnes about them back in 1989. Nevertheless, no effort had been made to inspect them that summer, when they still could have been legally collected. Then the legislature had passed the law making the records confidential, at least after 1990. If Toth et al. thought the records were important enough to subpoena in 2002, why hadn't Barnes back in 1989? That suggested that Barnes didn't think the records would provide any useful evidence, at least as to murder.

It turned out, in early 2003, that the only way Toth had even heard about the FCC records in the summer of 2002 was that someone who had worked at the FCC in 1988–1989, after seeing the news of Jeff's arrest on television in 2002, had blabbed about having counseled him back in 1988. That person in turn dropped the dime to Toth. Otherwise, it would never have come to light.

Baum was in Studio City when all this began to unfold.

After that, he was in Tampa, preparing for his Florida trial. That left his second chair, Andre Gammage, to cope with this new issue. As far as the defense lawyers could see, they didn't have any beef in the fight between the prosecutor and the FCC.

True, they didn't want Dvorak's people rummaging through the counseling records—who knew what they might contain, or what 16-year-old Jeff might have spouted off about back in 1988, or what some social worker fourteen years before might have thought about it? But what they mostly did not want was to disrupt their efforts to get the case dismissed on the speedy-trial claims, or at least require Chamblee to grant the long-sought bail.

So Baum and Gammage elected to sit on their hands, and watch the tennis match as the prosecutor and the lawyers for the FCC went back and forth over the confidentiality of the records.

On March 19, Judge Chamblee convened a hearing to sort out the counseling records problem.

"The state feels that the evidence leading up to the homicides is extremely important," Ducrring argued. "We now have people telling us what Bob Pelley said. We have people telling us what Dawn Pelley said in the weeks and days and even the day of the homicides, about what was going on inside that household, and the relationships and the fear and things like that. Unfortunately, due to the fact that Bob Pelley and Dawn Pelley are dead, that largely makes these statements inadmissible."

What some witnesses, like the Schafers or the Howells, claimed that Bob or Dawn had told them about Jeff and/or the prom was second-party hearsay, and not ordinarily admissible as evidence. But that wasn't the case with the written material—case notes and summaries and the like. The rules of hearsay recognized an exception for authenticated medical records.

"The statements that are contained in these records . . .

fall squarely within the hearsay exception—statements made for the purpose of medical treatment or diagnosis," Duerring contended. "And there's no other way we have— The state has no other avenue to get this kind of evidence in . . . It's not like we're dallying around, fishing for things . . . It's information that is critical, and really the only information we have that would be admissible, as to the nature of the relationship of these parties prior to the homicides."

The records were necessary for proving his case, he insisted. And even if there was nothing in the records showing that Jeff had explicitly threatened to kill his father, stepmother and two stepsisters, the broader background of the atmosphere in the Pelley household in 1988 and 1989, as depicted in the records, could be probative. That was the relevance, and as for the asserted privileges, there were grounds to deny that any existed, Duerring said.

It wasn't only that the records had been assembled before the social worker privilege law had been passed, and could therefore be legally disclosed, Duerring told Chamblee. There was also an exception in the law—if the records could relate "directly to the facts or immediate circumstances of [a] homicide," they could also be disclosed, even if Chamblee decided that the privilege was retroactive. This was the "homicide exception" to the social worker/psychologist/doctor/minister privilege, and Duerring thought it applied—the background of the Pelley family angst in 1989 was pertinent evidence as to the murders. Duerring contended that this homicide exception to the privilege should be wide-ranging, incorporating almost anything that came to bear on the atmosphere in the parsonage in 1988 and 1989. Any domestic difficulties were grist for the mill, in that they could have precipitated the murders.

Well, that was putting it backward, in a way. Duerring had no idea of what the records actually said—he was assuming, or rather hoping, that the would be relevant to the killings. Actually, he had to see the records to make the argument, but he couldn't see the records because of the privilege—Catch-

22. He proposed a solution: the judge could let him inspect the records, in camera, in the judge's chambers. Then he'd know how to frame his argument. He'd promise to say nothing of what he read to anyone until the judge made his decision. If the judge ruled against him, he'd keep his lips zipped.

Chamblee wasn't keen on this idea.

The only way to determine whether the "homicide exception" applied, Chamblee said, was for *him* to review the records. He asked whether any of the lawyers disagreed with that, and the lawyers for the FCC and Duerring shook their heads—they did not. Chamblee asked Gammage what he thought.

Gammage said he wasn't conceding that the counseling records were discoverable, in light of the FCC's argument that the social worker privilege should be construed retroactively. He thought Chamblee should first decide that issue, before actually looking at the records. Then Gammage made a verbal slip of the tongue: "And I think that's an argument that has been made on our behalf, or, on behalf of the Family and Children's Center."

Well, of course, *Gammage* hadn't made that argument on behalf of Jeff Pelley—he was only telling Judge Chamblee his opinion as to the proper sequence for handling the issue. It was the FCC's lawyers who'd said that the privilege should be retroactive, not the defense, and the FCC wasn't arguing on Jeff's behalf, they were trying to protect *all* their clients, only incidentally including the dead Pelleys.

If after uttering the word "or," Gammage had interposed something like "rather," or "I meant to say," he would have made himself clear.

This slip of the tongue would later be seized on by the prosecution to assert that the defense had "joined" the FCC's lawyers in their motion to quash. And that in turn would lead the prosecution to soon contend that the six-month and one-year clocks had stopped, because the defense had caused a delay in the proceedings—the motion to quash.

By "joining" the FCC's motion to quash the subpoena,

the defense had stopped the speedy-trial clocks—or so the prosecution contended. Sometimes the law resembles a high-stakes poker game—any "tell" is seized upon for ruthless advantage. *Aha!*, Duerring said to himself, *you blinked.*

Unaware of how the prosecution was construing his slip of the tongue, Gammage continued. Even if the judge found that the privilege wasn't retroactive, the defense wasn't conceding that the information in the records was admissible under the hearsay rule. That was a separate issue.

Chamblee agreed—admissibility was an entirely different issue from privilege. He'd take the sixty to seventy pages of the FCC records back into his chambers and pore over them privately to see whether the "homicide exception" applied to the counseling sessions, and try to decide whether the social worker privilege could be retroactively applied. But Gammage was right—the judge didn't need to read the actual records to decide the larger issue of whether the intent of the law was to go backward. The specifics in the records were irrelevant to that determination.

"For the record," Gammage said, "we object to the court making that [in camera] review."

"All right," Chamblee said. But he had to do it—he had to determine whether the homicide exception came into play, he said.

"There is no possible way that it can be done without somebody looking at the records. I'm the gatekeeper of the evidence. How can you object to me looking at them?"

"I realize that you may have to look at the information," Gammage said, "but I also have to object to that, for the record."

"Well, you have accomplished that, Mr. Gammage," Chamblee said.

The next day, March 20, Chamblee issued an order quashing the subpoena. The provisions of the social worker privilege law were retroactive, Chamblee ruled. Besides that, the information in the records did not relate " 'directly to the fact or immediate circumstances of . . . homicide' . . . whether that phrase is given a more limited meaning, or the more expansive meaning proffered by the state . . ."

In other words, Chamblee had read the records and had found they simply weren't relevant to what the state was trying to prove. They said nothing about murder, not even close, and besides that, the records shed little light on the pre-murder atmosphere in the parsonage, contrary to Duerring's assertions, or perhaps, wishful thinking. There could be no "homicide exception" to the counseling privilege.

"Judge Rules Counseling Records 'Privileged,'" the *Tribune* headlined on Saturday, March 22. "State Denied Access to Family Sessions." The paper's Marti Goodlad Heline caught up with Duerring for his reaction.

"It's unfortunate. But it's not the only avenue we have," Duerring told the reporter. "We are pursuing another way to get the records. The state feels these records are essential." But Duerring wouldn't say what his Plan B was.

"It's unfortunate the Family and Children's Center is being so obstinate," Duerring added. "They don't have to raise the privilege issue . . . these people [the Pelleys] went to this organization with a serious family problem. It obviously didn't work. Now they're dead, and the Family and Children's Center is blocking our attempt to get records to search for the truth of their deaths. It's ironic."

Chamblee picked up his Saturday morning newspaper and read the headline and became upset. The following Tuesday he sent a sharply worded letter to Duerring, chastising him for his remarks.

> The implication of your statement is that the Pelleys went to FCC to address some homicidal tendency on the part of the defendant Jeffrey Pelley, which effort failed, resulting in their death, and further, that the records which you sought would expose the truth of the defendant's involvement in their deaths. Whether intentional or not, your comments have now raised the innuendo that, notwithstanding the evidence which might be presented at trial, that the state, in these suppressed

> records, has further evidence of the defendant's guilt which could not be presented.
>
> Had those records contained evidence or disclosures related directly to the fact or immediate circumstances of the homicides in question, the records would have been disclosed. As I noted in my order of March 20, 2003, they do not, whether applying your interpretation of that phrase or some other . . .
>
> A determination of this case by a fair and impartial jury might be . . . facilitated if jurors are permitted to make that decision based on evidence presented at trial, without the specter that otherwise relevant evidence is being withheld.

Noting that the trial was just over three weeks away, and jury selection was imminent, Chamblee slapped a gag order on both sides. From this point forward, he advised Duerring and Baum, any new out-of-court statements by either side would be severely frowned upon, if not penalized, by Chamblee. And if Duerring wanted to take the judge on, he was free to do so "in open court," which meant a debate, with every news media outlet in attendance.

In a way, this was challenging Duerring to a public boxing match, and one in which the judge had the clear advantage—after all, he had the bench, the high ground. It was clear from this letter that Chamblee was irate—Duerring seemed to be setting him up. If Jeff Pelley was acquitted, Dvorak, et al., could say it was Chamblee's fault for withholding supposed key evidence. The fact that the evidence didn't actually exist was beside the point—this was just another attempt by a politician, Dvorak, to stick somebody else with the blame if things went wrong. Or so Chamblee believed.

Well, Chamblee wasn't going to take the gaff. His letter to Duerring was a warning—if Duerring wanted to take him on in "open court," Chamblee would humiliate him in front of the assembled news media, and, since he made all the rules, Chamblee knew that Duerring knew that Dvorak didn't want to get into a public squabble under those conditions. The message was clear: back off, especially with any more public statements that might tend to make the judge look bad.

But Duerring was already at work on Plan B.

CHAPTER 24

By early April, Duerring was even more determined to get the Family & Children's Center counseling records, Chamblee's order quashing the subpoena notwithstanding. Exactly why Duerring was so insistent is a bit puzzling. Chamblee had essentially assured the deputy prosecutor that there was nothing in the FCC material that helped the state's case. And when Duerring had seemed to contradict this in his remarks to the *Tribune*'s Marti Goodlad Heline, Chamblee had reproved him in very sharp terms, reiterating that there was no useful evidence to be found in the material. Didn't Duerring believe him?

Later, Baum formed his own theory of what happened next. He was convinced that Dvorak's group had no confidence in their case against Jeff—that they thought their case would blow up on the witness stand, that Jeff would be found not guilty, the jury would be appalled at the paucity of evidence, and that Dvorak and his assistants would then be the laughing stock of Indiana, all because Chris Toth had left them with a sow's ear, with the pre-election charging of a case that was unprovable and therefore unwinnable.

So, Baum said, Dvorak's side decided to make a desperate play for more time. Maybe, if they got more time, something else would turn up as evidence. In effect, this was the Michael Barnes 1989 strategy all over again—except now, as Baum thought, the speedy-trial clocks were whirling away, exactly as Barnes had feared back in 1989.

In any event, in a routine hearing on April 2, 2003, Duerring dropped a bomb on Chamblee, and by extension, the case of *State of Indiana* v. *Robert Jeffrey Pelley*. After Chamblee had disposed some ordinary matters of scheduling, Duerring advised the judge that he had a new matter to discuss.

"I have one more thing to throw into the mix," he said, and with that, passed over a petition requesting that Chamblee "certify" an interlocutory appeal of the counseling records issue to a higher court.

"Oh, my goodness," Chamblee said, as he scanned the petition. Then: "All right. Now that you've thrown that little monkey wrench into the mix, let's go back to Rule Four." What Chamblee wanted to know was whether the state's attempt to go over his head was a delay that would require him to let Jeff out of jail on his own recognizance under Rule 4(A), the six-month clock. Once the issue got to the higher courts, it might be years before the matter was resolved—far longer than six months, of which there was less than a month or maybe two remaining on that clock, anyway, depending on who was doing the counting.

Yes! Gammage was thinking. And once he heard what had happened, Baum, still engaged in his Florida trial, was certain that Duerring's move would require that Chamblee let Jeff out of jail, maybe even forthwith.

Chamblee questioned Duerring closely. He understood, didn't he, that any "interlocutory appeal," as such pretrial or prejudgment appeals are called, virtually guaranteed he'd have to release Jeff until the appeal was resolved? Duerring said he wasn't so sure about that—he'd talked to some people in the Indiana Attorney General's office (he was required to get them to approve an appeal if he had any chance of convincing a higher court to take it), and the attorney general's people in Indianapolis believed that any such appeal would stop all speedy-trial clocks—freeze them in mid-tick, so to speak.

Chamblee said he thought that was all wrong. As far as he could see, the prosecution's effort to go around his decision on the counseling records would be on their head—it had to count on the six-month and one-year clocks, which should keep on rolling. Chamblee made an obliquely disparaging remark about bureaucratic lawyers in Indianapolis who had little actual trial experience.

"I was somewhat instructed to do this," Duerring admitted. That made it sound like his Plan B had come down from Dvorak himself. As far as whether the attorney general was right about the speedy-trial clocks being "tolled," that is, frozen, Duerring acknowledged he wasn't sure himself.

"I just hope they know what they're doing," he said.

Chamblee said he was inclined to allow the prosecution to go forward with an interlocutory appeal of his order on the counseling records, as long as they understood what the stakes were. The Court of Appeals had thirty days to decide whether to take the case, and he was very sure that time would count against the speedy-trial clocks, no matter what someone in the state attorney general's office claimed.

If a higher court declined to hear the prosecution's appeal, the prosecution would be that much closer to having to let Jeff out—the hands of the six-month clock were nearing the witching hour. If something else happened to delay the trial before April 21—

"I assume you would rather have the evidence in and let the man out on his recognizance than to go forward to trial without the [appellate] question being answered?" Chamblee asked.

"Probably," Duerring admitted.

"Okay, just as long as you recognize— But as far as I've read the case law, if we don't try the case within X amount, the door opens. And you prefer to appeal [the order to quash the FCC subpoena]?"

"Yes," Duerring said. "I mean our— Yes. We are very serious about that."

Chamblee said he understood that he didn't have to "certify" the interlocutory appeal, and that if he didn't, the chance that the appellate court might accept it would be lessened. On the other hand, the appellate court might ignore his lack of certification and accept it anyway.

Duerring said his side was convinced that Chamblee's order quashing the subpoena raised a "substantial question of law," in that it improperly extended the social worker privilege back in time, and that resolving the issue would "promote a more orderly disposition of the case."

The legality of making the 1990 social worker law go backward, he said, was crucial: If Jeff was found not guilty, and the state then appealed Chamblee's quashing order and won, the result would be moot: due to double jeopardy, Jeff could not be retried. What if the social worker records showed Jeff had explained exactly how he was going to murder his family? Obtaining them after a trial without the records would be useless—a pyrrhic victory. This would cause substantial damage to the state's interest, which was in punishing those who commit murder.

But if the records before 1989 were not privileged, the state had a right to know that before trial started.

Now Duerring filled in a little more of the background. Some weeks earlier, an investigator for the prosecuting attorney's office had tracked down the FCC social worker. It turned out that she had made some off-hand remarks in a bar conversation, and those remarks had made their way to the prosecutor. The social worker told the investigator some of the things that Dawn had told her, back in 1988 and 1989; it appeared that some of these things were corroborated by what Dawn had told others that she had told the social worker. But much of the material was the social worker's own subjective feelings about what Dawn was saying.

Getting the actual records could put those feelings into better perspective, Duerring argued. Likewise, it would bolster the prosecution's effort to get more of the original Bob and Dawn hearsay statements into evidence. So could hearing from the social worker herself at trial. He wanted Chamblee to allow her to testify, and even be permitted to submit to further interviews, notwithstanding the order to quash, because Dawn, in telling others about her conversations with the social worker, had effectively waived the privilege, even if it existed before 1990.

This alarmed Gammage. The social worker shouldn't be

allowed to testify, he said. She should be covered by the judge's order quashing the FCC subpoena. Not only that, the prosecutors should be prohibited from asking her any more questions.

"Whatever they [already] got from her, it shouldn't even be used for purposes of any discussion about this issue of the interlocutory appeal," he said.

"I disagree," Duerring said.

Now Gammage and Duerring got into a hot debate about the social worker privilege, which Chamblee quickly cut off.

"I think we're done for the day," he said.

Chamblee was exasperated. Just as it looked like the trial was about to start, now there was this legal jack-in-the-box, leaping out and leering at everyone. The judge took Duerring's petition back into his chambers and opened his law books. It was much quieter back there.

Two days later, Chamblee certified the interlocutory appeal.

Five days after that, Gammage filed a motion for Jeff's release on his own recognizance. As far as he was concerned, the six-month alarm bell had sounded. And the one-year clock was turning, too. If Chamblee was correct, if the clocks still turned, there was a chance that Jeff might avoid a trial altogether, that is, if the higher courts couldn't resolve the question by the following December. As Chamblee had said, the delay was on the state's head.

In the meantime, Gammage and Baum would try to get Jeff sprung on the six-month rule, so he could finally make it back to Florida to see his wife and son. It had been a business trip with an unexpected layover that now threatened to derail his life—forever.

CHAPTER 25

Although the defense filed a motion asking for Jeff's immediate release from jail on April 9, 2003, Dvorak and Duerring weren't so willing to give up their captive. As Duerring put it to the *Tribune*, the prosecution believed that once out of jail, Jeff would bolt—head for some place that had no extradition treaty, although such places were increasingly rare in a world shrunken by the jet age.

Duerring was well aware of the reality: people facing the prospect of spending the rest of their life in a prison cell always have ideas about absconding—it's human nature. But Gammage kept insisting that if Jeff got out, he would attend every subsequent court hearing. He hadn't killed anyone, Gammage insisted on Jeff's behalf, and he wanted a jury to say so.

With the assistance of the attorney general's office, the prosecutors scoured Indiana case law for a precedent that said that the clocks *were* frozen for the purposes of an interlocutory appeal. That way, they could keep Jeff in the slammer.

Soon enough, they found one: *Cox* v. *Superior Court of Madison County, Indiana*, a 1983 case in which the state's Supreme Court held that the clock *did* stop on an interlocutory appeal—at least in terms of Rule 4(B), the seventy-day clock.

In that case, the defendant, who was in jail on a murder charge, filed several motions to preclude the state from introducing certain evidence, which the defendant thought might prejudice his right to a fair trial. The trial judge agreed to the limitations, the prosecutor appealed, and then, because the seventy-day clock ran out, the defendant demanded "discharge" under Rule 4(B). He filed a lawsuit to compel the discharge, the prosecutor opposed it, and the state Supreme Court eventually held that the cause of the delay belonged to the defendant, because of his motions to preclude the evidence—asking that the evidence be limited had initiated the delay, the court held. The *Cox* decision should control in the Pelley case, Duerring insisted.

But Chamblee disagreed—he said the seventy-day clock was different from the six-month clock. For one thing, the seventy-day clock mandated "discharge," not release on recognizance, as the six-month clock required. It was apples and oranges, he said. Release on recognizance didn't mean the state couldn't go forward—the charges were still valid. The only difference was, Jeff would be out of jail, but that hardly meant the state couldn't prosecute him.

That distinction didn't matter, Duerring argued. The standards of both rules were the same—if the defendant did anything to cause the delay, or failed to object, the clock stopped. And in the Pelley case, Gammage had done exactly that when he'd "joined" with the Family & Children's Center in the motion to quash the subpoena. If no one had moved to quash the subpoena, the prosecution would've gotten the records, and there would be no delay. It was the defense's own responsibility for "joining" with the FCC for the stopping of the speedy-trial clocks, Duerring argued.

But Gammage had actually done no such thing, except for his slip of the tongue, as the transcript of the hearing made clear. All he'd done was give Chamblee his view on the law, and that only when Chamblee had asked—that the judge should decide the retroactivity of the social worker privilege first, before reviewing the records for the possible homicide exception. The defense had filed no written briefs giving their researched opinion as to what should be done. Gammage had been dragooned into the discussion by Chamblee—the record on that was beyond dispute.

True, Gammage had objected to the judge reviewing the

files, "for the record," as he had put it. The judge had overruled him, and reviewed the records in camera—no harm, no foul, no delay. There was nothing in the record to support Duerring's contention that the defense had "joined" with the FCC's motion to quash.

And even if Gammage had lacerated his tongue with his incisors to say nothing, that hardly altered the fact that it was the FCC, not the defense, that had objected to the subpoena and was the party of record, and which would have done so no matter what Gammage had said, or not said. After all, there were multiple privileges involved—not just Jeff's, but also those of Bob and Dawn. It was a substantial legal question: did Jeff actually have the legal right, even if he wanted to, to waive his dead parents' privacy privilege? Probably not, as Chamblee agreed, and even Duerring conceded. The fact was, Dvorak's position, at least regarding the issue of whether the defense was responsible for the delay, was probably legally untenable.

But Duerring was only providing downfield blocking for his patron, Dvorak. Like one of the Seven Blocks of Granite of Fordham University lore—Vince Lombardi—he wanted his client, Dvorak, to run to daylight. Well, that's the way Lombardi, the legendary football coach, had put it. As Lombardi had it, winning was the only thing.

That applied to prosecutors as well as football teams, not to mention politics. Dvorak wanted Duerring to get rid of the troublesome foundling left on his electoral doorstep by the police-despised Toth—winning the Pelley case could only boost Dvorak with the St. Joseph County voters. Getting the counseling records might win the case, or so Dvorak thought. But to evade the Rule 4(A) and Rule 4(C) consequences, Duerring had to find a way to lay the blame for the delay on the defense.

To Duerring, blaming the trial delay—the interlocutory appeal—on the defense was only a matter of tactics. It bought his side more time, under the speedy-trial clocks. The Indiana Supreme Court's decision in the *Cox* case effectively penalized a defendant for exercising his right to a fair trial by charging him for a judicially approved delay, even though the prosecutors had initiated the objection, the appeal, and the delay. It effectively turned Rule 4(B) upside down—it made the defendant pay the price for defending himself.

It was, in Baum's view, yet another violation of due process, because it essentially penalized any defendant for exercising his constitutional rights.

But to Duerring, none of that mattered. If he could only freeze the speedy-trial clocks, he could run away to fight another day.

In yet another hearing on April 10, all these opinions were expressed, and eventually Chamblee grew exasperated again.

"It seems that every time I have what appears to be a brief hearing in this case, you guys take up the rest of my day reading cases," Chamblee grumbled.

But actually, the prosecution's position was even more complex. Because it didn't know whether the Court of Appeals would even accept the appeal of the counseling records, and if it did, whether that meant the clocks were stopped, it wanted to keep Jeff in jail until at least April 21, 2003, the day the trial was supposed to begin—if it began.

And, Duerring contended, because the defense had "acquiesced" to the sixty-day continuance for the gun testing, and had then agreed to the April 21 trial date, the six-month clock had at least stopped on January 17, and was frozen until April 21, when it could start up again—unless the Court of Appeals said it should be stopped as of the date of the appeal, April 4, 2003, or later, depending on if the court stopped the clocks when it actually accepted the appeal, if they did, which had to be within thirty days after April 4.

Good grief—the rules were ruining everything.

Chamblee tried valiantly to sort through the mess, holding numerous hearings throughout April and into early May, where each side argued their own version of the six-month clock. The problem was, by this point, nearly everyone had different sums. The prosecution kept arguing for a slower six-month clock, hoping that the appellate court would issue an order freezing the clock in the meantime, contending that Baum's "acquiescence" meant he'd stopped the clock from January 17 to April 21, which meant that the six-month rule ran even longer: any way you sliced it, the earliest Jeff could get out of jail, even assuming the Court of Appeals held that the clocks weren't stopped for Rules 4(A) and (C), would actually be in early May, Duerring argued.

The defense disagreed, Chamblee scratched his head, Duerring insisted, and court clerks scurried about, trying to assess the by-now hopelessly disparate speedy-trial clocks of the defense, the prosecution and the court.

It was a can of worms, all right.

"It all depends on how you do the math," Chamblee aptly observed, and as the various clocks ticked away, different people continued to have different ideas of how fast time really flew. It depended on where you stood, where you were headed, and how fast you were going there. But no one really knew. Like Einstein's theory, it was all relative.

And so it went over the next month, with Baum and Gammage striving to spring Jeff from the St. Joseph County can, and Dvorak and Duerring trying their utmost to keep him in. The discussion about the various speedy-trial clocks became increasingly arcane, with each side trying to find Indiana cases that supported their own side. The problem was, there were very few cases, and none with the same circumstances that encompassed Jeff Pelley's incarceration.

Throughout the end of April and through most of May 2003, Baum and Gammage filed motion after motion to force Jeff's release from jail, based on various interpretations of the six-month clock. They worried that something awful might happen while he was in custody. High-profile prisoners are frequently targets of other prisoners seeking notoriety, and the more widespread the publicity, the more likely it was that Jeff would become a target, for either accused murderers who had nothing to lose, or would-be snitches eager to sell him out in order to escape their own troubles. The sooner his lawyers could spring Jeff, the better. Already, at least one would-be snitch had come forward, claiming that Jeff had confessed to him. Gammage had had to spend at least a week beating that snake into submission.

At the same time, Duerring admitted he didn't want Jeff out—given that Jeff was facing the possibility of spending the rest of his life in prison, Duerring thought he might bolt, or simply change his appearance and hide out someplace—who could say? The stakes, at least for Jeff, were enormous.

But by May 28, 2003, Duerring ran out of objections, and Chamblee ruled that the six-month clock had finally run out, no matter how you calculated it, Newtonian or Einsteinian. Jeff was released on his own recognizance.

A defense investigator, Scott Campbell, picked him up from the jail—photographers were there to record the event—and drove him away for a long-delayed reunion with his wife and mother-in-law, Phil Hawley's sister. The next day or so, Jeff returned to southwest Florida, where Phil and Danny soon found him a job in one of the Hawley enterprises.

On June 16, 2003, the Indiana Court of Appeals formally accepted the prosecution's interlocutory appeal, and issued a stay in the proceedings, which meant everything ground to a halt—subpoenas, depositions, anything at all to do with the case. The court wasn't clear, however, on the issue of the one-year speedy-trial clock.

Was the one-year clock stopped? If it was, was it Jeff's doing? Or the prosecutors'? If the one-year clock was still ticking, exactly when did the state have to give Jeff his trial, or forever hold their peace? The trial record was unclear, and so was the appellate decision, but it seemed to be sometime in December 2003.

If Jeff didn't get his trial by then, under the one-year rule, did that mean he'd get to walk free? True, the trial had been "stayed" by the Court of Appeals, but did the stay count against the one-year rule, if the stay was the result of the prosecution's action?

Baum and Gammage were convinced that was the case, while Dvorak and Duerring vehemently denied it. So once again, there were two different clocks, depending on who was keeping time. Dvorak's side kept insisting that the state should not be charged for the time it had spent arguing in the higher courts with the FCC.

If there was any delay, Dvorak's team asserted, the blame was on the defense, not on them. At first, they said, the delay was the fault of the FCC—a non-party to the criminal case. But once the defense had "joined" with the FCC's motion to quash the subpoena, that made the Pelley side equally responsible for the delay. The clock issue lay there, unresolved, a ticking bomb under the case.

Chamblee set a new trial date for October 2003, thinking that by then the appellate court would have sorted everything out.

But by early October 2003, the appellate court still hadn't reached a decision on the counseling records, so Chamblee postponed Jeff's trial once again. The question of whose version of the clock took the rap for the delay still wasn't clear.

Then, in December 2003, the appellate judges ruled: the social worker privilege *did* run backward from 1990: Dvorak's team wasn't entitled to the records, just as Chamblee had held months before.

But that wasn't the end of the matter. In January 2004, Dvorak's side appealed the ruling to the Indiana Supreme Court. And there the matter sat for all of 2004 and well into 2005.

Then, in June 2005, the Supreme Court ruled that the Court of Appeals was wrong: while Chamblee had been right to review the records himself, he had been wrong to say that the privilege ran backward. And, the court said, when Duerring had asked to look at the records privately, in camera, Chamblee had been wrong to say he couldn't let him. The matter of the speedy-trial clocks wasn't addressed by the court.

By then, Duerring had left Dvorak's office, replaced by Frank Schaffer, a long-time ally of Dvorak, and a former prosecutor under Barnes. Ironically, Barnes had been elected to the Indiana Court of Appeals in 2000, although he did not consider the Pelley case as a justice. The Pelley case now became Schaffer's problem. But by then, another election was on the horizon.

CHAPTER 26

The long delay for the appeals had shoved the Pelley matter far back down the list of pending cases in St. Joseph County. But when the Indiana Supreme Court formally issued its opinion as to the counseling records in August 2005, Pelley jumped back onto the "front burner," as Chamblee put it. It had been three years from the time Jeff had first been charged by Chris Toth. After having spent almost 10 months in jail in South Bend, Jeff had had a little over two years of freedom with his family in Florida.

But with the State Supreme Court's decision granting the prosecution access to the counseling records, the stay in Jeff's trial was over. To some, that meant the one-year speedy-trial clock began turning again—that is, if Jeff didn't agree to a further delay.

The seventy-day clock wasn't an issue—the defense had shut that one down on January 17, 2003, when it had "acquiesced" to the prosecution's request for a sixty-day continuance to examine the shotgun found in the tree. Because Baum had had another trial at the end of March 2003, that clock had never been restarted.

The six-month clock had finally run out in late May 2003—that was why Jeff had been released on his own recognizance to go back to Florida. So that clock didn't come into play, either, since Jeff was already out of jail.

But the one-year clock—that was a different matter. When did it start? When was it suspended? When did it start up again? How many days counted on the one-year clock, and who had responsibility for them? These were all murky questions.

In late October 2005, Chamblee held yet another hearing on the Pelley case, this one to get everyone back on the same page—the two-year hiatus in the case demanded some sort of recapitulation as to who was who, and where they were. He made it clear that so much time had passed, so many other cases had come before his court after the 2002–2003 maneuvering, that his own memory of the Pelley facts was spotty. It seemed to him there was a lot of unfinished business left over from 2003, not least of which was Baum's motion to dismiss the case on the Fifth and Sixth Amendment claims.

Chamblee said he'd checked his records: while Baum had been arguing the dismissal under constitutional grounds, the issue about the counseling records had blown up and consumed everyone before the judge had reached any decision. He wanted to dispose of that—again, that had priority, because if he granted that, everything after that would be unnecessary. If Jeff's speedy-trial rights under the federal Constitution had been violated, he would walk—the law required it.

Baum now told Chamblee his side wanted to file a supplemental argument in support of dismissal under Indiana court rules as well as the federal constitutional claim. Baum did not then tip his hand, but he believed the one-year clock had run out. He intended to force Chamblee to "discharge" Jeff on the basis of Rule 4(C), the one-year clock. Baum made his argument in a written motion to dump the case:

> Rule 4(C) has no tolling provision for taking interlocutory appeals and the case should be dismissed . . .
>
> In our case, not only did the defendant not set the chain of events in motion, other than Mr. Gammage attending the hearing on the motion to quash and making a few comments when asked by the court a direct question, the defendant did not participate in the entire process . . . It was the state who set things in motion when they couldn't get their hands on records that they

believed relevant to their case . . . which was opposed by counsel for the [Family & Children's Center].

The prosecutors had finally reviewed the disputed material from the FCC, only to be disappointed, Baum noted. There was no smoking gun in the counseling records, exactly as Chamblee had advised them more than two years before. Not a single person from the FCC was named to the roster of the prosecution's proposed witness list. The interlocutory appeal and all its attendant delay meant absolutely nothing to the trial of Jeff Pelley, except insofar as it might affect a later appeal—Baum remained convinced that the only reason Dvorak's side had interrupted the April 2003 trial was to buy more time to investigate.

It was a sham, Baum believed, an egregious violation of the one-year speedy-trial clock, and an unconscionable violation of the Fifth and Sixth Amendments. Baum was certain that his client's right to a speedy trial had been grossly violated by the St. Joseph County Prosecutor's Office, simply to evade political responsibility for trying a case it had no confidence in.

Chamblee scheduled another hearing for the end of January 2006—that would be Baum's last chance to convince the judge that the murder charges should be dismissed for any violations of the speedy-trial guarantee. The charges against Jeff were more than three years old, and the crimes themselves were almost seventeen years old, Chamblee said. It was time, long past time, for the community, for the dead Pelleys, for the survivors and their relatives, to end the struggle, to find a resolution.

Chamblee set a trial date of July 10, 2006, and told everyone he wanted the whole thing to be over by the end of July, because that was when he intended to go on vacation. Baum agreed to the trial date—he was planning an overseas trip in late May. This agreement was crucial. In Chamblee's mind, this meant that Baum had stopped the one-year clock. Baum didn't see it that way, though—he thought that once he'd filed his one-year motion to dismiss, it didn't much matter if he'd agreed to a trial date that he thought would never come off. Neither side seems to have understood the other's position.

In the meantime, Chamblee said, he'd do some serious thinking about Baum's latest attempt to have the case dismissed for lack of timely prosecution, on the basis of the one-year clock.

Chamblee mulled Baum's motion to have the case dismissed for three months. Then, in early May, he ruled that the 4(C) discharge requirement did not apply to Jeff Pelley. Once the Court of Appeals had issued a stay in the case back in the spring of 2003, the one-year clock had stopped. This seems to have been a one-eighty from Chamblee's expressed opinion of April 2003, but then, the record wasn't exactly clear.

Then, he had said the interlocutory appeal would count on the state's six-month clock, and it did—he'd released Jeff from jail. But now he found that the one-year clock had been stopped once the Court of Appeals had issued a stay in the trial, which, Chamblee said, had effectively frozen everything, and the stay was maintained by the State Supreme Court's consideration of the counseling records matter.

In effect, the six-month clock was irrelevant after Jeff's release, while new rules applied to the one-year clock after the state's appeals. If it was apples and oranges with the seventy-day versus six-month clock, it was oranges and pears with the one-year clock. If Einstein had grown fruit instead of equations, it goes without saying that the world would be very different.

Chamblee agreed, however, that there were no Indiana cases that were directly comparable to the Pelley situation—so who knew? But he thought that once Baum had agreed to the July 2006 trial date, he'd waived the one-year rule.

Baum and Gammage now appealed Chamblee's rejection to the Court of Appeals, and then to the Indiana State Supreme Court.

For the better part of a month, the Supreme Court considered the defense argument that the one-year clock had somehow elapsed. Baum and Gammage were hopeful that their argument would prevail, and that the high court would order Jeff discharged, or at least, grant another stay in the trial to more fully consider the issue.

But then, on July 7, 2006, just three days before the trial was supposed to begin, the five justices voted unanimously to deny Jeff's demand for outright dismissal of the charges, or even a stay in the proceedings. The Indiana high court held that if Jeff was convicted, he could always appeal. Because of double jeopardy, he did not have the same risk as the state three years before.

The stage was finally set for Jeff's trial, more than seventeen years after the shotgun blasts that had wiped out a family.

IV. THE TRIAL OF ROBERT JEFFREY PELLEY

July 10, 2006–July 21, 2006

CHAPTER 27

Seven men and five women were selected for the jury that was to decide Jeff Pelley's fate. Ranging in age from the early twenties to the late sixties, they represented a cross-section of St. Joseph County—a retired elementary school teacher, the manager of a meat market, a claims adjustor, a homemaker, a counselor in a foster children's home, a retired truck driver, a banker—for the most part, working people, who had spent most of their lives in northern Indiana.

None had ever had very much contact with the police, or involvement with the courts. They were joined by four alternate jurors, two men and two women.

As Chamblee advised the empaneled, it would be their job to decide the facts—what was true, what was false, what the relationships were between the claims—in short, what was likely, and what was not, assertion compared against assertion. This was the jury system, in which adversarial declarations had to be weighed in the context of the totality. It was the American style of justice, rarely understood around the rest of the world, where power often flows down, not up. But this is the true American exceptionalism, not some high-flown rhetoric about democracy or freedom or liberty or republicanism, or even "free trade": in the United States, ordinary people, not politicians, not generals, not bureaucrats, not even those who are richest at any given moment, get to decide who is right and who is wrong—who is guilty, and who is innocent—in short, what is just, and just what the government can do to an individual. That ideal of American justice, of the people, and by the people—*for* the people—is the living heart of our liberty. It makes us all custodians of our freedom.

Almost all the chosen jurors had heard at least something of the Pelley case over the years, but every one of them swore that the publicity would have no bearing on their assessment—they were ready to decide the issue solely on the basis of what they heard in court, not what they had previously read or seen on television. By the time the jury was selected, after two days of intense questioning of a large panel of potential jurors, Baum pronounced himself content, even though he had once thought of asking that the case moved to another county because of the pretrial publicity.

"We've got a very fair-minded jury," he told the *Tribune*'s Marti Goodlad Heline.

The following day, July 10, 2006, Chamblee invited the chief deputy prosecutor, Frank Schaffer, to give the jury a summary of the evidence they would hear.

Schaffer's presentation was methodical. He avoided rhetorical flourishes, but simply summarized all the facts that the prosecution believed about the murders, and thought they could prove, beginning with the discovery of the bodies on Sunday morning, April 30, 1989, followed by the police attempts to establish the whereabouts of the principals on Saturday and Sunday. Schaffer contended that those facts alone proved that Jeff Pelley, and only Jeff, could have been the killer. As Ellen Corcella had said almost four years earlier, there was no alternative theory as to what had happened—it could only be Jeff, Schaffer contended.

Schaffer then went backward to the atmosphere in the Pelley household in the days before the murders: Jeff as a rebellious teenager, the grounding, the cancellation of the car insurance, the Saturday afternoon visit by Kim Oldenburg's group, and Matt Miller's observation of Jeff's Mustang at 5:10 P.M. or so, as Miller rushed toward the Holmgren house with the retrieved corsage. Other people had dropped by the Pelley house that evening, Schaffer recounted, only to find the doors locked, the curtains drawn, the Pelley cars in the driveway, the garage door down, but no one responding to knocks on the door. That showed clearly that Bob, Dawn and the two girls were dead by 5:30 P.M., he said, and in turn, that meant only one person could have killed them—Jeff.

He didn't have a videotape of the murders, Schaffer admitted. There was no last gasp from the victims accusing their murderer, nothing at all to prove exactly when the murders had occurred, or who had committed them. There was no way to positively prove that Jeff had pulled the trigger, no smoking shotgun, no eyewitnesses, no dying declarations. Though all he had were circumstances, Schaffer said, when assembled, they were very damning. It was up to the jury to consider those circumstances—how they fit together. It was like a jigsaw puzzle, he said. The jurors had to find how each piece fit into the frame. It was only when *all* the circumstances were assembled that the picture became clear—the pieces, once assembled in proper order, showed that Jeff Pelley, and only Jeff Pelley, could have brutally murdered his father, his stepmother, his two stepsisters—and just to go to his high school prom.

"And after we've presented all that evidence . . . over the next few days, we're going to ask each of you to go back in that jury room and we're going to ask you to find Mr. Pelley guilty of four counts of murder," Schaffer concluded.

Andre Gammage gave the opening for the defense.

"One of the things there won't be in dispute is that the Pelleys were killed in the home," Gammage told the jurors. "And that was tragic, it was a horrible thing. We're not here to dispute the tragedy of what happened."

What *was* in dispute was at the crux of the case, he said: who had done it. The state had the burden of proving that it was Jeff who'd pulled the trigger. It wasn't enough to say that Jeff could have done it, might have done it, or even probably did it. The jury had to be convinced that the facts showed, beyond a reasonable doubt, that Jeff had killed everyone.

The state, he continued, would present evidence from the

crime scene. But in evaluating this, the jury should be very wary.

"One of the things you will find out about the crime scene is what's lacking. What's *not* there. You will find no eyewitnesses. There is no weapon. You will hear about waddings and you will hear about shotgun [slugs], and you will hear about a lot of things. None of those things will be linked to Jeff Pelley." There would be no physical evidence to show that Jeff Pelley had shot anyone.

The state would contend that there was at least a twenty-minute "window" for Jeff to have committed the crimes, the time between when the Pelleys had last been seen, and Jeff had left to go to the Amoco gas station on Highway 31. The defense disputed that, Gammage said—the so-called "window" was actually much smaller—shorter. The facts would show that the time between when the four Pelleys had last been seen alive, and Jeff had next been observed, was less than half the twenty minutes claimed by the state.

"Now, I don't agree that there is a twenty-minute period of time," Gammage reiterated. But even if there was, the jurors should see from the evidence that the state's proposed timeline for the murders was stupid.

"Is the state really suggesting that a seventeen-year-old boy in 1989 committed these acts in twenty minutes, then left and went to the prom?" Gammage asked. No mere stripling of a teenaged boy, however angry he might have been at his father, could possibly have pulled off such a perfect crime, Gammage suggested.

For its part, the defense would present physical evidence—scientific evidence—that the murders could *not* have occurred during the time the state contended, Gammage added. They had to have occurred hours after Jeff had left the parsonage.

"Tell-tale signs of water evaporation . . . will show you that the crime could not have been committed when the state says."

Gammage did not elaborate, but this was an obvious reference to the moisture found Sunday morning in the bathroom. If Jeff had left the house at 5:10 P.M., even conceding the state's version of the timeline, was it likely there would still have been water drops on the bathmat and damp washcloths hanging over the tub almost seventeen hours later, when the bodies were found? How fast did water evaporate at the end of April, the beginning of May 1989? That was a question to which science had an answer, he said, and jurors would hear about it.

In trying to establish doubt about the time the murders had actually occurred, Gammage was also setting the stage for a later argument that there had been a murderous, if possibly fastidious intruder after Jeff had left to drive to the prom—say, someone from Florida: the dope dealers, or perhaps someone from Landmark Bank—someone who had washed himself off in the bathroom after committing the murders, if the Pelleys themselves hadn't used the tub hours after Jeff had left.

Well, Gammage didn't know who else might have done it—the point was, there were other people who might have wanted Bob erased, not just his unhappy son, and the moisture in the bathroom seemed conclusive: someone else had been alive in the parsonage well after Jeff Pelley had driven off with his tuxedo to the prom.

The jury had to think about all possibilities before jumping into the state's kettle of half-boiled conclusions, Gammage said. The case against Jeff Pelley was like a used car the jury was being asked to buy, he summarized.

"A car that looks nice on the outside, [that's] the package that has been presented to you thus far." [Gammage meant Schaffer's opening statement]. "A nice-looking package, a nice-looking car. You see that car, you go in and you buy the car. Drive it off the lot, and what do you realize? You've got a problem with the engine—it's the crime scene. You got a problem with the transmission—it's the timeline. You have a problem with the brakes—it's the evidence.

"You need to decide over the next few days whether you put your family in that car and drive it across this country. You're going to find the evidence is lacking, you're going to find yourself not comfortable with what's been presented.

You're going to find yourself wanting more. You're going to find yourself with reasonable doubt. And when you find yourself with reasonable doubt, you must find Jeff Pelley not guilty."

Just as it was Schaffer's goal to show the jury how all the pieces fit—that, once assembled, there could be no one else but Jeff who could have committed the killings—it was the objective of Baum and Gammage to pry the pieces apart, to show that the state's theory of the murders was a haphazard amalgam of spare parts and loose wires, barely held together with duct tape, to adapt Gammage's used-car analogy.

Over the next few days, as Schaffer called witnesses to establish the crimes—Stephanie Fagan, now grown up, then Dave Hathaway and Wilmot Tisdale, and after them, the initial investigating police officers, Botich, Rutkowski and Pavlekovich.

Baum and Gammage did their best to poke holes in the state's theory. Baum paid particularly close attention to how the crime scene had been processed by the detectives.

"Hollywood," Senter said later, with a slight sneer of contempt, and Botich agreed. To the two detectives who had spent their lives in the real world of northern Indiana, the idea that a slick, Gucci-clad lawyer from Tinseltown could come to their homeground and fault their work was ridiculous—in fact, to them, it was insulting. That Senter and Botich made no differentiation between Hollywood and Studio City—miles apart, culturally and economically—made no difference.

As the first days of the trial unfolded, Baum worked hard on his cross-examination, flaying the initial investigators, trying to show that they had jumped on Jeff as the prime suspect from the start, and had therefore overlooked potentially vital evidence. Had they found a single drop of blood evidence linking Jeff Pelley to the murders? No, the police admitted. They had sent the clothes found in the washing machine to the FBI for analysis, but the tests had found nothing. Baum asked if it wasn't likely that the killer had been spattered with blood from the victims, and Pavlekovich had to admit they had first thought it very likely, but hadn't found a single article of clothing of Jeff's with blood or brain matter on it.

Pavlekovich admitted that the police hadn't examined most of the parsonage for any fingerprints, because they expected to find only the Pelleys' fingerprints, and because Jeff was already the prime suspect. Finding Jeff's fingerprints in a house he had lived in would be useless—it proved nothing unless they were on the murder weapon, and the murder weapon was still missing after more than seventeen years. As Baum had anticipated, the old shotgun found in the tree years earlier could not be connected to the crimes.

"Who made the decision that fingerprinting [of the house] wasn't necessary?" Baum demanded of Pavlekovich.

It was by common consent of the four detectives, Pavlekovich answered—Botich, Rutkowski, Pavlekovich and his assistant, John Kuhny, informed by Mark Senter's assessment of Jeff's viability as a suspect. The railing from the stairwell to the basement had been removed that Sunday evening, and a few days later, it was dusted for fingerprints, but none were found.

But it didn't much matter, Pavlekovich testified—most of the time, more than 90 percent of the time in all cases, recovered fingerprints are so smudged as to be worthless. So much for another canard of detective fiction—first the exact time of death, now the fingerprints. Agatha Christie would have been chagrined—nothing in the traditional English country house murder novel would have been useful in real life.

"So, the railing leading from the main floor to the basement was the only thing in the entire house that was dusted for prints?"

"Yes."

"And that was because a lot of time fingerprints are smudged?"

"The majority. That was our decision."

"Is that how you're trained in crime-scene investigation? 'Don't bother taking prints, because they might be smudged'?"

Baum was starting to get under Pavlekovich's skin with his obvious sarcasm.

"Well, counsel, you know, every crime scene is different, okay? You know that yourself." Any time a police officer refers to a defense lawyer as "counsel," it's clear he's beginning to get angry.

"So a lieutenant, two sergeants and you discussed whether we should bother to take prints in this quadruple homicide crime scene, and it was decided, 'No, let's not bother, because they might be smudged'?" Baum demanded. Baum tossed his pen down on the counsel table in an unmistakable sign of disgust and dismissal.

"That wasn't just the reason."

"What other reason was there for not taking prints that might lead to evidence?"

"Because at the time we were looking at Jeff Pelley."

CHAPTER 28

Of course, Baum knew as well as Pavlekovich that it was extremely rare to find useful fingerprints at any crime scene, let alone at a bloody quadruple murder where no weapon, and not even a bloody shoeprint, had been found. But that wasn't the point he was trying to impress on the jury. He wanted Pavlekovich to admit to a rush to judgment—the detectives' assumption, as Baum saw it, as early as Saturday afternoon that Jeff had to be guilty, before all the facts were in.

Baum scored another point when Pavlekovich confirmed that the bathroom seemed to have been used. The washcloths hanging over the side of the tub were damp, one more so than the others. And there, on the videotape that Pavlekovich had recorded, were obvious water droplets still glistening on the rubber mat inside the tub. The question was—when had the water run in the bathtub?

Was it after Jeff had driven away from the parsonage in the Mustang?

Baum wanted the jurors to think about what that water meant, because he would come back to it later. He was sure this was solid evidence that someone had taken a bath or a shower in the tub, hours after Jeff had left for the prom—which meant that either the Pelleys had been alive on the evening of April 29, 1989, or, if they were dead, the killer had cleaned himself up. Baum believed the droplets should have evaporated long before Pavlekovich had recorded them with his video camera on Sunday morning or early afternoon, if indeed they had been left around 5 P.M. on Saturday.

He intended to try to prove this scientifically, and in Baum's mind, the moisture in the bathroom was hard evidence that Jeff could not possibly be the killer.

This would be the linchpin of the defense case—the water droplets and the wet washcloth proved that the Pelleys had been alive and well after Jeff departed for the prom sometime between 4:50 and 5:10 P.M. Which in turn meant that Bob had given Jeff permission to drive the Mustang, go to the dinner, attend the after-prom party and then go to Great America with his friends. The water in the tub meant all the talk about Bob's grounding was so much gossip, just gibber-gibber talk—it had to mean that Bob's bark was worse than his bite.

Hadn't that been exactly what Jeff, Jacque and even Jessica had always maintained? And who would know better than the surviving family members themselves?

No—Baum was sure he could show that the police focus on Jeff from the very beginning had blinded them to others, possibly bad guys from Florida, who wanted Bob dead. Dawn and the girls were simply collateral damage, in Baum's conception of the case.

And there was more: Hoover's autopsy had shown that all the Pelleys had eaten something only hours before they were killed—fruit in the case of the little girls, popcorn in Bob's case. And the anecdotal evidence seemed to be, Bob only ate popcorn in the evening. The crime-scene photos appeared to show a Tupperware canister of popped popcorn on Bob's desk in the basement. The failure to make the biological tests as to time of death was looming larger and larger.

In Indiana, jurors are permitted to submit written questions to witnesses through the judge. (Rather oddly, they are also permitted to talk to one another about the case as the trial goes forward, just as long as they don't speak to anyone who isn't on the jury. Many states compel jurors to keep their mouths shut, even with one another, until all the evidence is in.)

One of the jurors posed a question to Pavlekovich that Baum thought was very pertinent. Had the police ever investigated anyone other than Jeff? Pavlekovich said he didn't know. As far as he was aware, the police had believed Jeff was the killer almost from the start. Baum thought this would bear fruit later—the fact that at least one juror was thinking outside the prosecution's box was very encouraging to him.

"Pelley Defense: Police Slanted Probe," the *Tribune* headlined succinctly the following day.

The next witness was Dr. Hoover, the pathologist who had performed the autopsies on the victims. All had been killed by lead deer slugs fired from close range, Hoover said. There was a lot of blood, as well as brain matter all across the basement floor, forced out of the victims' heads from the shots. The shooter had been standing within six inches to a foot or so from little Jolene when he'd fired. The 6-year-old was lying on the basement floor at the time—it was an execution, pure and simple.

No one asked Hoover, who had been trying to learn about blood spatter before coming to the parsonage, if in his opinion the shooter's feet and lower legs would have been spattered with blood and brain tissue from the victims.

Talking heads on television often use the word *splatter* to describe the spray of blood from a murder victim, but the word used by experts is *spatter*, without the *l*—as in liquid material forced out in small droplets from a relatively flat surface, similar to a spray of material from a frying pan to a stove surface. Those who use the word *splatter* instead of *spatter* are in error. But even Baum used *splatter* in his subsequent cross-examinations—once a word enters the popular culture, it becomes almost impossible to get rid of.

The failure to ask Hoover about "spatter" on the shooter's feet or legs was an oversight, as it turned out. If the shooter was really within a foot or two of the downstairs victims, he almost certainly would have had some blood or possibly brain tissue spattered on his lower limbs, as even a St. Joseph County crime-scene expert later admitted. Yet, as Baum had already established with Pavlekovich, no one had ever found any clothes or shoes associated with Jeff Pelley that had the slightest trace of blood or brain tissue on them.

The police had searched Jeff's Mustang, Pavlekovich admitted, but they hadn't looked for blood, tissue or even gunshot residue there. True, they had hoped to find a shotgun and shell casings, or even bloody, brain-spattered clothing, but had found nothing—not even a reasonable time frame in which Jeff could have dumped them. Baum was trying to impress the jurors with the idea that the police were so eager to solve the murders by naming Jeff as the culprit that they hadn't performed even the most basic procedures—if not a single speck of blood or brains had been found on Jeff, on any of his clothes or in his car, why was he still the cops' prime suspect?

Surely, if Jeff Pelley was the killer, the one who had blown out the brains of Dawn, Janel and Jolene from close range with a shotgun, why did he seem to be so bereft of blood?

When Hoover took the witness stand, Schaffer knew that Baum would try to make the point that no one had established a time of death for the Pelleys, so he tried to head this off. He asked Hoover if he had been able to establish an accurate time of death.

"The only time that time of death is actually done accurately, is on television," Hoover told Schaffer. "And it's one of those medical fantasies that don't hold up in real life."

Agatha Christie, Erle Stanley Gardner, Rex Stout, Dorothy Sayers, Ngaio Marsh—all authors of classic murder mysteries, the very best of the genre in the last century—none of them knew what they were talking about, Hoover seemed to suggest. In the real world, no one could accurately pinpoint the time of death, even within hours—it was a nice device for a detective story, or a TV cop show, but it just wasn't the way things were in the real world.

But just as Schaffer had anticipated, Baum still pressed Hoover on the time-of-death issue. He asked Hoover why no effort to examine the bodies had been made while they were still at the parsonage. Hoover said that wasn't his job that day—he was only there to examine the blood spatter. When Baum asked about rigor mortis, lividity, liver temperature and other such biological indicators of time of death, Hoover said they weren't always reliable indicators. In any event, he hadn't actually looked at the bodies until the next day at the autopsies, and this was after they had been refrigerated.

The fact was, no one could say for sure when the Pelleys had been murdered—the evidence was only circumstantial, and contradictory. For every fact that suggested they'd been killed around 5 P.M., there were other facts to suggest that the murders had happened much later—water droplets in the bathtub, the damp washcloths, popcorn in Bob's stomach, the church socks on the tables in the living room, bowls of what appeared to be breakfast cereal in the kitchen and in the living room, all of which might suggest an early morning hour for the murders.

An attempt to make a scientific assessment of the time of death, whether on Saturday afternoon or early Sunday morning, would have been very useful. But as Hoover said, sending a pathologist to the scene of a murder wasn't standard operating procedure in St. Joseph County—in fact, it was rare almost everywhere else in the country, too.

On the other hand, there was the testimony of those who had come to the parsonage between 5:30 and 6:30 P.M., who had seen the Pelley cars in the driveway, the curtains closed, the doors locked, and who had heard no response to their knocks. While some evidence seemed to indicate that the Pelleys *might* have been murdered hours after Jeff had left, still other evidence suggested that the Pelleys were dead before 5 P.M., and that, when Jeff had started up his supposedly disabled Mustang, he was already leaving behind a life that he hated.

Schaffer next called Steve Diller, who in 1989 owned a gun shop in Lakeville. Diller told of trading a Mossberg 500 pump-action shotgun to Bob in late December 1987. In exchange, Bob had given him a .44 magnum Smith & Wesson revolver, claimed that Bob had paid him the difference, although that was odd—the revolver was worth far more than the shotgun. Still, this established that at one time, at least, there had been a pump-action shotgun at the Pelley house.

Diller added something else: on Saturday morning, April 29, 1989, Bob had been in the shop looking at handguns. Exactly why Bob had been looking at pistols on the weekend of his murder was another mystery—but then, as one of Bob's old friends put it later, Bob "loved guns."

Brenda Hale, who had been Jeff's supervisor at the McDonald's back in 1989, was the next witness. Brenda was also a member of the Olive Branch Brethren church. It had been Brenda who had promised Jeff the $50 gift certificate for dinner at the Emporium. She had been at the church on Friday night, cleaning it, along with Jeff, Bob, Darla and several other people. That evening, Jeff had told her he was going to be allowed to attend the prom and the dinner, but that he was a little short on money. That was when she promised to give him the gift certificate. Brenda told Jeff she'd give it to him the following morning, when they started their shift at the McDonald's. Jeff told her he'd pay her back later.

Then, as she was leaving the church, she had a short conversation about Jeff with Bob. Bob told her that Jeff was going to be allowed to attend the prom—the prom only. She did not tell Bob about the certificate, she testified. Nor did Jeff hear Bob's assertion that Jeff would only be going to the dance, not the dinner, not the "after-prom," and not the trek to Great America.

Neither Schaffer nor Baum asked Brenda Hale why she didn't tell Bob about the gift certificate, which obviously wouldn't be needed if Jeff wasn't allowed to go to the restaurant. It might well have been that Brenda simply didn't distinguish between the various events—that to her, "the prom" was the whole kit and caboodle, dinner and all, and that when Bob had told her Jeff was going to be allowed to attend "the prom," she assumed that Bob meant everything. Although Brenda still left with the impression that Bob was going to do the driving.

The next night—Saturday, April 29—Brenda had returned to the church just after 6 P.M. She had a child who was desperately ill, and she wanted to pray. She saw both Pelley cars parked in the driveway, but Jeff's Mustang wasn't there. The garage door was down—unusual, she thought. She went into the church—Bob always kept it unlocked—and found it empty. She half expected Bob to come in, because he kept a close watch on the church, and often talked to people who dropped by, just to see how they were. She prayed for about twenty minutes. Then she thought she heard the front door of the church close. Brenda thought it might be Bob, but no one came into the sanctuary.

"I sat up and I looked around," Brenda said. "And, I don't know, but I just got kind of an eerie feeling, so I left. And I was going to go over to the parsonage on my way out, but I didn't. I just got in my car and left." This had been sometime between 6:30 and 7 P.M., Brenda said. She'd seen no one else, and no other cars at the church that evening.

Baum now asked Brenda if it was true that she'd once told police she knew of threats that had been made against Bob—this was an attempt to get to the rumors that Jeff had talked about so long before, in reference to the Herczeg brothers. He showed her a police report in which she'd apparently told an investigator about the rumors.

But Schaffer wanted to head this off. He demanded a sidebar conference out of earshot of the jury. He objected to any discussion about the Herzceg brothers as potential assassins of the Pelley family.

"What he's getting into is a situation having to deal with the defendant doing a bunch of stealing and—"

"Slow down," Chamblee told him. "With the defendant—what?"

Schaffer tried to explain. It all had to do with Jeff's ill-fated career as a petty burglar, he said.

"Apparently there were some other young men in town, and Mr. Pelley and these young men were apparently stealing from each other and stealing from other people, and threats started going around because of it," Schaffer told him. If Baum wanted to ask about the supposed "threats," he should be allowed to ask Jeff about his own career as an outlaw.

Chamblee asked Baum why he wanted to ask Brenda about the supposed threats.

"It's to show incompetent police investigation," Baum said.

"How so?"

"Well, if the police had received information that some people other than Jeff Pelley threatened his father, the victim, I think that's relevant. I mean, I can inquire of police officers, and it's foundational, as to whether or not the police did anything to follow up on this."

The lawyers had been whispering at the bench for several minutes, and it was clear to the jurors that something intense was in dispute. Chamblee decided to send the jurors back to the jury room, so the lawyers could speak in normal voices. At least some of the whispering was slipping by Chamblee's comprehension. The jurors filed out of the courtroom, and the judge invited the lawyers to try again to explain their argument.

Once he grasped what was at stake, he suggested that Baum show the old police report to Brenda to see if it refreshed her recollection of what the police officer had reported she had said. If Brenda had no recollection, there would be no need for anyone to ask any more questions, at least of Brenda.

Brenda read the report, and said she had only the vaguest recollection of the matter—something about Bob having told her that he had photographs of things the brothers were supposed to have stolen—and then a non sequitur: that Bob had told her he and Jeff had gotten into a fistfight. Was it because of the supposed photographs, or because of the stealing? Brenda couldn't make this clear—the link between the stealing and the supposed fight between father and son was never explained, and no one asked.

The fact was, Baum didn't want to go anywhere near any supposed fisticuffs between father and son. How could that help convince the jury that Jeff hadn't done it? He realized this whole subject was going to cause as many problems for Jeff as it raised problems for the prosecution. He withdrew the question.

Not so fast, Schaffer said. He wanted the judge to admonish the jury—tell them that they weren't to consider Baum's mention of the supposed threats, since no evidence of any external threats would now come in. Schaffer didn't want any tinge of alternative theories seeping into his case—he wanted the jury to think only of Jeff, Jeff and Jeff.

Baum agreed to back off—he had something else in reserve as to alternative theories.

CHAPTER 29

Over the next three days, Schaffer put on witness after witness to establish that Bob and Jeff had been squabbling, and that Bob had been adamant about driving Jeff and Darla to the prom, even as late as Saturday afternoon. Roger and Joyce Schafer, Vera Howell, and Christina Keb all testified, as had Brenda Hale, that in grounding Jeff, Bob had taken his car away—that was why Brenda Hale had given a ride to Jeff to their work shifts at McDonald's on Saturday morning, April 29—Bob didn't want Jeff driving, and the Mustang was still disabled.

No one could remember Bob saying he would drive Jeff and Darla to South Bend to attend the dinner at the Emporium, for which Jeff had obtained the gift certificate from Brenda, or for that matter, to the after-prom at the bowling alley, let alone Great America on Sunday morning. To all of these witnesses, Bob had been intent on constricting his rebellious son's freedom of movement, at least for a time.

Kurt Schafer, the son of Roger and Joyce, and Jeff's friend, testified that he'd seen Jeff washing the Mustang at some point on Saturday afternoon. Then, some hours later, he'd been with a friend, hunting for mushrooms along Mulberry Road, when he'd seen Jeff's Mustang speed past.

Well, this was odd—Jeff had told Botich, then Hemmerlein that he'd driven east on Osborne Road, not west; that he'd taken Osborne to Maple to Route 4, then south on Highway 31 to Casey's, or the Amoco, or both. But Kurt Schafer's sighting of the Mustang on Mulberry Road was to the west—in the opposite direction of Jeff's claimed route to the Amoco. This seemed to show that Jeff was lying about his route—but why?

Schaffer called an insurance agent, who had the records: liability coverage for Jeff had been cancelled by Bob on April 12, 1989, and a note in the file indicated that it wouldn't be restored until the fall. Another note indicated that about a week after the murders, someone had called to reinstate the coverage—but the records clearly demonstrated that Jeff was an uninsured driver on the night of the prom.

Would Bob have allowed Jeff to drive uninsured? That was doubtful, given Bob's usual obsessive attention to detail. The testimony was devastating to Jeff's side of the story—the idea that Bob would have allowed Jeff to get behind the wheel of the Mustang without insurance seemed highly improbable.

Schaffer called other witnesses to nail down the timeline. Kim Oldenburg testified that her group had visited the Pelleys for fifteen or twenty minutes, then left to go to Chris Holmgren's house between 4:45 and 5 P.M., arriving there, about a half-mile away, right around 5. Kim also said that she was surprised when Jeff had asked to sleep over at the Oldenburg basement on the night of the prom, then accompany everyone to Great America—as far as she knew, as of prom night, Jeff wasn't allowed to do either.

Matt Miller told his story: how he'd arrived at the parsonage while the Oldenburg group was still there, remembered the corsage, and immediately raced back to La Paz to get the flowers. Jeff had been in the parsonage, dressed in blue jeans when Miller was there for his brief encounter, Miller said. When, after retrieving the flowers, he had come racing back, past the parsonage about 5:10 or 5:15 P.M., the Mustang was still parked on the grass near the church basketball hoop, as it usually was.

Then, when he and the Oldenburg group had passed the parsonage on their way to pick up their limo in Lakeville about 5:30 P.M., the Mustang was gone.

Crystal Easterday told of expecting Bob and Dawn to come to the Easterday home that day around 5:30 P.M., so she could show Bob her prom dress—Bob had said he and Dawn would come. When they didn't show up, Crystal and her date went instead to the parsonage. They found all the doors locked and the drapes closed, and no one responded to their knocking—this was about 5:45 or 6 P.M., Crystal said. This was highly unusual for Bob and Dawn, Crystal said. The doors of the parsonage were almost always unlocked when Bob and Dawn were at home. The Pelley cars were parked as usual in the driveway, but the garage door was down—this, too, was unusual, Crystal said: the garage was almost always open.

Randy Brackett, the neighbor just to the west of the Pelley house on Osborne Road, had returned from a funeral around 6:30 P.M. He'd begun mowing his lawn. At no time did he see Bob, Dawn or the girls, or notice anyone arriving or departing the house. He often saw the little girls playing around the house in the evening, he said.

Brackett seemed to have missed Brenda Hale's visit to the church to pray—but then, he wasn't paying much attention to who came and went from the church parking lot. Still, if someone had fired a shotgun five or six times in the parsonage that evening while he was mowing the lawn, he probably would have heard it, Brackett said.

Dennis Nicodemus told of seeing Jeff arrive in the Mustang at the Amoco station just after 5:20 P.M. He had known Jeff from school. He was very clear on the time, because he'd looked at his watch just before Jeff pulled in—from Quinn Road, the back side of the gas station, which seemed to contradict Jeff's assertion that he'd driven in from Highway 31, at the front of the gas station. Those coming from Highway 31 had to drive over a pneumatic bell—bing! bing!—which was supposed to alert attendants to customers, and there had been no bing with Jeff. That seemed to show that Jeff had driven down Mulberry Road from Osborne, just as Kurt Schafer had testified. It was the only way Jeff could have arrived at the gas station without running over the alarm bell.

The time of Jeff's arrival at the station had become firm in his mind, Nicodemus said, because he was irritated. He'd looked at his watch at exactly 5:17 P.M., because his relief at the station, Jeff Roberts, was supposed to have shown up at 5, but was late. As far as Nicodemus was concerned, Amoco, or maybe Roberts, owed him at least a quarter hour's time.

When Jeff pulled in to the station, a few minutes after 5:17, maybe five minutes, Nicodemus had first thought it might be Roberts. The next thing he knew, Roberts had appeared, and was helping Jeff with his car.

As Nicodemus later learned, Jeff asked to borrow a screwdriver from the station. Roberts had found one, and Jeff worked for a minute or two on the Mustang's engine, then made a telephone call, Nicodemus remembered. Jeff pulled out at maybe 5:25 P.M., or perhaps 5:30.

Mark Berger, Lynette Greer's date, testified that Jeff had arrived at the Greer house in La Paz around 5:30. After changing into his tuxedo for the prom, Jeff and Darla set off to pick up Jenny Barton and Eric Gockle in the Mustang. Berger next saw them at the Emporium for the dinner shortly after 6 P.M. He said they were slightly late—maybe ten or fifteen minutes after the time of the dinner reservation, which had been for 6 P.M.

All of these times, the accounts of Bob's adamancy about driving Jeff and Darla to the prom, coupled with the cancellation of the car insurance and the fact that Jeff had driven the car anyway, along with Crystal Easterday's inability to rouse any of the Pelleys in the parsonage between 5:30 and 6 P.M., constituted strong circumstantial evidence against Jeff—taken together, as a jigsaw puzzle, as Schaffer had urged the jury, it suggested that Jeff had killed all four Pelleys between 4:50 and 5:10 P.M. The window of time for murder was that narrow—just twenty minutes. But that was only if one accepted the belief that the Pelleys had actually been killed on Saturday afternoon.

And here, the absence of the definitive time of death was an evidentiary black hole—no light was available.

Without time-of-death information established by science, and considering the water in the bathtub, the cereal bowls, the church socks, the fruit, the popcorn, the lack of corroboration of the Pelley visitors on Saturday afternoon, of the clothing worn by the family when later found dead, the notion that the murders could have been committed between 4:50 and 5:10 P.M. was debatable, in fact, subject to possible reasonable doubt. But that was what Schaffer had to work with.

Although it seemed impossible, there it was—it was, he contended, the only logical explanation for what had actually happened on April 29, 1989: Jeff Pelley had murdered four people with a shotgun within twenty minutes, just to go to a dance.

There was little Baum could do to blunt the effect of these witnesses' testimony. True, he could try to induce the witnesses to hedge their estimates about the times. But the best that could be achieved here for the defense was the point that the times were all just their best guesses.

The whole thing turned on a matter of minutes, and there was far too much slack in anyone's guess as to the actual time of anything that had happened. There was no precision, no time clock. No one was punching in, or using stopwatches, clicking off the events, one by one, writing down the times. And, after all, everything had happened more than seventeen years before.

Who could say for sure where exactly they had been on Saturday, April 29, 1989, at 4:52 P.M.? No one could, it was impossible. It didn't happen in real life, not like in murder mysteries, where clocks chimed, bells rung, on-time buses came and went, or whistles blew. The real world was far fuzzier when it came to clocks.

In the real world, most times are simply estimates, usually accompanied by the all-purpose "-ish" around the number: "5-ish," or "6-ish," "about," "around," or "nearly," "just before," or "just after." The fact is, none of us is watching the clock—in real life, we have other things to do.

It "could be," it "might be"—these were slim reeds to hang someone on, Gammage and Baum believed. The inexactitude of time was reasonable doubt. As far as they could see, it was entirely possible that Kim Oldenburg, et al., had left the parsonage a minute or two before 5 P.M., and it was also entirely possible that Matt Miller might have arrived at the Holmgren house a bit earlier than he'd estimated. That way, instead of having twenty minutes to commit the murders, Jeff might have had less than ten.

If Nicodemus was right about Jeff pulling into the gas station just after 5:20 P.M., and if it had taken Jeff ten minutes to get from the parsonage to the gas station, that meant Jeff had to have left at around 5:10 . . . a seemingly impossible period of time to shoot everyone, pick up the shell casings, put his clothes in the washer, take a shower, put on new clothes, lock all the doors, close all the curtains, put the gun and the shell casings in the car along with his tuxedo, and start for the Greer house. That is, if Kim's group had left a minute or two before 5.

And then, the kicker: just when had Jeff had time to get rid of the gun and the shell casings? That had to have taken some minutes, and despite all the searches, with frogmen and horsemen, no one had yet found them, even after seventeen years. In terms of human endeavor, it seemed improbable, actually impossible. On paper, it seemed patently ridiculous.

Which left the question: if Jeff hadn't done it, who had?

Baum would try to answer that question for the jury as the trial unfolded. But at this point in the trial, the ball was on Schaffer's side of the net—it was his obligation to try to convince the jury that it was reasonable to believe that Jeff Pelley was a cold-blooded killer, and that the circumstantial facts proved it could only have been him.

As far as Schaffer could discern, what he had to do was convince the jurors that it was certain that Jeff had had enough time between 4:45 and 5:15 P.M. at the outside to have committed the killings. If he could do that, Schaffer figured, he was home free. Because as far as Schaffer could see, there was only one person who had the motive to kill Bob and Dawn Pelley—Jeff.

Let Baum and Gammage whine and moan about 4:45 as opposed to 4:58—what difference did it really make? Who was the one person who was angry at Bob Pelley? Who might have had access to a shotgun? Who had access to the bedrooms of the house? Who had driven his car after it had been disabled and uninsured?

Jeff, Jeff, Jeff and Jeff. That's how Schaffer saw the situation.

The truth was, each side was trying to use the murder clock to try to prove its own version of the facts. But the clock didn't stand up—the half hour between 4:45 and 5:15 was impenetrable, in 1989 as much as in 2006. Schaffer was counting on the jury looking at the whole picture, not just the clock, while Baum and Gammage were intent on showing that not only was their client incapable of murder—hey, he was just a kid—he also didn't have enough time. To them, it was as simple as that.

On the third day of the trial, Schaffer called Darla Emmons as a witness.

This was high drama—the teenage siren of 1989 who had supposedly, if inadvertently, incited Jeff to murder, if the prosecution's theory was correct. Over the years, Botich and Senter had made many visits to Darla in an effort to find out if Jeff had said anything to her that might indicate his culpability, reasoning that if Jeff was going to confess to anyone, it might be Darla.

But Darla, over the years and through many tears, had insisted that Jeff had always claimed he hadn't done it. Now, seventeen years later, she was in her midthirties, a wife and a mother. Taking the witness stand to tell of her teenage romance with Jeff Pelley so many years before was the last thing she wanted to do.

But Darla was forthright. And she had at least a part of the story to tell: on the Friday night before the prom, while they were cleaning the church, Jeff had told her he was going to be allowed to attend all the prom activities after all, including the dinner, as well as the trek to Great America.

"By Friday night he said his dad was going to let him go to everything," Darla testified. "He just told me not to mention it . . . it was a sore subject, and to keep it to myself." So Darla kept quiet, not wanting to get further enmeshed in the struggle between Jeff and his father. The fact was, in some ways Bob generally intimidated her.

Now this information was potentially significant: it suggested that Jeff had been planning to attend the prom events despite his father's restrictions, that he wanted Darla to know he would be with her, but to keep his father in the dark about his intentions. In some ways, even, it might constitute support for the notion that Jeff had been planning the murders the day before they had taken place.

After leaving the parsonage Friday night, the next time she saw Jeff was when he arrived in the Mustang at Lynette Greer's house "probably five-thirty," as Darla put it. Then the group left for the dinner and the prom, with Jeff again driving the Mustang.

Darla described the events of the evening and the trip to the amusement park the following day. She came to the time when Jeff had said he had "a bad feeling."

"There was a point where he was really quiet, and I asked him if there was something wrong," Darla said. "And he just said he had a bad feeling. And I said, 'What kind of bad feeling?' And he said, something, just a bad feeling about something. But he didn't know what."

Schaffer asked if she had tried to find out any details. No, Darla said.

Darla told of being contacted by the police at the park, then taken to the Gurnee police station to await the arrival of Botich and Rutkowski. She was separated from Jeff, and at some point someone told her that Jeff's parents and stepsisters were dead. After the detectives arrived, the couple was put in the back of the police sedan and driven back to South Bend.

"How was he acting in the car on the way back?" Schaffer asked.

"Very sad."

"When you were in the car with Jeff, did you talk about what had happened to his parents at all?"

"I didn't, but he did."

"What did he ask you?"

"He just told me he didn't do it."

"Did you say anything to him?"

"He asked me if I believed him, and I just said I didn't know."

Schaffer returned to the days before the prom. Did Darla know that with the grounding, Jeff's father had said he would drive them both to the prom?

Yes, Darla said.

"Did you want to do that?"

"No."

"Did you let Jeff know that?"

"Yes, I did."

She had told Jeff that, rather than let Bob drive them to the prom, she'd just meet Jeff there. She still intended to go to the dinner, the after-prom and the amusement park with the others, even if he couldn't go. She told Jeff he'd still be her date for the dance, though.

This was a very effective series of questions by Schaffer, because Darla's answers implied that Jeff might have been so upset by the prospect of his girlfriend having a good time with others that he might have been driven to desperate measures.

On his cross-examination, Baum asked Darla whether Jeff had told her as long as a week before the prom that Bob was slowly relaxing the restrictions on Jeff—first, that he couldn't go to the prom at all, then he could go, but Bob would drive them, to Friday night, when Jeff had told her that his father would let him go to everything.

That was true, Darla said—Jeff had told her his father was easing up on him as the day of the prom approached. Baum wanted the jury to consider the possibility that what Jeff had said to Darla on Friday night was quite likely the case—that the restrictions were being progressively eased by Bob.

Baum asked Darla to describe Jeff's demeanor after the police had told him about the murders.

"He was heartbroken. He was very sad. He was not himself."

Baum asked Darla if she had commiserated with Jeff.

"I did not say anything . . . I talked to my parents. They told me to get in the car and not say a word, and that's what I did."

"In that ride back in the police car, did Jeff tell you whether or not the police had accused him or questioned him about him being the one who had done this?"

"Jeff told me he didn't do it."

"But did he tell you that the police had suggested or asked him if he had?"

"I think he presumed that, otherwise he wouldn't have said, 'I didn't do it.' "

Schaffer's final witness for the day was Jessica Pelley, now called Jessie, 27 years old, and a wife and mother herself. Jessica told the jury that there *had* been a shotgun in the rack in Bob and Dawn's bedroom, right up until the day—Friday, April 28, 1989—when she'd gone to spend the night with her friend Holly in La Paz. Jessica couldn't remember her friend's last name. It was too long ago. The testimony about the gun in the rack was good for Schaffer's side: up until Jessica's testimony, there had been no evidence that there were any firearms in the Pelley house on April 29, 1989.

For some reason, Schaffer did not ask Jessica any questions as to how Jeff had been getting along with his father and Dawn before the murders. But then, Jessica had originally told the police that her first thought, on hearing about the murders, was that Bob had killed everyone because Dawn had been contemplating a divorce—this seemed to show that Dawn had confided in her oldest child that she wasn't happy with the marriage to Bob. And, in fact, Jessica had told the original investigators in 1989 that as far as she knew, there was no bad blood between Bob and Jeff. Others, including Christina Keb, had already testified that Jeff was "very protective" of the little girls. But neither Schaffer nor Baum followed up on this—that is, the relationship between Bob and Dawn, or Jeff's relationship with Janel and Jolene, at least as seen by Jessica.

Perhaps neither thought it relevant to the issues at trial, when it was obvious, from the absence of the shotgun, that it could not have been a case of murder-suicide.

But—that wasn't to say there weren't other issues between Bob and Dawn that might be relevant, even if not related to a murder-suicide scenario. In fact—was there something in Dawn's previous life with Huber that might have made her the target, not Bob?

The fact was, despite Corcella's assertions back in 2002, no one had ever looked very hard at any other possibilities—just as Baum had tried to show, the police believed Jeff was the killer from the start. And from then on, almost all of the taxpayer-funded effort had been invested in trying to prove that. But Jessica, who had only been 9, almost 10 years old at the time of the murders, wasn't likely to know of any reason why someone would want to kill her mother and little sisters.

For Jessica, the whole thing was inexplicable—something that had happened in her life, that had marked her forever. It was only by chance that she had escaped. She had moved on with her life, but was left with a loss that no one could recompense. As she put it, she'd barely known Bob Pelley before he and her mother and sisters were murdered.

"I only lived with them for two years," she said.

When it was his turn to cross-examine, Baum asked Jessica if it was true that the police had asked her, that day at the church, where to locate her stepsister Jacque and her stepbrother Jeff.

She didn't remember telling the police how to find Jacque, she said.

"Do you remember telling any officers that Jeff was at Great America?" Baum asked. He had a police report from 1989 saying that Jessica had said exactly that, to Botich.

"Yes, I do remember that," she said.

Jessica said she'd been brought back to the parsonage from La Paz by her friend's mother after the discovery of the murders, sometime just before noon. Police had taken her in hand, and asked her questions about the whereabouts of Jeff and Jacque. She remembered being taken to a Lakeville park, some distance away from the church.

"And some police officers wanted to know if you knew where Jeff was, right?" Baum asked.

"Yeah," Jessica said.

"And you did, you knew that Jeff was at Great America?"

"That's what I had been told, yes."

"When had you been told that Jeff was at Great America?"

"Before I left."

"On?"

"Friday."

"That he was going to be going to Great America?"

"Yeah, that he was going to be there."

"Who told you that?"

"I think it was my mother."

Wow! This was a major hole in the state's theory of the crime—that Jeff, obsessed with going to the dinner, the prom, the after-prom, then to Great America, had murdered four people in order to be able to drive his car to all those events. While the state had been insisting from the beginning that Bob Pelley had grounded Jeff, was insistent on driving his son and his son's date to the prom and picking them up, that there was to be no dinner, no after-prom, no Great America—here was Jessica, the then–10-year-old survivor of the massacre, testifying that she'd known Jeff was going to Great America, and that she'd known that on Friday night.

And that she had heard this from her mother, Dawn.

So much for the idea that Bob wasn't going to let his son attend all the prom festivities. Here was testimony from Jessica that directly contradicted what Bob had supposedly told the Schafers, the Howells, Brenda Hale, and others. Jessica's own dead mother, Dawn, had told her that Jeff had been liberated from the grounding, and this, hours before Bob had discussed the situation with the Schafers and Howells on

Saturday. And Jessica had not the least reason to make up such a story to help Jeff—after all, she barely knew him after so many years.

Both Schaffer and Baum were taken aback by Jessica's testimony.

"It was a gift," Baum said later. Both lawyers realized it punched a sizeable hole in the state's theory of what had happened. If Dawn had told Jessica on Friday that Jeff was going to be allowed to go on the amusement park jaunt, why was Bob telling Brenda Hale something different Friday night, or the Schafers and the Howells something different on Saturday morning and afternoon?

For Baum: was Bob telling his parishioners one thing, and his family something else? For both: had Bob and Dawn argued over how to deal with Jeff, with Dawn telling Bob to lighten up, and Bob refusing? For Schaffer: had something else happened between Bob and Jeff on Friday night or Saturday, which led to a reimposition of restrictions?

It was a puzzle. Schaffer made no attempt to salvage the situation, and Baum, happy for the gift, asked no further questions. Baum thought the jury had to be thinking: if Bob had relented, and had let Jeff drive himself to the prom and to all the other activities, where was the motive for murder? Why, if Jeff had been freed from the restrictions, would he have done such a thing?

Later, the prosecutor's office tried to characterize Jessica's surprising testimony as merely the faulty memory of a girl who was, at the time of the murders, only a month shy of being 10 years old. But if Jessica was wrong about how she'd known that Jeff was at the amusement park, was it also possible that she was wrong about seeing the shotgun in the gun rack? And if so, was that also "reasonable doubt"?

CHAPTER 30

The next day, Schafer called two more St. Joseph County police officers, John Kuhny and Ron Nowicki. Kuhny described removing the jeans, shirt and socks from inside the washer, and attempting to test the clothing with luminol, a chemical that reacts in the presence of blood. But since the chemical also reacts to phosphate—some detergents contain phosphate—the mild reaction to the luminol meant nothing.

Just why Schaffer bothered to call Kuhny as a witness wasn't clear—he may have been trying to demonstrate to the jury that the police had been careful and conscientious, despite Baum's "rush to judgment" insinuations. For his part, Nowicki testified that he'd sent the clothing, and some of the shotgun wadding, to the FBI lab for analysis. The results from the FBI were inconclusive as to the presence of DNA.

Baum asked Nowicki, a crime-scene expert, if, had he been at the parsonage the day the murders were discovered—Nowicki didn't join the department until some years after 1989—he would have expected that the proximity of the shooter to the basement victims meant that the killer would be spattered with blood. Nowicki said yes, he would have expected that. Now Baum was trying to use the state's own witness to bolster the defense.

Schaffer next called an FBI firearms expert, Douglas Murphy. Murphy had inspected the shotgun shell waddings found with the victims, and concluded that two different types of shells had been fired—one that used cardboard for wadding, and another that contained plastic. One of each had been found, downstairs and upstairs. But without the shells themselves, he could not say for sure whether all the shells had been fired from one weapon, or more than one. In fact, he couldn't even say how large the shells had been—some shotgun shells were two-and-three-quarters of an inch in length, and others were three inches. The Mossberg 500 pump-action shotgun could hold four of the longer shells, and five of the shorter ones.

By inspecting the waddings and the slugs, Murphy was confident that the slugs had come from a 20-gauge shotgun, similar to the Mossberg, but could not say for sure exactly what kind of shotgun had been used. There were many manufacturers of 20-gauge shotguns.

This was an important point to Baum—he believed he could account for seven different blasts from the shotgun: two upstairs at Bob, one on the way down the stairs that had wound up in the book, a fourth that had hit Dawn in the hand and severed her finger, a fifth that had hit Dawn in the head, and one each in the head for Janel and Jolene. That made seven shots, not five. The information that there had been two different types of ammunition, upstairs and downstairs, one with plastic wadding, and the other with cardboard, supported the inference that there was more than one person firing at the Pelleys—two shooters, seven shots, two different shotguns. Then, afterward, the killers had picked up all the casings, and disappeared, taking the shotguns and casings with them. That was why the police had never been able to find the murder weapon(s), despite their intensive searching by horseback, on foot, and in the ponds. The killers had taken two shotguns and their casings away with them.

Schaffer was able to establish that at most there had been only six shots—Baum was counting one twice—the hand and the head to Dawn, which might well have been a defensive wound as she'd thrown up her hand to block the shot to the head.

But Baum's contention was that even that depended on the killer using the smaller size ammunition and reloading at least one slug, if Murphy was right about the five-shot maximum that could be loaded in the pump-action shotgun. Since no casings had ever been found, not even that could be determined with certainty.

Still, on redirect examination, Murphy admitted that a single shooter could have mixed both types of ammunition, some with cardboard wadding, others with plastic. And while no one said it—Jeff's career as a burglar meant he could well have stolen mixed ammunition—the slugs didn't necessarily have to come from one box, as Baum's questions suggested. They could have been leftovers, residue from other boxes. In fact, Jeff could have stolen the slug shells from Kurt Schafer—he'd already told Botich, years earlier, that he'd once fired shotgun slugs with Kurt. Jeff could have hidden the mixed shotgun slugs for a future, if fatal day.

Now Schaffer called Harold "Irish" Saunders, the Pelley neighbor immediately to the east.

Saunders and his wife, Sheila—Bob had married them on the back deck of their house in 1988—had last seen Bob about noon of Saturday. Saunders had to meet some people in Plymouth, and as he left, Bob drove by, apparently after picking Jeff up from the shift at the McDonald's. Saunders returned home about 9:30 P.M., just after Sheila had also gotten back to the house from her job, he testified. Both Saunderses noticed a light burning in the basement bedroom used by the three girls. They thought it was a little strange—normally the girls were in bed by 8:30 or so.

Sometime during the night, Sheila rose and went into the Saunderses' bathroom, which faced the east end of the parsonage. She noticed that the light in the girls' basement bedroom was still on, even after midnight. She again was struck by the oddity.

On Sunday morning, the Saunderses got up early, around 7 A.M.—Irish worked for Hoosier Racing Tire, a major employer in Lakeville. They were scheduled to attend a race at a track in Kalamazoo, Michigan. Sheila asked Irish to telephone the Pelleys to see if they would let the Saunderses' dog out for the day. Irish called the parsonage, but there was no answer. Sheila told Irish that he had to have dialed the wrong number. Irish called again, and there was still no answer. The Saunderses looked out the window, and noticed that the Pelleys' own dog was outside in its dog run. Normally, the Pelleys let the dog out in the morning, so the Saunderses concluded that the Pelleys must be up. But they concluded that the Pelleys must have gone somewhere—all the drapes were closed, and normally the Pelleys opened them in the morning when they let the dog out. Shortly before 8 A.M., the Saunderses left for Kalamazoo. But sometime a little after noon, Saunders' boss approached them to inform them of the murders. They were not to worry, she said—the police had already decided there was no danger from a roving lunatic. But the police wanted them to return to Lakeville as soon as possible. They wanted to ask them questions about what they might have seen and heard on Saturday.

Sheila Saunders confirmed her husband's testimony, but added something further. A few days before the prom, Jeff had asked her if he could borrow her car, a late model Pontiac Trans Am, to take to the prom. At first Sheila had said yes, but then learned that Bob had disabled the Mustang to keep Jeff from driving.

Then, on Saturday morning, Bob had asked her not to let Jeff drive the Trans Am—the implication being that the no-driving restriction was still in place on Saturday morning, despite Jeff's reassurance to Darla the night before.

Baum objected to the testimony. It was disallowable hearsay, he said. Chamblee sustained the objection, and instructed the jury to ignore Sheila's account of her conversation with Bob—but the damage was done to Jeff's credibility.

Still, the defense believed they had made headway in blunting the circumstantial evidence against Jeff. The *Tribune* agreed: "Evidence Fails to Link Pelley to 1989 Murders," its headline read. The paper quoted Baum: "I think the truth is coming out . . . That is what this is all about—seeking the truth."

The Sunday edition of the *Tribune* put it even more

starkly: "Prosecution Faces Tough Climb," the paper's headline read. Reporter Patrick M. O'Connell, in a piece labeled "analysis," wrote:

> With no murder weapon, no fingerprints, no bloody clothes and no eyewitnesses to a crime 17 years old, the prosecution in the Jeffrey Pelley trial is fighting an uphill battle.
>
> Forensic evidence from the gruesome crime scene has done nothing to tie Pelley to the murders, and witness testimony about Pelley's calm, seemingly normal demeanor the weekend of the killings has not lifted the prosecution.

One of the major difficulties with the case, Schaffer admitted in an interview with the newspaper, was the long time gap between the events of the murders and the reinvestigation that had led to the charges in 2002. So much time had elapsed that people had lost track of various details. The problem was compounded by the transition between the regimes of Toth and Dvorak.

Baum, for his part, again contended that the police had "rushed to judgment," and that they had failed to investigate viable leads that could have unearthed suspects other than Jeff.

"There were areas that should have been investigated as a matter of course and there was information they received that they didn't follow up on," Baum told the paper. "I'm cautiously optimistic that the jury will reach the right verdict."

But Schaffer was about to bring up his heaviest artillery: John Botich, and then Brent Hemmerlein.

Botich had come a long way from the day in April 1989 when he'd first viewed the Pelley crime scene. A detective sergeant at the time of the murders, the lead investigator in the case, he was now assistant chief of the St. Joseph County Police, and in charge of the county jail, the warrant section and the detective bureau. He had been only peripherally involved in the reinvestigation by Toth's regime, and since then had made himself available to Dvorak's group, but in the main, the charges against Jeff were the result of the "cold case" unit of the metropolitan homicide squad, which hadn't existed in his day as a detective.

Schaffer began by asking Botich about the search of the Pelley property and the areas leading away from it toward La Paz, as well as the times and distances between the parsonage and the Greer house. Botich admitted that the searches had proved fruitless. Then Schaffer came to one of his main objectives in calling Botich as a witness.

Had he interviewed Jeff Pelley on the morning of May 1, 1989?

Yes, Botich said.

"Was this statement taped in any way?"

"Yes."

Schaffer now moved to play the tape—actually by now transferred to a DVD—for the jury.

Baum objected, renewing his motion to have the judge throw the statement out as a violation of Jeff's Fifth Amendment rights, the old in-custody interrogation issue from 2003. Chamblee denied the motion. The DVD was played for the jury.

When it was finished, Schaffer passed the witness to Baum—Schaffer believed that the tape spoke for itself. He thought the jury might be put off by Jeff's calm, occasionally even jovial demeanor during the interview. Baum, too, thought the tape spoke for itself: Jeff was polite throughout, and answered every question put to him by Botich, without hesitation. To Baum, Jeff hardly seemed like a person who was guilty of having committed four bloody murders—there was no dodging, no weaving, no dissembling, not even an evasion of eye contact. In short, there was nothing on the tape, at least visually, that seemed to show that Jeff was guilty.

On his cross-examination, Baum asked Botich about all the searching that had been done in the days immediately following the murders. He had Botich dismount from the witness stand and draw on a map all the places that had been searched. Baum wanted the jury to get the point that the searches had been extensive, and despite all the effort, no one had ever found a thing that came to bear on the murders. That dovetailed with Baum's argument about the time element: Jeff simply didn't have enough time to ditch the evidence where it wouldn't have been found by the diligent searchers. Ergo, the real killers had taken the weapons away with them.

Baum began to work his way into the area where he believed Botich's testimony would be most vulnerable—the rush to judgment, as he thought of it.

"Did you or any member of your investigative team secure the records, or the names of all the members of the congregation, at Reverend Pelley's church?"

"I did not, and I don't know if it was done."

"Well, as the lead investigator, could we expect that you would know, and be getting periodic reports from what was going on in this broad investigation?"

"Let's just say I should have, yes."

"To the best of your knowledge, there was no effort to secure the names of the members of the congregation to investigate any of those people to see if they had any kind of sordid background, or if there was something there that might be of interest, correct?"

"Correct, yes."

"Do you know if Reverend Pelley's records, his files, were reviewed to see whether there was anything in there that might indicate some trouble he was having, or any threats, or anyone who might have reason to kill?"

"I don't recall that, no."

"To this day, have you ever seen any of Reverend Pelley's records that were actually taken into police custody for a review to see if they would shed any light?"

"I don't believe so, no."

Well, Baum went on, wasn't it true that in the very beginning, just after the murders, the police had been told by Pelley family members of other possible people who might have had motives to kill Bob?

True, Botich said.

"As part of that, you were provided information by the family concerning some trouble that occurred in Florida when Reverend Pelley was working in the banking business?"

Schaffer jumped to his feet.

"I want to object," he said. He demanded a sidebar conference out of the hearing of the jury.

"I don't know of any information that has ever come up that there were banking problems," Schaffer told Chamblee at the sidebar. "I heard there were rumors, but that's it."

"I don't care whether it's true or not," Baum retorted. "The point is, this investigator and others were told very early in the investigation that, well, the Pelley family was living in Florida, and he was working at a bank. There was a middle-of-the-night phone call. There was a million dollars found to be missing from the bank. The bank was— The [St. Joseph County] police were told that the bank was put under investigation as possibly laundering money by the DEA, and within twenty days, the Pelley family uprooted from Florida unexpectedly, and moved to South Bend. And I think this information was provided to the police, and they did nothing about it."

"That's not true at all," Schaffer said.

"Well, slow down," Chamblee said. "Let me at least understand. Are you saying that information was given to the police?"

"By both— By Jacque Pelley, the sister," Baum said, "and at later time, by Jeff as well."

"Jacque is the fourteen-year-old that he referred to in his statement?" Chamblee tried to clarify for the record, if not Schaffer. "Are you saying that Jacque, at fourteen years old, told the police about this money-laundering, the DEA stuff, in Florida?"

"Yes, sir," Baum said.

"And you say that is not true?" Chamblee asked Schaffer. "You called it a rumor. He's asking [Botich] the question: was he given information? What do you call it? Do you know what he's talking about? I assume you do, Frank [Schaffer]. I don't mean to make you concede, I'm simply trying to figure out what your objection is. You're saying it's rumor. [Did Botich] get information? Did he follow up? If that's his point, what's your objection?"

"Well, I guess I'm going to have to bring rebuttal in, to go after this hare again," Schaffer mumbled.

"What?" Chamblee said. "I didn't hear what you said."

"I didn't hear what he said, either," Baum said.

"Something about rebuttal," Gammage put in.

"The only information I've received is that there was nothing going on down in Florida," Schaffer said. "He wasn't involved in anything. He left to become a minister. So if this is what is going to be thrown out there, I will have to bring in rebuttal to back it off."

"Rebuttal saying what?" Gammage asked.

"There was nothing going on in Florida, that Mister Pelley— He wasn't involved in anything to begin with."

"I think we can cross that bridge when we come to it," Baum said.

"Do you have somebody in mind to do that?" Chamblee asked Schaffer. "I take it you have somebody that you are intending to call [in rebuttal] to do that. We're not talking about doing it two weeks from now?" Chamblee had scheduled his vacation for August, and had told the jury that they could expect to be done with the trial in two weeks. Now this threatened to wreck the schedule and Chamblee's vacation if Schaffer had to drag someone up from Florida to deny the rumor about Bob—the "hare," as Schaffer had described it.

"No," Schaffer said. He didn't want to deal with the issue at all, but if he had to, he certainly didn't want to give Chamblee the idea that it would be difficult to refute.

"The court will allow the inquiry," Chamblee ruled.

The lawyers returned to their counsel tables. Baum wanted to confer with Gammage.

"May I have just a moment, Your Honor?" Baum asked.

"Sure," Chamblee said. But after a pause, Chamblee called them back to the bench. "Gentlemen, can I see you for just a moment?"

When the lawyers assembled once again at the bench, Chamblee said he was changing his ruling.

"I'm actually having some second thoughts on allowing the inquiry into what may have been, or whatever," Chamblee told Baum, referring to Baum's question to Botich about Florida. "I know part of your defense is that there is a lack of proper investigation. But tell me what—how does what they did *not* do bear on the question of whether it's more likely than not that he did it [the murders]? All you will be doing is raising suspicion and innuendo about the thing in Florida. Do you understand the thrust of my question to you?"

"I understand, Your Honor," Baum said. "It's in the context of the rush to judgment in this case, which was testified to by Pavlekovich."

"Your phraseology, not his," Chamblee pointed out. "He simply said they saw him as a suspect and followed that exclusively, and I understand, that's the thrust of your case. My point, in essence, is in terms of what evidence gets tossed out here . . . whether there was or wasn't this information given to the police . . . the specifics of it, more accurately. I think it really doesn't do anything to prove that it's more likely or not likely that he committed the crime. It [only] proves they didn't do anything [about it]."

If it didn't prove that it was less likely than not that Jeff had committed the murders, what was the value of the question? Without any hard evidence, that had to be a separate question from the matter of guilt or innocence, Chamblee said.

"It's more than that," Baum insisted. "It's the fact that, in a very real sense, there may have been a reason for the murders, and there may have— And it goes back to the situation in Florida."

"And I guess that is speculation on your part as to the truth and the veracity of that . . . ?"

"If the family hadn't picked up and moved," Baum said, "if all we're dealing with was just some rumor that there was some problem in Florida, then it might be more tenuous. But I think the unusual circumstances leads to at least an arguable inference that something was going on there. And by the way, Your Honor, there is one other bit of evidence. The police were told that—"

"Let me do this," Chamblee interrupted, receiving a note from the clerk from a juror. "Let me kill two birds with one stone. They [the jury] need a break. Let me do that right now, and we can talk a little louder at that point."

"Crew," Chamblee addressed the jury, "rumor has it from Julie [the clerk] that it might be a good time to take a brief recess. I'm not going to say where that note came from, but we're going to act on it. So we're going to have you in the jury room for a couple of minutes and then we don't have to whisper, and you can kill two birds with one stone. You know what I mean. We will have you back out here in a couple of minutes."

At least one juror wanted desperately to go to the bathroom before the lawyers gabbled on another minute.

With Baum's attempt to question Botich about what the police had done about Bob's past in Florida, the trial had reached a crucial turning point. If Chamblee permitted Baum to question Botich about what he knew of the Pelleys' old life in the Sunshine State, he would be opening the door to the possibility that someone other than Jeff might have had a motive to kill Bob.

Establishing a viable alternative theory of the crime was reasonable doubt. If supported by factual evidence that there indeed *was* someone other than Jeff out to murder Bob, the jury would likely have to acquit Jeff. That's one reason Schaffer wanted to head this off. He knew the Indiana police had done very little to investigate Bob's past life in Florida, and he knew that he'd have to find some way to rebut the insinuation. Right then, he couldn't think of what it might be—that's why he'd called it a "hare," that is, a wild story.

But the fact was, he didn't know anything for sure—no one in Indiana had spent much time trying to investigate Bob. For the Indiana authorities, it had always been Jeff, right from the start.

The question was, was there evidence behind the rabbit? Was the alternative theory really viable?

But here Baum was handicapped by his own lack of information about Bob's past. All he had were the vague stories told by Jacque and Jeff—one from a girl who was only 12 at the time of the supposed Florida incident, the other from the defendant. He knew nothing of Harry William Stewart, the Hawleys, John Guise or the murder of C. Eric Dawson—or even of the Florida investigations that had led to the various indictments, or their denouements. He knew virtually nothing about Landmark Bank, or even the details of the money-laundering scandal of 1984–1985. Neither, for that matter, did Schaffer.

But it was irrelevant that he had no hard evidence, Baum insisted to Chamblee. The point was, the police had been told about the Florida situation, admittedly in vague terms, but the police had made no effort to look into it. That was all he wanted Botich to tell the jury from the witness stand.

Baum told Chamblee that Jacque had told Investigator Whitfield about the bank in 2002, before the charges against Jeff were filed. She said it was her understanding that Bob, who had been in charge of the bank's computers, was supposed to find the missing million. And that shortly after receiving the midnight telephone call, the family had packed up and moved to Indiana. Jeff had told Botich himself about the bank in April 1990, on one of his visits to Botich's house in Lakeville. It also appeared that Jacque had first mentioned the bank story to police as early as May 1989. Yet no investigation was ever undertaken, Baum contended. That was all evidence of the rush to judgment, he said. The failure of the Indiana police to consider other possible motives and killers was the fatal flaw of the charges against Jeff.

There was more, Baum told Chamblee. A witness interviewed by Whitfield in August 2002 told of having seen a white limo in the area of the parsonage on the day of the prom in 1989, and the limo had Florida license plates. This was the same information the police had in 1989, but it had never been explored.

It was all hearsay, Schaffer said, double or even triple hearsay. If Baum really wanted to get into the matter, he should first call Whitfield as a witness, then Jacque, or the person who had reported the limo, not ask Botich.

But Chamblee wouldn't even go that far. The whole problem, he told Baum, was the reliability of the information. If all he had were the stories of Jacque and Jeff, it was "too attenuated. Because all it is, is utter speculation and [it] does nothing, I think, in the substance of the case, other than add to your theme."

Chamblee sustained Schaffer's objection. There would be no more talk of Florida. But, he consoled Baum, at least he'd made a record in case of appeal.

Baum was chagrined. This was one of his major wedges, a blockbuster he needed to crack the case apart—clear evidence showing that the police investigation had been incompetent, or at least lax, for the failure to look south. But Chamblee wouldn't allow him to ask the question.

CHAPTER 31

The following day, Schaffer called his final witness: Brent Hemmerlein.

Hemmerlein had been a supervising lieutenant of the South Bend Police Department's detective division back in 1989. He hadn't been to the murder house, but was briefed on what Botich, Rutkowski, Senter and others from the county police knew or believed about the murders. The deputy prosecutor, Jack Krisor, had asked him to "interview" Jeff, he testified. Hemmerlein was still under instructions to avoid any reference to the abortive polygraph test.

Under questioning by Schaffer, Hemmerlein related Jeff's responses to his pre-polygraph questions. Jeff's answers matched almost exactly what he had told Botich in the taped interview of the morning. Hemmerlein initially disclosed little to the jury of how he had conducted this pre-polygraph interview—his own demeanor, for instance, or whether he had taken an aggressive posture with Jeff, as Jeff had claimed in 2003, which had blurred the roles between examiner and closer. Then Hemmerlein's account of the discussion had Jeff departing somewhat from what he'd told Botich that morning on tape.

Hemmerlein said that Jeff had told him that the police believed he was the killer because of the physical confrontation he and Bob had had, "on the Saturday prior to the death of his family," as Hemmerlein described it to the jury. This was about the "fistfight" of Saturday, April 22, 1989, although

Hemmerlein didn't make the date of the fight clear in his testimony.

"He and his father had gotten into a confrontation in the front yard, and his father had struck him and knocked him to the ground," Hemmerlein told the jury.

Jeff had told him this, Hemmerlein said, because people had seen it, and he knew they would be telling the police about it. So he'd wanted to come clean—he didn't want the police to think he was concealing anything from them, but it certainly didn't mean he'd killed his father, or anyone else, Jeff had said.

Well, Hemmerlein's description of this statement by Jeff was inartful, to say the least. Did "the Saturday prior" mean Saturday, April 29, or Saturday, April 22? Both Saturdays were "prior to the death of his family," strictly speaking, but one was hot, only hours before the murders, while the other encompassed an obvious cooling-off period. There was a week's worth of difference, at least as to motive, between the circumstances, but Hemmerlein's testimony seemed to make the earlier Saturday seem like the later one. The implication from Hemmerlein's testimony was that Jeff had retaliated against Bob for the knockdown by blowing him away with a shotgun.

But this was wrong—the "fistfight" could not have occurred only hours before the prom, as Hemmerlein knew. Since Brenda hadn't seen Bob after Bob had picked up Jeff at the McDonald's about 11 A.M. on Saturday, April 29, the fight couldn't have taken place on April 29—how else could she have known about it from Bob? She hadn't talked with Bob since the night before, and never would again.

Nevertheless, the imprecision of the dates left the jury with the idea that just hours before the Pelleys were murdered, Jeff and Bob had been in a violent, even physical altercation, which wasn't the case. It was only later, when the jury submitted its written questions through the judge, that Hemmerlein acknowledged that the supposed fistfight hadn't taken place on the day of the prom, but a week earlier. Both lawyers, prosecution and defense, had missed the implication of Hemmerlein's imprecise testimony, which seems to stand as proof that the Indiana practice of allowing jurors to submit written questions is a good thing.

The story Hemmerlein claimed Jeff told him now swerved even a little further from the early morning account. Jeff had told him he'd stopped at Casey's, the gas station halfway between the parsonage and the Amoco station on Highway 31. There he'd borrowed a screwdriver to fix the car. This was also what he'd told Botich in the videotaped morning interview.

"At this point," Hemmerlein now testified, "I had been supplied some information by the investigators, and I asked him [Jeff] specifically if he had stopped at any other place than Casey's, and he said no, he had not . . . so I asked him, if I had information that he'd stopped at the Amoco . . . what he thought about that."

Jeff told him that he hadn't stopped at the Amoco station, Hemmerlein said, so he asked Jeff what he would say if he was told that Darla said he'd called her from there.

"At that point he got pretty nervous and upset, and he then acknowledged that he forgot that he had been at the Amoco station." Jeff then said he'd stopped at both places—Casey's didn't have a screwdriver, so he'd gone on to the Amoco.

"At that point in time I— I pressed him a little bit with his discrepancy," Hemmerlein said. "I told him that in a situation where four of his family members were dead, killed violently, there was no such thing as a small discrepancy or a little lie . . . That there's something wrong with his story, that I believed he had been telling me a story, that he intentionally left that information out for some reason." Hemmerlein was convinced that Jeff had been concealing the stop at the Amoco. His suspicion was that Jeff had dumped some evidence there.

Hemmerlein said he'd told Jeff that his story didn't make sense: if he'd been "running late," as Jeff had put it, why did he make two stops? Jeff then told him that he had bought a soft drink at Casey's, then stopped at the Amoco to fix the car.

"At that point in time, I told him that I thought he had some involvement in the death of his family," Hemmerlein testified. He'd told Jeff that he believed Jeff had made up the story about Casey's in order to account for his whereabouts at the time of the murders, and that Jeff hadn't wanted them to know about the stop at the Amoco.

"What was his reaction at that point?" Schaffer asked.

"He began to get upset. He was getting very nervous and upset about the situation. I told him that I thought that what he had done was killed his family. He had a short period of time to cover his tracks. That he had cleaned himself up, cleaned up part of the crime scene, grabbed his prom outfit, jumped in his car, locking up the house and leaving, knowing that he's not coming back, and that he locked up the house so no one would find his family before he started his prom activities to establish his alibi . . .

"He was pretty upset at this point . . . and he then asked me a question, a kind of threefold question. He asked me if he could see his girlfriend tonight . . . if he would go to jail tonight, and if he would get the electric chair."

Hemmerlein said that as he'd asked these questions, Jeff had slumped down in his chair, with his head down and his hands covering his eyes. Jeff's body language at the time of the evening interview, Hemmerlein suggested, indicated guilt.

The interview had ended shortly after that, Hemmerlein said. Altogether, from the time that Jack Armstrong and Jeff had arrived at the police station to the end of the interview, about four hours had elapsed.

But on subsequent analysis, Hemmerlein's version of his conversation with Jeff made little sense. Jeff had been under visual observation by the two Amoco attendants the entire time he was at the Amoco station—all of five to ten minutes, if Dennis Nicodemus's estimate was correct. He'd had no opportunity to dispose of any evidence there, and neither

Nicodemus nor Jeff Roberts had said he was ever out of their sight. Nor had any of the police ever found any evidence at the station, despite their search.

True, he might have disposed of the shotgun before arriving, somewhere along the road, but if so, no one had ever found it, and it had to be within searching distance of the route, either down Maple or Mulberry Roads.

This was why the police had been so interested in 2002 in the shotgun-in-the-tree situation—besides matching the kegger-party story, it was on the route from Osborne to Mulberry to Route 4, although not Quinn Road, unless Jeff had doubled back to the west. But it was a single-shot shotgun, not a pump, and the blood on the barrel matched none of the victims' DNA.

If Jeff had really reached the Amoco from Quinn Road via Mulberry, as Nicodemus' testimony suggested, it wasn't likely that he'd been on Route 4 at all.

Even if he'd ditched the shotgun and the shell casings on the way to the Amoco, Jeff had no reason to lie about stopping *there*. How could it misdirect the police? There were two witnesses to his appearance.

Also true, he might have had a reason to conceal the stop at Casey's, but he'd told Botich about that one himself. So how could lying about either stop help Jeff cover up? Why would Jeff want to conceal the stop at the Amoco? Perhaps he didn't want the police to interview Jeff Roberts, who had helped him adjust the idle spring on the Mustang with the screwdriver and the cardboard.

If Bob had disabled the Mustang, one of the easiest ways to do it would have been to remove and hide the idle spring. Perhaps Jeff had taken one of the idle springs from Bob or Dawn's car, found it was the wrong size, and stopped at the Amoco to make an on-the-fly adjustment. The police had no evidence that either of the Pelley cars had no idle spring—but on the other hand, they hadn't bothered to look.

The chances were, Jeff had just gotten confused between the two gas stations, naming Casey's when he meant Amoco.

Then, when Hemmerlein confronted him about the "discrepancy," Jeff had realized that Hemmerlein was bent on using the mistake to accuse him of murder. Jeff then had told Hemmerlein that he had stopped at *both* places, even if he hadn't, one to get a soft drink, the other to borrow a screwdriver. But then, he was only 17 at the time of the interview—a kid trying to cover his honest mistake, perhaps terrified of the consequences of his small error.

But that had only made Hemmerlein more confrontational, and when Jeff realized where this was all headed, he'd put his head in his hands and asked if he might get the electric chair.

It would be up to Baum to try to pry all the kinks out of Hemmerlein's testimony, to straighten things out.

But Baum simply asked Hemmerlein if he'd viewed the taped interview Botich had recorded in the early morning before sitting down with Jeff. Hemmerlein said he had not, but that the main points of the morning conversation had been summarized for him by Botich, Rutkowski and Krisor.

Baum asked only one other question: had there been a confrontation between Jack Armstrong and the police as Jeff and Jack were leaving the police station that night?

"No," Hemmerlein said.

That was it for Baum's cross-examination of the prosecution's final witness.

In retrospect, the brevity, if not paucity, of Baum's cross examination of Hemmerlein is difficult to fathom. There were some obvious "discrepancies" on Hemmerlein's part—the imprecision over the day of the fistfight, the unlikelihood that Jeff was trying to conceal the stop at the Amoco station, the possibility that Jeff's remark about the electric chair was simply an emotional response to Hemmerlein's browbeating technique as a "closer," using the polygraph test as the club.

And, as already noted from the hearing three years earlier, Baum could have once again hammered Hemmerlein with his published letter excoriating Toth for his "political prosecution" of Jeff, or the fact that Michael Dvorak, the beneficiary of the letter, had hired him for his staff.

All of these problems with Hemmerlein's testimony could have been exploited to undercut Hemmerlein's credibility and bias, yet Baum did not pursue them. Why?

One possible explanation is that Baum believed he had his own witness to undermine Hemmerlein—Jack Armstrong.

But first, Baum made yet another effort to have the case thrown out.

"I have a motion," Baum told Chamblee.

"Fire away, sir," Chamblee said. Chamblee often used that phrase with lawyers.

Baum formally asked that Chamblee enter a judgment of acquittal based on the evidence that had been presented by the state. When the evidence was insufficient to support a conviction, the court was required to find a defendant not guilty under Indiana law, Baum said. The only thing the state had proved in their case was the fact that four murders had occurred. There was no credible evidence of motive, of opportunity, of physical evidence to show that Jeff Pelley had committed the crimes.

Chamblee asked Schaffer what he thought about Baum's motion. Schaffer said he believed that his side had presented enough evidence to let the jury decide the case without interference from the judge.

Chamblee said he agreed with Schaffer.

"I'm going to deny your motion, Mr. Baum," he said. Of all the laws of the state, he added, "that is probably the least-used rule in the judiciary in the state of Indiana." The reason was simply that the jury had already put in more than a week listening to witnesses, and he simply wasn't willing to substitute his judgment for that of the jury members, twelve members of the community, as he pointed out. Chamblee didn't add that most were also voters, and voters selected judges. He didn't have to.

"And call it cowardice, call it the unwillingness to weigh the evidence myself, I'm going to leave this to the jury to decide, not whether there's a scintilla, but whether there's enough to prove guilt beyond a reasonable doubt, and we'll wait their decision."

Jeff Pelley would have to put on a defense.

Jack Armstrong took the witness stand as the first defense witness the same day. Jack, of course, was Jeff and Jacque's maternal grandfather, the father of Joy Pelley, their natural mother, who had died in 1985, which made him Bob Pelley's former father-in-law. In earlier years, there had been minor friction between the older Armstrongs and Bob. He'd had relatively little contact with the Pelleys after Bob had married Dawn in late 1985—maybe a visit or two a year. Bob had been moving on—no tears for Joy.

Under questioning by Baum, Jack told of receiving the horrifying news of the murders while at home in Burlington, Kentucky, and how he and his wife, Mary, had immediately packed bags and rushed off to Lakeville, arriving at the church in late afternoon. They had picked up Jacque, then waited for Jeff to arrive with the police late that night. They'd checked into the Holiday Inn in South Bend, then had arisen around 3:30 A.M. for the summons to the police station for the first formal interview. They had sat for that interview, the one that had been videotaped, then left.

Baum soon moved on to the second interview, the one with Hemmerlein that night.

Jack had picked Jeff up at the track meet, and had taken him to the police station at the request of the police, and after a short conversation, had left him alone in a room with the door closed, he said. He sat down in a chair along a corridor, and a man he did not know—Hemmerlein—had walked past him without a word, entered the interview room, and shut the door.

Jack said he guessed that the discussion might last a while, so he asked a woman who worked at the police station if there was someplace nearby where he could go to eat.

"And her comment was, she says, 'You do not want to go out here after dark.' " So Jack returned to his chair and sat down again.

Just a few minutes later, Jack said, the man who had gone into the room with Jeff came out again and summoned Jack.

"He just walked by me and said, 'Jeff wants to see you.'"

Jack said he went into the interview room to see what Jeff wanted.

"And what did you see when you went into where Jeff was?"

"Jeff was— He was sitting there crying. He said, 'Grandpa, he never asked me a question. He just come at me and chewed me out.' And he said, 'I did not do it.' I said, 'I believe you, come on, let's go.' And we went out of the room."

Jack and Jeff walked down the hall to where Hemmerlein was speaking with Krisor. Jack Armstrong was a somewhat pugnacious, or at least forthright, type, someone Dave Hathaway would have recognized as a kindred spirit—they were about the same age—and had had somewhat similar life experiences. Jack asked Hemmerlein if it was true he'd accused Jeff of the murders without asking any questions.

"And he shook his head up and down, yes. And I looked at him again, and I said, 'You're stupid.'" According to Jack Armstrong, Hemmerlein put his head in his hands, and shook it in a manner of derisive disbelief. Then Krisor put his arm on Hemmerlein's shoulder, and said something that Jack couldn't hear. Jack thought they were mocking him.

"And I left," Jack added. "And before I went out the door, I said, 'You don't talk to us no more, we'll have a lawyer when you do.' That was the end of it."

By Jack's reckoning, the entire encounter with the police that night had unfolded in a matter of a few minutes.

This was a rather large "discrepancy," as Hemmerlein would have called it, given the fact that he'd just testified that the interview with Jeff had lasted three to four hours.

Baum asked no further questions of Jack Armstrong.

Schaffer's objective was to undercut the reliability of Jack's testimony and bolster the credibility of Hemmerlein. He induced Jack to admit that he couldn't remember what time they had arrived at the police station, or what time they left.

"How long were you there at the police station?" Schaffer asked.

"I doubt very much we was there even fifteen minutes."

"Okay, it wasn't a four-hour interview?"

"No, sir, it was not."

Schaffer asked Jack where he and Jeff had gone after leaving the police station. Back to the hotel, Jack answered.

Now the jury submitted written questions through the judge. Most of the questions were about Jeff's living arrangements after the murders. It seemed that the jurors were trying to judge just how close Jeff and his grandfather were as a means of assessing Jack's credibility. But one question jumped out, mostly because of Jack's response.

"Do you know where his sisters lived after the death of Reverend Pelley and Dawn and the girls?" Chamblee read.

"His sister?"

"Well, the question is 'sisters,'" Chamblee said. "And I guess they're referring to both Jacque and Jessie [Jessica]. If you know."

"Yeah," Jack said, "she lived with us."

"Which sister lived with you?"

"Jacque's the only sister he's got," Jack said. It was as if Jessica, Janel and Jolene had never entered Jack's mind as part of Jeff's family. In a way, that answered the credibility question—for Jack, only Jeff and Jacque were family. Dawn, Jessica, Janel and Jolene were just names.

The defense now called a witness they thought would be very effective for Jeff—Lois Stansbury, the neighbor who had been to the Kmart with her daughters on Saturday afternoon, and who once had the time-stamped receipt to prove it.

Lois had lived for years on Osborne Road, two houses east of the parsonage. Her elderly father lived in another house west of the parsonage, at the northeast corner of Osborne and Mulberry Road. As a girl, she had attended the

Olive Branch Brethren church, although she was no longer a member. On Saturday afternoon, she'd taken her two daughters to the Kmart on Highway 31 and Ireland Road, on the South Bend city border.

"Do you recall what time it was when you left Kmart that day?" Andre Gammage asked her.

"Four-oh-three," Lois said.

"How is it you're so certain about the time?"

"By the receipt that Kmart gave me."

Gammage established through his questions that it might have taken Lois and her daughters some minutes to get to her car in the Kmart parking lot, in part because one of her daughters was confined to a wheelchair and mostly immobile. Once they were in the car, the wheelchair stowed in the trunk, Lois exited the parking lot and drove south some miles on Highway 31, then stopped at a roadside business, Country Gardens. Inside the store she purchased the window covering she'd promised her elderly father. That took about ten or fifteen minutes, Lois estimated. When she emerged from the store, one of her daughters was talking to a friend, and that took another five minutes.

Lois testified that she and her daughters had then turned back onto Highway 31, driven another mile or two south, then turned right—west—on Osborne Road. At the intersection of Osborne and Mulberry Road, just west of the parsonage, Lois stopped at her father's house, again leaving her daughters in the car. She went in, hung the window covering, and chatted for a few minutes with her father. That took about fifteen minutes, she testified. Then she left.

Gammage asked her what happened next.

"I got in the car and drove [east] down the road back toward my house and stopped in front of the parking lot of the church."

"Why did you stop?"

"There was Canadian geese resting on the peat moss across the street from the church. And I stopped to show my daughter the geese."

"When you stopped there to look at the geese, did you notice anyone at or in front of the Pelley home?"

"Not in front of the home, but in the church parking lot."

"Who did you see out there at that time?"

"Bob."

"Bob Pelley?"

"Yes."

"Was he talking to someone?"

"Yes."

"Did you know the person that Mr. Pelley was talking to?"

Lois said she did not.

"Okay, did you get Mr. Pelley's attention in any way when you saw him there?"

"I blew my horn at him."

"What was his response?"

"He turned part way around and waved behind his back at us."

"Did he greet you in the normal way he would greet you?"

"Not really."

"Did he seem preoccupied?"

"Yes."

"Do you know about what time this was?"

"I'm not really sure. I'm guessing around five o'clock. I don't know."

If Lois had really seen Bob Pelley alive at 5 P.M., that narrowed the window even further—if she was right, Jeff would have had less than ten minutes to murder four people and clean up, in order to get to the Amoco by 5:20. And if the jury believed Jeff that he'd left around 4:50, that meant Jeff couldn't be the killer—he would have left ten minutes before Lois had seen Bob.

Now, Gammage asked, did she turn her information about seeing Bob around five o'clock over to state police Investigator Mark Senter in early May 1989?

She had, Lois said. She'd told Senter that she thought she'd seen Bob "a little before" five. She had also told Senter that she'd seen a black pickup truck in the church parking lot. She'd given the Kmart receipt to Senter, she said.

Why had she done that?

Because, Lois said, she'd read in the newspaper or heard on television that the police had fixed the time of death as of Saturday afternoon, and she wanted them to know they were wrong.

CHAPTER 32

It was difficult, maybe even impossible, to parse Lois's testimony. By her account, they'd checked out of Kmart at 4:03 P.M., spent perhaps five minutes going to the car, getting in, loading the wheelchair, then another two or three minutes turning south onto Highway 31. Another four or five minutes driving to Country Gardens, probably arriving there just after 4:15 P.M.

Lois had spent perhaps ten, maybe fifteen minutes in the store, buying the window shade, and another five minutes while her daughter talked with her friend—that meant the clock was up to 4:30 or 4:35 P.M.

Another one or two minutes leaving the store and driving south to Osborne Road. Maybe five or six minutes driving to Lois's father's house at Mulberry and Osborne. Ten to fifteen minutes inside to hang the window covering and chat—and now the clock was up to 5 P.M.. She had not seen the Kim Oldenburg group leaving, which suggested that she'd passed the parsonage after they had left—4:45 at the earliest, a little before 5 at the latest.

All she saw after leaving her father's house was Bob, in the parking lot, talking to an unknown man. Bob had been holding a shovel, and there was a black pickup truck in the church parking lot. She had given her Kmart receipt to Mark Senter within a few days of the murders—this wasn't some years-after-the-fact discovery, like the kegger party, or the shotgun in the tree. This was real-time information.

But was it possible that Lois had simply mixed up the days

she had seen Bob with the shovel? That she had actually seen him on Friday, not Saturday? That seemed hard to believe: she had a receipt from Kmart, and the receipt was time- and date-stamped.

But where was the receipt? In the years since the murders, it had gone missing.

If Lois really had seen Bob around 5 P.M., that would have given Jeff Pelley only around ten minutes, maybe a minute or two more or less, to commit the murders, with all the activity the crimes entailed—the shower, the drapes, the loading of the car, et cetera—and still get to the Amoco gas station by 5:20. And meanwhile: who was the unknown man, apparently associated with the black pickup truck, who seemed to have preoccupied Bob?

Was he the real killer? Had he arrived after Jeff had left—if, as Jeff had said, he'd left at 4:50, just after the Oldenburg group had departed, wasn't it possible that the unknown man was the real killer, if in fact the Pelleys had really been murdered between 4:45 and 5:30 P.M., as the state insisted, albeit without firm, scientific evidence of the time of death?

Who was the mystery man? And why hadn't the police ever identified him?

Lois Stansbury's evidence didn't fit the picture the police investigators had formed in their minds, Baum and Gammage believed. When it didn't fit, they'd simply tossed it: they wanted Jeff to be the killer, because it was simple—obvious. And then the receipt had been lost. It was yet another example of the rush to judgment, or, as Jacque later called it, "tunnel vision."

Those were the questions the defense wanted to leave in the minds of the jurors. To Baum and Gammage, it was more than ample reasonable doubt.

Because Lois Stansbury was as close to an eyewitness as the Pelley case ever had, Schaffer wanted to carefully examine the significance of her observations. It was true, wasn't it, that she had originally estimated that she'd seen Bob with the unknown man at some point between forty-five minutes and an hour after leaving Kmart?

Yes, Lois said.

Okay, said Schaffer. Did she see anything else that day?

Yes, Lois said. Sometime after she'd gotten home, she'd seen a person in a brown car arrive at the church parking lot. She couldn't tell if the person was a man or a woman, or if he or she had gone to the church or the parsonage. She wasn't sure of the time, but it had still been light out. After some minutes, the person had driven away.

Had anything else happened?

Yes, she'd heard another car drive by her house.

At this point, Gammage objected, and demanded another sidebar.

"Judge, I'm objecting to what I anticipate she might say," Gammage told Chamblee. In taking a deposition from Lois some years earlier, Lois had said that when she'd heard a car go by her house, she'd thought, "There goes the pastor's son," because of the distinctive sound of Jeff's Mustang and the way he often drove it. But she hadn't actually seen the Mustang, so Gammage was now arguing that she had no basis to testify that it was Jeff going by. The significance of Lois's car-witness testimony about the Mustang and "the pastor's son" was that it might have proven that Jeff had left the parsonage sometime after Lois had seen Bob alive around 5 P.M. That contradicted Jeff's assertion that he'd left the parsonage at about 4:50, just after Kim's group had left.

If Jeff had left before 5, and Lois had seen Bob after 5, then heard Jeff's car after seeing Bob, it suggested that Jeff was lying. So the defense didn't want the jury to hear that. All this was in contradiction to Kurt Schafer's testimony—why would Jeff's car be rushing past Lois's house when Kurt had testified he'd seen the Mustang racing down Mulberry Road, in the opposite direction? Either Jeff had driven east past Lois Stansbury's house, or west, then south on Mulberry Road, as Kurt had testified. There just wasn't enough time for Jeff to have driven in two directions—even the prosecution admitted that.

Chamblee sustained Gammage's objection, at least as to "the pastor's son" part. Schaffer tried it another way.

When she'd heard the car go by, was it before or after she'd seen the brown car in the parking lot?

"Before," Lois said.

So the sequence was: she'd seen Bob Pelley about 4:50 to 5 P.M., and honked her horn at him; then she'd driven home. Sometime later she'd heard a car drive by her house, and sometime after that, she'd seen a brown car pull into the church parking lot. Someone had alighted, and after some minutes, the brown car had left.

Yes, Lois agreed.

Now there was a sort of order to Lois's observations. If one assumed that the driver of the brown car was Crystal Easterday and her date, arriving around 5:45 P.M., or even Brenda Hale, on her visit to the church at about 6 P.M., and the car that had earlier passed her house was Jeff's Mustang, it seemed to show that Jeff had left the parsonage *after* 5 P.M., not at 4:50, if indeed Lois had seen Bob about 5.

If so, that meant Jeff was lying. Or so Schaffer thought he could demonstrate in his closing argument.

The jurors seemed to be very interested in Lois's testimony, judging from their written questions.

Did Lois notice what the mystery man looked like?

No, she said.

Was Jeff's car in the parking lot when Bob had waved at her from behind his back?

"I don't know," she said.

Where was the black pickup truck parked? Was it in the Pelley driveway?

"I can't remember anymore."

Did she remember what kind of pickup truck it was?

No.

She couldn't remember whether it was a large pickup truck or a small one?

"Not anymore, no."

Had she ever seen the pickup truck at the Pelleys' before?

"I don't know."

The judge asked Gammage if he had any more questions for Lois.

"Did you hear any gunshots that evening?" he asked Lois.

"No."

For his part, Baum thought these were all excellent questions—questions that should have been asked back in 1989, when Lois might have remembered, when the impressions were still fresh in her mind. It was, to him, direct evidence of what happens when investigators focus too soon on a suspect: potentially valuable information gets lost.

The defense called Jeff's sister, Jacque. Now grown up, married to a minister, and a mother, Jacque had been waiting outside the courtroom for more than a week, in support of her brother.

Baum knew that Jacque had never seen the video of Jeff's interview with Botich. But he wanted the jury to hear Jacque's take on Jeff's seeming lack of emotion as he had responded to Botich's questions years earlier.

"If I were to tell you that in that video, Jeff does not appear to be sobbing or crying or extremely emotional, would that surprise you?"

"No."

"Why not?"

"Because that's the way we were raised. We weren't allowed to cry." Jacque told the story of the death of her mother, Joy, and how her father had told them that life goes on.

Baum asked about guns in the house. As far as she knew, Jacque said, all the guns had been removed a month or two before the murders. A friend of Bob's had come to take them away. She couldn't remember who it was.

Now Baum asked questions intended to show that night had fallen before the Pelleys were murdered. When did Bob always enjoy his popcorn? As the girls were going to bed, Jacque said, and that was usually between 8 and 8:30. That was usually bath time for the girls on the night before church—as far as Baum could see, this was evidence that the water found in the tub had been deposited well after Jeff left the parsonage.

What about discipline? Jacque said it wasn't unusual in the Pelley household for her father to "ground" the children with heavy restrictions. You didn't argue with him, but merely accepted them, Jacque said. Then later, after Bob calmed down a bit, you could negotiate some reasonable compromise. That's what had been going on with her brother and father in the week before the prom.

By Friday, Jacque said, Bob and Jeff had reached a compromise: if Jeff was allowed to drive his own car to all the prom events, he would agree to extend his grounding period—again, no car—for an additional period of time after the prom.

"They were negotiating different options for Jeff to go to prom," Jacque said. "He was—in the negotiations, I remember Dad saying that he could go to prom alone and have some additional time added on to the end of his grounding—he would just lift it for the prom activity . . . he could go to the entire prom activities, and he could have more time added on to the end of his grounding."

Baum now tried to ask Jacque about the Florida rumors—the bank, the money-laundering, the missing million. But Schaffer objected.

In another sidebar conference, he said that Jacque's recollections were unreliable, that she'd only been 10 or 11 years old at the time, that she couldn't possibly know anything about banking—and in short, any talk about what had caused the Pelleys to leave Florida would only confuse the issue. Baum shot back: Jessica's testimony about the shotgun, when *she* had only been 10, ought to qualify Jacque's recollection at the same age, insofar as the Florida fiasco. One 10-year-old's testimony qualifies another's, Baum said—it's all equal.

Well, said Schaffer, if the judge was going to allow Baum to ask about Florida, he should be entitled to ask Jacque about what she'd said at the church the day of the murders—this was an apparent reference to Jacque's supposed statement at the time that Jeff might have been capable of the murders.

Just as the two lawyers seemed set to go into an extended, even vitriolic argument, Chamblee cut them off. He sustained Schaffer's objection. Baum said he had no more questions. He believed that he had established grounds for appeal.

There was little Schaffer could do with Jacque on his cross-examination. He certainly couldn't treat her with overt hostility or sarcasm—the jury would see it as beating up on one of the victims. He simply asked her if she'd been home on Friday night, whether she was privy to any conversations between her father and brother Friday night or Saturday morning.

No, Jacque said—she'd been visiting at Huntington College. Schaffer's point was that Jacque had no way of knowing whether Bob had retracted his permission for Jeff to drive himself and his date to all the prom activities after she'd left on Friday afternoon. Of course, Jacque did not. She had no idea of what had happened between her father and brother on Saturday, April 29, 1989.

The following day, Wednesday, July 19, 2006, Baum called his star witness. This was Roy Otterbein, an expert in air-conditioning systems, and particularly, in the physics of water evaporation. He held masters' degrees in both physics and mechanical engineering, and operated a private consulting business in Phoenix, Arizona.

Baum had employed Otterbein to conduct tests of the rates of water evaporation of two of the three washcloths found hanging over the side of the Pelley bathtub on the morning of April 29, and to determine whether a similar rubber bathmat would still have had water droplets on it more than seventeen hours after the Pelleys had supposedly been murdered.

This all had to do with "dew point"—just when the moisture in the air might condense and fall to the earth. This was a matter of some interest to the farmers of northern Indiana, and people there tended to understand the atmospherics of moisture extremely well—they had lived most of their lives in a place where the relationship between water and soil was critical. The physics of water evaporation—when, how, where—was part of the jurors' lives.

For the Pelley defense, the obvious implication was, if the washcloths found in the bathroom were still wet when videotaped by Pavlekovich on April 29, or the droplets on the mat were obvious, someone had to have used the tub and the washcloths well after 5 P.M., after Jeff had left the parsonage. How else could they have gotten wet?

Baum showed Otterbein several photographs of the Pelley bathroom. One of the photographs showed a furnace vent quite close to the washcloths. With this, Baum meant to suggest that the furnace might have even accelerated the drying, although Baum never actually tried to make that claim—there was no evidence that the furnace had been on at the time of the murders. Still, as Baum knew, sometimes a picture is worth a thousand words, especially when you're trying to save a client from wrongful conviction.

Baum asked Otterbein how he'd conducted his evaporation tests.

First he'd totally saturated the washcloth that had been identified as the wettest by the police and weighed it, Otterbein said—the cloth and the saturating water together. Then he'd draped the dripping cloth over the edge of a plastic box similar in dimensions to the side of the tub. Then he'd timed how long it took for the cloth to stop dripping. Two hours, he said. When the dripping ceased, that was when evaporation into the air began.

Every few hours he'd weigh the assemblage, Otterbein said, and record the time. Eventually the cloth was completely dry.

"And how long, starting from saturated, from dripping wet, how long did it take for the washcloth to be completely dry?" Baum asked.

"To be dry to the touch, it was about twenty hours at most." But if the washcloth had been wrung out, it would have dried much faster.

Had Otterbein conducted evaporation tests with rubber bathmats?

He had, Otterbein said. He'd found several rubber bathmats that appeared to be identical to the one depicted in the crime-scene video. He'd used them as "replicas" of the bathmat shown in the police crime-scene tape.

"What was your conclusion, based upon your testing of the replica bathmat?"

"That water will not remain on a bathmat in a shower stall after ten hours, maximum."

Ten hours! If Otterbein was right, that meant someone had used the shower late Saturday night, nearly midnight, at the earliest, seven hours after Jeff had left for the prom, or even possibly early Sunday morning.

This was the scientific evidence Gammage had promised the jury in his opening statement.

"I have no further questions," Baum said, with the air of a magician who had just made someone disappear.

Schaffer had to do something to cast doubt on Otterbein's findings. He began by asking if Otterbein had ever actually been inside the Pelley house to inspect the bathtub. Otterbein admitted that he hadn't. And, wasn't it true that he'd conducted his experiments in Phoenix, Arizona? A place notorious for its dry atmosphere?

Well, yes, said Otterbein, but he'd adjusted his experiments for the environment.

What if the cloth hadn't been wrung out? Well, it would have added more hours to the drying time, Otterbein said. And would the washcloth have dripped water into the bathtub itself? Schaffer was trying to show that the droplets on the bath mat could have come from the washcloth—that over a period of time, the droplets would be replenished, rather than having been available for evaporation all at once.

Otterbein admitted that at least some of the moisture in the washcloth might well have run down onto the rubber bathmat.

Was this the first time he'd ever done tests of washcloths and bathmats?

Yes, Otterbein said, although he'd done similar tests with other materials, mostly for corporations trying to make their air-conditioning systems more efficient. But this was the first time anyone had ever asked him, in a court of law, in a criminal case, to estimate just how fast a washcloth or bathmat ordinarily dried.

After Otterbein, the defense called one more witness—Rebecca Greer, Lynette Greer's mother. Rebecca said that as far as she could recall, Jeff had arrived at the Greer house at 5:30 P.M., just as he'd said, and as Mark Berger, Darla Emmons and Lynette had all confirmed. Then Rebecca added something new: customarily in the Greer house, all clocks were set ten minutes fast. That meant Jeff had actually arrived some minutes before 5:30. Well, that was another problem with clocks—not everyone had them set to the same time. Dennis Nicodemus said he'd looked at his watch at 5:17 P.M., when he was mad at Jeff Roberts' tardiness; Lois Stansbury had a receipt stamped at 4:03; other people wore watches, but the plain, inescapable fact was, none of them were synchronized. April 29, 1989, wasn't D-Day, and the various clocks were all humming along in different temporal realities. Einstein would have enjoyed the conundrum—too bad he and Agatha Christie never compared notes.

Jeff Pelley did not take the witness stand in his own defense.

Schaffer had two rebuttal witnesses: former deputy prosecutor Jack Krisor, who said he'd watched the interviews with Jeff, and the one with Hemmerlein *had* lasted hours, not just minutes; and Botich. Botich said he, Rutkowski and Krisor had watched the Hemmerlein interview through a one-way mirror into the interview room. He thought Jack Armstrong had been with them at the time, also watching through the glass. This seemed to be the kibosh on Jack's version of the Hemmerlein encounter.

"How long did the interview last?" Schaffer asked.

"Quite a while," Botich said.

Baum and Gammage had no substantive questions for Botich.

The case was finally ready for closing arguments.

CHAPTER 33

Schaffer began by saying he didn't think it was his job to "prove" anything. All he had to do was present the facts, and that's what he'd done. All the witnesses who had come forward had the facts, and it was up to the jury to decide if those facts proved the case. Of course, he believed the facts *did* prove the case. Otherwise, he wouldn't have prosecuted it.

Schaffer spent almost an hour summarizing all the testimony—who had said what, and what they had observed. Only when taken as a whole could the pattern be seen, he said. There was the grounding, the disabling of the car, the withdrawal of the insurance coverage. There was no break-in in the house, no evidence of ransacking or robbery. And the inescapable fact was, after 5 P.M. at the latest, no one had ever seen the Pelleys alive again.

"I think the state's main contention in this case is the timeline," he said. "I think everyone can see that." And there, the key was Matt Miller: if Jeff had left the parsonage at 4:50 P.M., as he contended, how come Matt Miller had seen Jeff's Mustang parked at the parsonage at least twenty minutes later? It was obvious—Jeff had to be lying, and if he was lying, he had to be guilty.

"Because, the most important thing to remember in this case is, where is Jeff Pelley during that time? Because from five-thirty on, Dawn, Bob, Jolene and Janel are never seen alive again. They are never talked to, they're never talked to on the phone, they're never seen walking, they're never seen talking after that time. And the only person who had contact with them in that time [before that] was the defendant. The only person who had the means, the motive and the opportunity was Jeff Pelley . . .

"There is a lot to this case. I never tried a simple case yet. But I ask each of you to go back in that jury room and use your common sense . . . On April twenty-ninth, 1989, Jeff Pelley gunned down Bob, Dawn, Jolene and Janel. That's what the evidence shows, that's what the testimony shows. Use your common sense . . . go back in the jury room and find Jeff Pelley guilty as charged in this case."

Baum agreed with Schaffer that it wasn't the prosecutor's job to "prove" the case. The prosecutor's job was bigger than that, he said. The prosecutor's job was to find the truth.

"And no prosecutor that I've ever tried a case with has ever come into court and said, 'You know what, I didn't prove my case, so you ought to go back there and find the defendant not guilty.' You don't see it on TV, even, and you sure don't see it in a real courtroom. His job isn't a search for the truth. His job is to convict Jeff Pelley."

Any objective analysis of the crime scene, Baum went on, had to show that there were two shooters in the parsonage—"sometime in the evening of April twenty-ninth or in the early morning hours of April thirtieth," as Baum put it.

The ballistic evidence was clear, Baum said: there were two types of shotgun slugs used, one with cardboard wadding, the other with plastic wadding. Who would load one shotgun with two different types of ammunition? And there was evidence that six or seven shots had been fired, when a pump-action shotgun, like the Mossberg, could hold only four or five rounds, depending on the length of the round—either two-and-three-quarter–inch, or three-inch.

If there was only one shooter, he would have had to reload, and if he'd had to reload, why were the bodies in the basement so close together? Didn't it make sense that someone would try to run away before the last fatal, reloaded shot or two? But if there were two shooters, no reloading would be necessary, no one could have gotten away and it explained why there were two different types of ammunition.

Baum now suggested a possible two-shooter scenario: one shooter was in the basement with Dawn and the girls, while a second was upstairs, perhaps searching for something in the Pelley house. The downstairs shooter had herded Dawn and the girls into the basement, perhaps firing a shot that hit the wall of the stairwell, one that ricocheted off the floor of the basement and wound up in the book, while the second man had contained Bob upstairs.

Then the upstairs gunman had fired a shot that hit Bob in the chest, knocking him on his back. The second shooter had then joined the downstairs gunman in the basement, and after that, Dawn, Janel and Jolene were shot by both shooters, accounting for both types of ammunition, plastic and cardboard wadding. Afterward, the original downstairs gunman had gone upstairs and shot Bob in the neck and chin as a "coup de grace," as Baum put it. That had to be why there were two different types of ammunition—plastic wadding and cardboard wadding—found in both places.

Baum pointed out that Bob had been wearing shoes when he was shot—the Pelleys had a rule of no shoes in the house, they had to be left in the kitchen. The fact that Bob was wearing shoes in the bedroom hallway—what did that mean? Baum put it out there without elaborating on its possible significance. He wanted the jury to focus their attention on the total number of shots, which in his mind seemed to show that there had to have been two shooters.

"Why would there be six or seven shots fired, when a normal twenty-gauge shotgun holds five? Why would there be one plastic wadding downstairs and one upstairs? Why haven't they [the police] answered any of these questions?"

Baum went on to suggest that the police were so eager to charge Jeff that they hadn't paid much attention to the anomalies.

"I think part of it is, they simply didn't care," he said. "They didn't care because, at one o'clock on Sunday afternoon, before they had spoken to anybody about the prom, before they had spoken to anybody about grounding, before they had spoken to anybody about anything, when they had four dead people, they decided that Jeff did it."

The police might have been prejudiced against Jeff from the start, Baum suggested.

"Jeff had been around Lakeville, he had been around. These cops knew Jeff. They probably didn't like him very much. You heard Jeff got grounded. He had gotten into some trouble . . . you didn't hear any evidence of what that trouble [was] . . . But, it is a small community, and I wouldn't be surprised if some of these cops didn't like Jeff.

"So—what did they decide, at one o'clock on Sunday, before they knew anything about [the] prom and grounding and Amoco and Casey's? This is what they decided, at one o'clock on Sunday, when all they have is four dead bodies."

What they had decided only three hours after the murders were discovered was that Jeff had done it, Baum said.

Baum blasted the police for their failure to look for fingerprints—it showed, he argued, that they had already concluded Jeff had to be the killer, and were so set on that conclusion, from the very beginning, that they hadn't even bothered to do the minimum.

Baum scorned the authorities for the failure to establish a time of death scientifically. Dr. Hoover had been at the parsonage, and he certainly knew how to conduct the appropriate tests.

"I suggest how critically important time of death is, because we all know, Mr. Schaffer knows, everybody knows, that Jeff left the house sometime around five o'clock . . . I mean, all they have to do is determine that the time of death is six P.M., seven P.M., eight P.M., nine P.M., ten P.M., et cetera, et cetera, et cetera. And then we wouldn't even be here, because Jeff is with his friends, clearly from sometime around five-thirty. So we wouldn't even have a trial, he never would have been charged, not even in 2002. It's just so basic. It's so unfair. It's so unfair that they treated this case the way they did."

There was the expert's testimony about evaporation, Baum

continued. The undisputed facts that the washcloth was still wet and droplets on the bathmat showed that someone had used that tub hours after Jeff had left the house. Then, too, there was the likewise undisputed fact that no one had ever found any physical evidence linking Jeff Pelley to the murders—no blood, no DNA, nothing—while even the state's own crime-scene expert had said he believed that the killer would be spattered with blood. Nor had the police ever found a murder weapon, although they had looked very hard.

"And they were so hoping to find something. They knew how far off the road he could have gone. I mean, he's only got a few minutes. They searched everywhere. They didn't find anything, because there wasn't anything to find. Not because they couldn't find it, it wasn't there. Because the shooters, the murderers took their guns and their evidence, [and] whatever else it was they were there for, with them.

"We don't know what the back story is here, and that's what makes it a murder mystery. Our problem is, Jeff didn't do it. And not only did he *not* do it, they don't have any evidence that he did."

It was true, as Schaffer had said, that the state had built its case around the timeline, Baum continued. But the state's timeline was itself built on a foundation of sand. No one was clocking any of the events. Everything was an estimate, compromised by "about," or "near," or "maybe," or "-ish," and still further compromised by the passage of so many years since the murders. The only documented instance of a time was Lois Stansbury's receipt. And the police had lost that.

Schaffer had it right, in the beginning of the trial, when he'd told the jury that the case was like a jigsaw puzzle, Baum said. And with that, Baum dramatically produced a jigsaw puzzle contained in a cardboard box—"*C.S.I.*" for the popular television show, *Crime Scene Investigation*. Baum showed the cover of the box to the jury.

"It says here, seven hundred fifty pieces," Baum said, pointing to the cover. "But when I opened the box, there were only four pieces." Baum opened the box, and sure enough, there were only four pieces. "That's Bob Pelley, that's Dawn Pelley, that's Jolene, and that's Janel.

"The only thing they proved is that these four people were killed. I don't see the picture here. So yeah, you've got a jigsaw puzzle, and you've got four pieces. He's innocent. He's not just 'not guilty.' He's innocent. I know you know that."

But Baum's argument elided over some of the most critical evidence—primarily, the fact that Bob had been shot from the bedroom end of the hallway. Why would a strange gunman have been in that part of the house? If someone was really gunning for Bob, for his allegedly mysterious Florida past, wouldn't it have been much cleaner to have hit Bob outside the house—say, while he was driving to Huntington College, or anywhere else on the rural roads of St. Joseph County? The configuration of the shooting powerfully suggested that the gunman had to have been in the house before the shooting started—which pointed directly at Jeff Pelley, along with all the other circumstantial evidence, such as the insurance withdrawal, the lack of a tuxedo at 4:45 P.M., the dissonance of where Jeff had said he had stopped on the way to Lynette Greer's house. Baum did not address these problems in his argument. Perhaps he thought the jury would overlook them.

But in trying to address the facts as presented by Schaffer, Baum may have missed a viable, perhaps even vital, alternative theory.

What if there were *three* assassins? One outside—the mystery man seen by Lois Stansbury, and two inside, who had gained access while the mystery man kept Bob at bay, either with a threat or a gun? Perhaps there was one inside man to maintain control of Dawn and the girls, while a second searched for something Bob had in his possession—say, evidence of a past crime, or evidence of the supposed missing million.

Perhaps this murderous trio had arrived *after* Jeff had left, but before Lois had looked at the geese, and had then seen Bob around 5 P.M., being preoccupied by the mysterious stranger.

Then, perhaps, after Lois had driven on, something had gone wrong. While the upstairs man was searching, maybe Dawn had tried to escape, trying to get herself and the girls into the back bedroom in the basement, there to shut the door. The man guarding Dawn and the girls might have chased her into the basement, firing one shot that ricocheted off the stairwell and then the floor, the slug perhaps hitting her in the hand, before winding up in the book.

Then Bob, hearing this shot, had raced into the parsonage, pursued by the mystery man, only to meet the upstairs man coming out of the Pelley bedroom after his search. The upstairs man fired one shot as the tennis shoe–wearing Bob rushed toward him, hitting him in the chest. This was why Bob had been wearing shoes—he'd been outside, but was trying to save Dawn, and had run toward the bedroom, the shoes rule being meaningless at that point.

Then, as Bob lay dying in the hallway, the mystery man and the upstairs man descended the stairs, where both gunmen executed Dawn and the girls to get rid of the witnesses. After that, the downstairs shooter ascended the stairs to fire the last shot into Bob's neck and face—as Baum had argued, accounting for the two different types of ammunition found by Hoover in Bob's body.

Then, after that, all three had raced away in the black pickup truck, past Lois Stansbury's house. It hadn't been the "pastor's son" at all, but the assassins—maybe even assassins from Florida.

Schaffer was fast on his feet. Baum's visual demonstration with the puzzle had to be countered.

"Mr. Baum is right," he said, as he began his final remarks to the jury. "There is a big piece missing. The big piece is Jeff Pelley, between five o'clock and five-fifteen."

Baum was also right about Lois Stansbury's importance as a witness, Schaffer said. "But it's not Mrs. Stansbury who is the most important witness in this case, it's Matt Miller. Because Matt Miller was the only one to drive by that house between five and five-thirty, and he sees Jeff's car parked in the driveway at five-fifteen, and he's not supposed to be there."

Schaffer reiterated all the circumstantial evidence: the suspension of the car insurance, the fact that Jeff wasn't already in his tuxedo when the Oldenburg group came calling, Crystal Easterday's unanswered knock at 5:45, when both Pelley cars were still in the driveway, the locked doors, drawn drapes.

"Why did he say to Officer Hemmerlein, 'Can I get the electric chair if I talk to you?' Why would you say that if you innocently went to the prom and didn't do anything wrong that night?

"This case comes down to one thing—that twenty minutes from five to five-twenty. Because the most important thing from this [witness] stand was what you didn't hear the last ten days. You didn't hear one person who saw the Pelleys alive after five-fifteen. And there was only one person who was in that house before five-fifteen. He sits right there." Schaffer gestured at Jeff.

"Only he knows."

He knew it was a hard case, Schaffer went on, especially since the murders were seventeen years in the past. But it was the jury's responsibility to make a decision, maybe a tough decision.

"The most difficult thing in the world is to go back in that jury room and [then come out] and state to someone, 'You are guilty for doing this.' To follow through on that. Because that twenty minutes is gone, and that twenty minutes cost four people their lives. Only one person knows about that shotgun and knew how to get it out of there. Only one person had a premonition, only one person made a comment about getting the electric chair."

Schaffer urged the jury to examine the gory crime-scene pictures "very, very closely.

"Remember what happened to those little girls in the basement," he said. "Imagine what those little girls went through and what that family endured. They scream to you for justice . . . Find Mr. Pelley guilty of all four counts of murder. Not because the law demands it, not because justice says it's what needs to be done in this case, but because it's the right thing to do."

On that emotional plea, the jury retired to deliberate.

CHAPTER 34

The jury began its discussions just after 4 P.M. on Wednesday, July 19, 2006. They worked until 11 that night reviewing the evidence, trying to put it into some sort of coherent order. The next morning, they began again. The review lasted most of Thursday. At the end of the day, the foreperson sent a note out to the judge: they had completed their review, and wanted to begin actual deliberations on Friday morning.

The jury deliberated all that day and into the evening hours. Chamblee began contemplating the necessity for bringing the jury back the next day, a Saturday; he didn't think allowing the jury to take the weekend off would be a good idea. So the deliberations went on, and on, and on.

Then, just before 9 P.M., a note was delivered to Chamblee from the jury foreperson: they had reached a verdict. The panel had considered the case for almost thirty-one hours.

Chamblee's clerk notified the lawyers. Within a few minutes, all had assembled in the courtroom. Jeff settled in at the counsel table, the tension apparent on his face. His sister and wife sat behind him. Before he called the jury in to receive the verdict, Chamblee asked both sides to "respect the system and the process, and the fact these twelve people busted their butts . . . That's not really eloquent, but . . . busted their butts for the last three days to try and give their best judgment . . . so whether you side with the verdict or you don't, I hope you can respect the fact that these folks have given it their best, and that's what this process is all about."

The jury came in. Few looked directly at Jeff. Baum had a

sinking feeling—Friday night verdicts were always trouble, and when the jury doesn't want to look at the defendant, that's a bad sign.

After commending the jurors for their willingness to serve, Chamblee asked the foreperson to pass the written verdict forms to the clerk. The clerk passed them to Chamblee. There was a silence as Chamblee read each of the forms to himself, then put them down. He spoke in his usual laconic style:

"Folks, each of the four verdict forms, which are dated July twenty-first, 2006, and signed by the foreperson, make a finding that Robert Jeffrey Pelley is guilty of the murder charged in each of the four counts."

Jeff flinched, then began to weep. His wife rushed forward, sobbing. They held each other, crying, and whispering to each other. Baum could only look at the floor, shaking his head slowly.

Chamblee polled each of the jurors individually at Baum's request. Each said the verdict was correct, and their own decision. Chamblee excused the jury, then permitted Jeff, Baum, Gammage, Jacque and Jeff's wife to meet privately for a few minutes in another courtroom.

Then Jeff was handcuffed, and taken to jail.

Afterward, Schaffer was ecstatic.

"We knew we had an uphill battle the whole way, because of the age of the case," he told reporters for the *Tribune*, one of whom asked him if he considered the verdict a vindication. "I think more than anything else, it's kind of a vindication for the families and the victims."

Baum was devastated.

"Two weeks ago I was asked why I didn't request a change of venue in this case," he told the reporters, "and I said it was because I believed the people of St. Joseph County would be fair, and judge the case on the facts. Now I'm sad that I said that. This is not fair. This is absurd. There's no evidence. I'm speechless. I don't have anything more to say."

CHAPTER 35

On October 17, 2006, Chamblee called a hearing for the imposition of Jeff's sentence. Under the law in effect in 1989, Chamblee had the power to sentence Jeff to the mandatory minimum sentence of 30 years on each count, and to make the sentences run concurrently, which meant Jeff had a chance at parole eventually. But before he imposed the sentence, Chamblee wanted to give the families a chance to speak.

John Hanson, Dawn's brother-in-law, went first.

"There are no words we know that can be used to express the loss of Dawn and Bob, Janel and Jolene," he said. "There's such pain in our hearts that will remain for the rest of our lives. Nothing will take it away, for we remember what was lost and think of what will never be. Dawn and Bob raising their children, enjoying being a part of their grandchildren's lives. So much was taken away from us. Because of what Dawn and Bob believed and lived, we do ask for grace and mercy for Jeff."

Jessica spoke next. She missed her mother and her sisters very much, she said—she'd had to grow up without an immediate family, and that had been very hard. It made her very sad, because her mother and her sisters never had the chance to meet her own children and her husband. While people talked about "closure," they didn't really understand.

"There will never be an actual closure," she said. "It will always hurt." And now, Jeff's son would have to face the same kind of hurt—missing his father as he grew up. Jessica felt bad for Jeff's son.

Jeff's aunt, Bob's sister, Jon Boso, came forward. She was just getting to know Dawn when she'd been killed, she said. They were just becoming friends. She hadn't known at the time that Dawn had been an A student in high school, the prom queen, and the school's athlete of the year. It was only after she was gone that Jon had come to realize what a remarkable person she had been.

But her brother, Bob—Jon admired him for his religious devotion, which was enfolded in such joyful enthusiasm.

"My brother loved people. He had enough love for the whole world. He loved children. That's why he adopted Jessica, Janel and Jolene. We have beautiful memories of Bob. Yes, he was strict, but that's the way we were raised, and that wasn't a reason to shorten his life. He might have been the one that was able to change Lakeville, Saint Joe County, who knows, the world, for the better with God's help, because he lived so close to God.

"They say suicide is a permanent solution to a temporary problem, but I think, in this case, it was murder that was the permanent solution to a temporary problem. I know that my brother had told Jeff that he had to wait until he was eighteen on his birthday in December to leave home. But he told me at spring break, 'Jeff's in Florida now. I won't be surprised if he comes home and says he has a job waiting for him. And I believe we'll tell him, "You can go after graduation." ' That was only six more weeks."

Jon said she believed that Bob and Dawn and Janel and Jolene were all in heaven, pulling for the families to put aside any bitterness.

"Our family doesn't have to be divided. No greater love has any man but he would lay down his life for a friend. I believe my brother would have laid down his life that Jeff could know Him as his personal savior." God was forgiving of everyone who was sincere in his repentance, she said—it did not matter what evil anyone had done, as long as they truly believed in God.

"His love can fill your soul and you will see that it was best for Him to have His way with you. Because God has forgiven me, Jeff, I forgive you."

That was the prevailing sentiment from the side of the family that believed Jeff had committed murder—sorrow, and forgiveness for Jeff, pity for his wife and son.

But the tone was different from the side that believed Jeff had been wrongly convicted.

First to speak for Jeff was Phil Hawley, who had come from Fort Myers.

Phil first read a letter to the court from his son, Danny, who extolled Jeff as a good Christian, and a fine employee. Danny noted that Jeff had gone to work for him after the murders:

> That was when I learned that both sides of Jeff's family, for the most part, shunned him and that he was left only with the clothes on his back. Jeff became hard-working and a very good employee.
>
> Your honor, as you can see, I have known Jeff almost his whole life. I've watched him grow into a successful Christian and God has big plans for him. If for one second I thought that Jeff could have anything to do with his family's murders, I would be the first to help him be punished for what he did.
>
> I am reminded of the stories of Job, Daniel, Paul and others of the Bible that have wrongly been accused and in that light, God will prevail. I'm also reminded of the reasonability that we have as citizens of this country. I understand the importance of a jury but more importantly, I understand the importance of a Judge. You bear a huge burden to just not hide behind the decisions of a confused jury but for justice for all. Jeff's life has been temporarily turned upside down, and it's in your hands to bring him back to his feet. I hope when the defense team gets the evidence, they will be able to find justice for the Pelley family murders. It is not Jeff. Jeff is not a threat to society nor has he ever been. Please,

Your Honor, do whatever in your power to right this injustice.

Thank you,
Danny Hawley

Now Phil asked to say a few words of his own.

Phil began by saying Bob had been his best friend, and because of that, Phil had known Jeff since the age of 5.

"Jeff was a good child, a normal teen and became an outstanding man despite many setbacks and problems that have come his way. I say this from knowing Jeff, knowing his father, knowing his mother, knowing his stepmother and all of his sisters. I also speak from knowledge of raising boys and teenagers. I have raised five of my own sons, and I took in and helped raise three other boys when they were troubled as teens and they had problems in their home, and their parents elected to either put them out or, for some reason, they were turned over to me by the court."

All of his sons, natural and adopted, had grown into good Christians, Phil said, as had Jeff. Jeff was successful in the computer field, and very active in his church. The notion that Jeff could have murdered anyone was simply outlandish, Phil said.

"It is so out of character, knowing Jeff so completely, that I cannot believe we are here for this type of hearing," Phil said. Somehow, the justice system had broken down.

"So out of character, yes, it's so out of character, it's so much out of character that this case has made me think deeply, because Jeff Pelley has become a victim of the system we call justice. So out of character, that when Jeff was convicted of this heinous crime—I have thirty-five years' experience as an investigator. I began doing an investigation. And with my investigation, I have come across proof that I will be able to . . . prove Jeff one hundred percent innocent of this heinous crime."

Phil sat down. Chamblee thanked him. He didn't ask Phil for his proof, and Phil didn't offer it.

Now Jacque addressed the court. The conviction of Jeff had devastated her. She believed with all her heart that her brother was innocent, and what was more, that he'd only been accused to further a political agenda. To Jacque, the whole process was corrupt, self-serving. Now all those feelings came pouring out in a torrent of anger.

She started by describing how her father was supposed to have picked her up on Sunday.

"My life was forever changed that weekend. I became an orphan. I lost my dad, my stepmom, three sisters and my brother. You see, those of us that were still living no longer lived together. I lost my house and many of my belongings, and I never have considered myself a victim. I've always seen myself as a survivor. I was supposed to be there that weekend, but by the grace of God, I wasn't."

There was only one other person in the courtroom who understood how she felt about what had happened at the parsonage, and that person was Jeff.

"Jeff, you're the only person who can possibly understand how I feel having lost Mom, Dad, Dawn, Janel and Jolene. You've been through it with me. However, I can't imagine how you must feel, because not only have you had to deal with this great loss, but you've been accused and convicted of killing the four of them. When I look at you, Jeff, I don't see what they see. I've read all the police reports, at least all the ones that have been filed and turned in.

"When I look at you, I see a fall guy, an easy way out, a scapegoat. They had to have somebody to use to climb the political ladder, and they chose you. When I look at you, Jeff, I see Jesus. When the jury was sent out to begin deliberating, I watched you. You moved from the defendant's chair to the benches behind you. And I sat there and I watched you share your faith. I watched you twice, during deliberations, share your faith. Your priority of sharing the gospel and being an ambassador of Christ.

"Although I'm not able to comprehend how you must feel, Jesus can, because he was persecuted for the sins of others as well. So while I can't be there with you every step of the way, I'm praying for you. I love you, and I'm proud to be your sister."

Since the murders, Jacque continued, she had felt fear every night of her life. She could never escape the feeling that someone was out there, intent on doing her and her family harm.

"The farther away from South Bend I get, the safer I feel," she said. "Now most of you sitting in this courtroom today probably feel safer. You probably feel some sense of relief and satisfaction to know that Jeff has been convicted. I don't. My fear still lives on because somewhere out there is the person or persons that killed my family. You have a sense of closure, and for us, the battle has just begun. Now, I finally feel like a victim. We have been victimized by people who [were] slack on the job, who decided not to fingerprint a crime scene because the fingerprints might be smudged, or because the crime scene contaminated itself.

"But it doesn't take Sherlock Holmes to figure out that the killer closed at least four doors in that house without any blood near any one of them, and there was plenty of opportunity to try to fingerprint. A jailhouse confession was ignored as well as a warning that the murders were going to occur days before they ever did. We are victims of campaign promises and shoddy police work.

"Your Honor, you sat through trial and I believe, in your heart, you feel the same way I do. I realize that there isn't much that you can do, but I'm begging you to please impose the lightest sentence possible so that my brother may be reunited with his wife and son as quickly as possible. Not only is Jeff a victim here, but so are his wife and son. I personally know how painful it is to grow up without your father, and my nephew does not deserve to endure that heartache."

Jeff's wife spoke last.

"I love you," she told Jeff.

She told Chamblee she wanted to read her statement, because otherwise she would not be able to get through it with breaking down. She'd known Jeff most of her life, she said, and Jeff was a good father, a good husband, a kind and gentle man.

> "I know without any doubt that he did not do this crime that he's being sentenced for—that he's being sentenced for. I know the grief that he has gone through over the loss of his family. I know how much he has wished his dad were here to see our son grow up. I feel his pain in that. I also feel his pain every day when I have to deal with our son crying because his dad is not home playing with him, helping him with his school and just being there to give him love. Our family did everything together."

The evidence simply did not support conviction, she said. And like Jacque, she, too, believed that the charges had been motivated by politics.

> "This arrest was based on political ambitions. I never knew politics could have such an effect on your life. I have a hard time believing in politics. I have a hard time believing in the police and in the judicial system at this point in my life."

The police had rushed to judgment, she said. They had picked out Jeff as the culprit without thoroughly investigating, and had even ignored information that showed Bob was still alive after Jeff had left for the prom.

Like her uncle Phil, Jeff's wife believed that there was proof that Jeff hadn't committed the crime.

> "Your Honor, there is information on who else could have done this, and I hope some day it will come out, with many details."

She asked that Chamblee use his power as a judge to void the conviction, or at the least, give the lightest possible sentence.

"Do you believe in your heart that the evidence supports the verdict? I don't. So I ask, please, Your Honor, use your God-given powers as an honorable judge to, in your mercy, help us. Thank you for your time. I'm sorry for crying."

Schaffer now addressed the court. The murders, especially of the little girls, were so heinous that the prosecution believed that the aggravating factors far outweighed any possible mitigation, he said. The judge had the power to make the sentences run consecutively or concurrently. The state favored the former—each sentence to be served, one after the other. Not only that, the judge should impose a harsher sentence than the 30-year minimum for each conviction.

Baum rose to address the court.

"My comments to the court will be brief and will be made by me, not as an attorney, so much as a friend of the Pelley family. In 2002, when Jeff was arrested in Los Angeles, I went to see him, and I have been a part of this case ever since. I know that it's a mistake for an attorney to personalize a case, and I've tried in thirty-eight years without much difficulty not to do that.

"But this case poses a unique exception to the rule. The Pelleys have been in my home. I have been— I have been more than a lawyer, I think. I hope. A defense attorney's worst nightmare, Your Honor, is defending someone that's innocent, going through trial and that person being convicted. We take personal responsibility for that, even though we may have done the best job, given what we had. But it's a nightmare. I can't even imagine, knowing what I've felt since the verdict in this case, what Jeff and his loved ones are going through . . . can't even imagine. I just pray that Jeff and his family will find the strength to endure and perhaps even understand the injustice that has been done in this case by a verdict of guilt. And that they will keep that faith in their hearts until that injustice is eventually undone, and he's free again."

Like Baum, Gammage said he'd come to know Jeff Pelley over the preceding four years, and everything he now knew about Jeff told him that Jeff was a kind, compassionate, law-abiding citizen who had put up with a horrendous situation with grace and dignity. Gammage, too, said he believed Jeff was innocent. But, he added, the judge should remember one thing: the crimes had happened when Jeff was 17. Gammage asked the judge to consider who he was now sentencing—a 34-year-old man in the prime of his life. Gammage asked that the judge sentence Jeff to the minimum 30 years, and asked that the sentences run concurrently.

Chamblee now asked Jeff if he had anything to say. Jeff rose.

"My deepest regret in life is that I was not home that afternoon, as maybe— maybe I could have done something," Jeff said. "My family tells me I probably would have been killed, too. I think that would have been okay. I loved my family dearly, and I have spent my life trying to pattern myself after my father and furthering his ministry and his love for people. I would not and could not, I *did* not do this.

"My father, my sisters, my stepmother were ripped away from me and my sisters, and now my family is having me ripped away from them. I don't know what your power is, Your Honor. I just know that I am innocent."

Now it was up to Chamblee to impose the sentence.

Despite what Phil Hawley, Jeff's wife, Jacque and others might believe, he said, he had no power to undo the verdict. It didn't matter what he believed about the evidence, whether the police work was shoddy or not, or the charges were politically motivated. All that was irrelevant—under the law, the jury was the finder of facts, and the jury had found that Jeff had committed the murders. It was just as simple, and as immutable, as that.

The only question was whether he should sentence Jeff to concurrent or consecutive sentences, and what the term of those sentences should be, whether 30 years or the maximum of 40 years. And the next issue was whether each murder deserved its own consideration for sentencing purposes.

"I am going to find that, as a practical matter, the law also acknowledges that every wrong deserves its own separate consideration," Chamblee said. "And Mr. Pelley is not convicted of killing one person or two people or three people, he's convicted of killing four people. Each of whose lives had a dignity and a value worthy of its own consideration.

"Mr. Pelley, on the jury's finding that you're guilty of murder in the four counts charged in this information, you will be sentenced on each of those counts to the standard presumptive advisory sentence of forty years in the Indiana Department of Correction.

"The sentences will be ordered to be consecutive to each other . . ."

Jeff had just been sentenced to serve 160 in the penitentiary.

Jeff had the right to appeal, Chamblee advised him. Did he want to appeal?

"Yes," Jeff said.

"All right. Good luck, Mr. Pelley."

V. AFTERMATH

The conviction and sentencing of Jeff Pelley wasn't the end of the matter, not by a long shot. As expected, Jeff appealed his conviction to the Indiana Court of Appeals. His appellate lawyer, Stacy Uliana, contended that Jeff's conviction should be thrown out, first, because the prosecutors had violated Rule 4(C), the one-year speedy-trial clock, by their pursuit of the counseling records of the Family & Children's Center; second, because the judge had allowed hearsay evidence to come in about Bob's supposed statements about Jeff and the grounding, while not permitting Baum to present evidence that other people might have wanted to kill the Pelleys; third, that the evidence presented by the prosecution was insufficient to warrant a conviction; and fourth, that Chamblee had erred in not appointing a special prosecutor.

The state attorney general's office opposed the appeal, and argued that the conviction and sentence should stand.

The Court of Appeals received the appeal in the spring of 2007. There it sat for more than a year, while a three-judge panel considered the claims.

Then, on April 8, 2008, the three-judge panel voted 2–1 to sustain Jeff's claim that the one-year speedy-trial clock had been violated by the prosecution. It threw Jeff's conviction out.

"Because we find the first issue dispositive, we need not address the remaining issues. We reverse and remand," the majority held. The dissenter said that dismissal of the case was far too drastic a penalty for something that was neither party's fault. In fact, it was pretty much a freak occurrence, and would probably never happen again.

But the majority's opinion meant the case would come back to Chamblee, who would have no choice but to grant the defense's demand for dismissal for the lack of a speedy trial.

The Indiana Attorney General promptly served notice that it would appeal the Court of Appeals' decision to the Indiana Supreme Court, and so the battle went on. In August 2008, the Indiana Supreme Court accepted the state's appeal.

In Feburary 2009, the state's highest court reversed the Court of Appeal's reversal of Jeff's conviction. In a unanimous decision, the five justices held that the one-year trial clock had indeed been stopped when the prosecutors appealed Judge Chamblee's decision on the family counseling records. To count the state's pre-trial appeal against the speedy trial clock would effectively bar the state from ever making such appeals in the future, which would be unfair to the prosecution. The court also held that, while all the evidence against Jeff was circumstantial, it was nevertheless sufficient for the jury to have convicted him. As for Jeff's claim that Judge Chamblee had erred in refusing testimony about possible other suspects in the murders—the Florida bank stories—the court agreed with Chamblee: it was just too "attenuated."

Thus, as the spring of 2009 arrived, 37-year-old Jeff Pelley was halfway through the third year of his 160-year prison term, buried behind concrete walls for crimes he still asserts he did not and could not have committed. One hundred-sixty years—ticking away, the slowest clock of all.